WILLIAM
N. BENDER

DARLENE
CRANE

RTI in MATH

Practical Guidelines for Elementary Teachers

Solution Tree | Press

a division of
Solution Tree

555 North Morton Street
Bloomington, IN 47404
800.733.6786 (toll free) / 812.336.7700
FAX: 812.336.7790

email: info@solution-tree.com
solution-tree.com

Visit **go.solution-tree.com/rti** to download the reproducibles in this book.

Printed in the United States of America

14 13 12 11 10   2 3 4 5

FSC
Mixed Sources
Product group from well-managed
forests and other controlled sources
Cert no. SW-COC-002283
www.fsc.org
© 1996 Forest Stewardship Council

Library of Congress Cataloging-in-Publication Data

Bender, William N.
  RTI in math : practical guidelines for elementary teachers / William N. Bender, Darlene Crane.
    p. cm.
  Includes bibliographical references and index.
  ISBN 978-1-934009-54-3 (perfect bound) -- ISBN 978-1-935249-32-0 (library edition)
  1. Mathematics--Study and teaching (Elementary) 2. Curriculum planning. I. Crane, Darlene Barrientos, 1948- II. Title.
  QA135.6.B458 2010
  372.7--dc22
                                        2010020707

Solution Tree
Jeffrey C. Jones, CEO & President

Solution Tree Press
President: Douglas M. Rife
Publisher: Robert D. Clouse
Vice President of Production: Gretchen Knapp
Managing Production Editor: Caroline Wise
Senior Production Editor: Suzanne Kraszewski
Copy Editor: Rachel Rosolina
Proofreader: Elisabeth Abrams
Text and Cover Designer: Amy Shock

Acknowledgments

Over the years, I find that the more I write, the more supportive my wife, Dr. Renet Bender, becomes. When I'm up at 2:00 a.m. with an idea I just have to write down, or when I stay inside on a beautiful spring day to do what I love, she is always understanding. As always, I thank her for her support, her kindness, and her love.

—William N. Bender

Daily I am humbled by the blessings I have been granted. I am eternally thankful for my husband and best friend, Lawrie, and our three beautiful daughters, Rachel, Mackenzie, and Alayna, who have each been sources of encouragement and support during this adventure. I also want to thank Dr. Bender for the opportunity to work on this project—thank you for valuing my classroom experience and love of teaching!

— Darlene Crane

Solution Tree Press would like to thank the following reviewers:

JoAnn Cady
Assistant Professor of Mathematics Education
University of Tennessee
Knoxville, Tennessee

Kelly M. Costner
Assistant Professor, Department of Curriculum and Instruction
Winthrop University
Rock Hill, South Carolina

Saul Duarte
Special Education Specialist
Los Angeles Unified School District
Los Angeles, California

Jennifer Falor
Math Resource Specialist
Shawnee Mission School District
Shawnee Mission, Kansas

Linda Larson
Math Coach
Puyallup School District
Puyallup, Washington

Laurel Marsh
Assistant Principal
Longfellow Elementary
Columbia, Maryland

Gale Yanish
Elementary Math Specialist
Sage Elementary
Spring Creek, Nevada

Table of Contents

appendix

About the Authors

William N. Bender, PhD, is an international leader in instructional tactics with an emphasis on differentiated instruction, response to intervention, brain-compatible instruction, and classroom discipline. He is an accomplished author and presenter who consistently receives accolades for his workshops from educators at every level.

Dr. Bender began his education career teaching in a junior high school resource classroom, working with adolescents with behavioral disorders and learning disabilities. He earned his doctorate in special education from the University of North Carolina. He has taught at Rutgers University in New Jersey and Bluefield State College in West Virginia, and most recently he served as a professor of education at the University of Georgia. He consults full time, writes professional development books, and presents workshops for educators throughout North America. Bender has written over sixty research articles. His numerous best-selling titles include *Response to Intervention: A Practical Guide for Every Teacher*; *Beyond the RTI Pyramid: Solutions for the First Years of Implementation*; *Differentiating Instruction for Students With Learning Disabilities* (second edition); *Introduction to Learning Disabilities* (sixth edition); *Relational Discipline: Strategies for In-Your-Face Kids* (second edition); and *Reading Strategies for Elementary Students With Learning Difficulties: Strategies for RTI* (second edition).

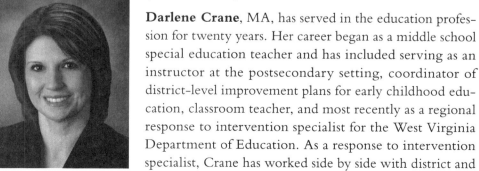

Darlene Crane, MA, has served in the education profession for twenty years. Her career began as a middle school special education teacher and has included serving as an instructor at the postsecondary setting, coordinator of district-level improvement plans for early childhood education, classroom teacher, and most recently as a regional response to intervention specialist for the West Virginia Department of Education. As a response to intervention specialist, Crane has worked side by side with district and school leaders and classroom teachers as they work to implement the tiered instructional model to support student achievement.

In addition to her experience as a classroom teacher and RTI specialist, her work has included the development of support strategies for students with ADHD and learning disabilities at the postsecondary setting, coordinating regional-level parent involvement for parents of children with special needs, and training hundreds of teachers and administrators on various elements of implementation of response to intervention in the areas of math and reading. Crane's passion for supporting educators as they work to provide high-quality educational experiences for all students arises from a combination of personal and professional experiences.

Preface

Newly devised response to intervention (RTI) procedures are transforming primary and elementary classrooms across the United States as teachers gear up their efforts to provide this intensive instructional support to students (Bender, 2009a). The RTI process involves targeting specific areas in which students are struggling and applying increasingly intensive research-proven interventions until the threat to learning is alleviated (Bender, 2009a). Nearly all of the research on RTI has taken place in the area of reading, because reading and literacy have been major national priorities since the Clinton presidential administration (Bender, 2009a). However, teachers are now beginning to use RTI procedures in mathematics. One 2009 survey of educational administrators indicates that over 50 percent of U.S. districts are currently implementing or soon intend to implement RTI for mathematics instruction (Spectrum K12 School Solutions, 2009). It is critical that teachers understand the similarities and differences in RTI implementation between reading and mathematics.

> It is critical that teachers understand the similarities and differences in RTI implementation between reading and mathematics.

This book addresses the immediate need for information on how RTI procedures might be implemented in primary and elementary mathematics. It is intended for various groups of educators in the kindergarten through upper elementary years, including:

- **Teachers** seeking practical guidance on how to implement an RTI process for a student who may be struggling in mathematics

- **Administrators** seeking to enhance schoolwide educational endeavors and more adequately address state mathematics standards

- **Professional learning communities (PLCs)** providing leadership on the RTI process in mathematics

In most of the chapters, we focus on implementation issues for RTI procedures in mathematics at the classroom level. In chapter 1, however, we provide some background on RTI and the development of RTI procedures themselves. Both chapter 1 and chapter 6 focus on implementation at the school district and the school level, and they provide guidance for PLCs or other leadership teams to assist in guiding the RTI implementation process. More specific information on each chapter follows.

In chapter 1, we discuss the overall RTI process and provide a brief description of the existing research on RTI procedures in mathematics. We present the RTI pyramid as the basis for supplemental interventions in the general education classroom. After a brief history of RTI, we describe problems many students today encounter in mathematics and how RTI procedures can address these problems. Next, we describe an RTI procedure and discuss progress-monitoring issues in a variety of mathematics areas. The standards of the National Council of Teachers of Mathematics (NCTM) as stated in their *Principles and Standards for School Mathematics* (2000) and the report of the National Mathematics Advisory Panel (NMAP), *Foundations for Success* (2008), provide the basis for this discussion of mathematics instructional techniques. We conclude chapter 1 by identifying issues that arise from implementation of RTI procedures in mathematics, including the primary issue of teacher time.

Because a solid foundation in mathematics is critical for subsequent success in math, the instruction students receive in general education is also critical. In chapter 2, we describe Tier 1 instruction appropriate for the general education classroom. Universal screening and benchmarking of mathematics performance in the general educational classroom are likely to become the responsibility of the general education teacher. We then describe how mathematics teachers might use the RTI process in the context of differentiated instruction and scaffolded instruction in mathematics. Finally, we present a variety of practical instructional ideas for enhancing Tier 1 mathematics instruction.

In chapter 3, we focus on early mathematics readiness in number sense and initial mathematics skills and the RTI process as implemented in kindergarten and first grade. We also discuss several curricula that may be appropriate for those grades. After a brief discussion on the brain basis for learning mathematics and number sense, we explore a case study of an RTI procedure addressing early mathematics skills. Finally, we discuss using the RTI process to diagnose learning disabilities in mathematics during the early school years.

In chapter 4, we focus on various mathematics areas in the upper elementary grades and discuss several curricula that may be appropriate for those grades. In this chapter, we also provide case study RTI examples in various elementary mathematics areas, including several areas stressed by NMAP's 2008 report. Because that report emphasizes automaticity with math facts and intensified instruction in fractions, we present RTI case studies in these areas. We also discuss how teachers might use RTI procedures in the middle and upper elementary grades for diagnosis of learning disabilities in mathematics.

In chapter 5, we discuss RTI procedures and intervention strategies for teaching problem solving. The field of mathematics has witnessed an increased emphasis on problem solving, as various national reports have identified problem solving as one area that consistently proves challenging for many students. We present a variety of instructional procedures (such as specific learning strategies and project-based learning) for teaching problem solving at the Tier 1 and Tier 2 levels. We place these instructional procedures into the context of a case study on RTI that focuses on solving story problems.

In chapter 6, we provide information for a PLC, a district-based leadership team, or a schoolwide RTI task force to assist with RTI planning and implementation in mathematics at the school level. We also include useful tips and descriptive notes on helpful websites and various forms for planning and implementing the RTI procedure in mathematics.

Visit **go.solution-tree.com/rti** for downloadable versions of the reproducibles found in the appendix as well as for live links to the websites mentioned in text.

The RTI Process in Elementary Mathematics

The instructional process referred to as response to intervention (RTI) has quickly taken root in the United States (Buffum, Mattos, & Weber, 2009; Kavale & Spaulding, 2008; Spectrum K12 School Solutions, 2009). In fact, proponents of RTI, as well as several advocacy groups and educational support organizations, have indicated that RTI may represent a fundamental paradigm shift in education (Fuchs & Deshler, 2007; Fuchs & Fuchs, 2007; Gersten & Dimino, 2006). For example, the National Association of State Directors of Special Education (NASDSE, 2006) indicates that RTI represents a "dramatic redesign" of general and special education. RTI has been implemented in reading and literacy in school districts across the United States, and in a survey of directors of special education, over half of the school districts reported implementation of RTI in mathematics as well (Spectrum K12 School Solutions, 2009).

Clearly, there is a great deal of emphasis on RTI, and RTI is resulting in a refocusing of educational endeavors. Furthermore, fundamental changes in teaching practices are stemming from the RTI initiative, and these changes will probably impact most teachers in kindergarten through grade 12 (Bender, 2009a; Kame'enui, 2007; Spectrum K12 School Solutions/Council of Administrators of Special Education [CASE], 2008). For that reason, these changes must be considered carefully by school leadership teams and PLCs within the school as educators move into RTI implementation in mathematics.

This chapter presents an overview of the RTI process in mathematics, with a focus on advocacy for RTI as a school improvement initiative. While this book is not primarily an introduction to RTI or a review of research on the RTI process, leadership personnel serving as proponents of RTI in mathematics will need some understanding of the research basis that provides the rationale for RTI procedures. We will also address questions, concerns, and problems that have arisen in the implementation of RTI in the areas of reading and literacy; these issues are likely to arise when RTI is implemented in mathematics as well. We introduce these issues here to suggest possible solutions.

What Is RTI?

Response to intervention is a network of support intended to assist all students in their learning by providing increasing levels of intensive, research-proven instructional interventions targeted to the needs of the individual student (Kame'enui, 2007; NASDSE, 2006). For students who are struggling in any academic area or struggling behaviorally, the RTI process results in timely interventions that should assist in overcoming those threats to learning and development (Gersten & Dimino, 2006; Kame'enui, 2007). During the RTI process, student progress is monitored repeatedly in order to document how students respond to instruction. That evidence is then used for data-based decision making relative to students' educational programs. Through the practice of universal screening, which is typically conducted at least three times each year, it is likely that the recent emphasis on RTI for meeting mandated standards will impact every student in the public schools.

> *Response to intervention* is a network of support intended to assist all students in their learning by providing increasing levels of intensive, research-proven instructional interventions targeted to the needs of the individual student.

The Three-Tier RTI Pyramid

In most of the literature on RTI, as well as in most state department of education guidelines, the RTI process is depicted as a pyramid of increasingly intensive, specifically targeted instructional interventions—referred to as intervention tiers—such as those presented in figure 1.1 (Berkeley, Bender, Peaster, & Saunders, 2009). Each tier within the pyramid contains more specifically targeted interventions. The pyramid shape suggests that fewer students require the more intensive interventions that appear at the top. This three-tier pyramid of interventions model was first used in the public health arena (Kame'enui, 2007), but has since been adapted to various areas in education, including reading interventions such as the national Reading First initiative, and interventions to reduce problem behaviors in schools (Bender, 2009a).

While various states have adopted slightly different models, the most commonly used RTI model is the three-tier RTI pyramid (Berkeley et al., 2009; Howell, Patton, & Deiotte, 2008; NASDSE, 2006; Spectrum K12 School Solutions, 2009). For example, in a 2008 survey on RTI among special education administrators, 73 percent of the respondents indicated that their state had implemented a three-tier RTI pyramid (Spectrum K12 School Solutions/CASE, 2008), whereas only 22 percent of respondents indicated that their state had implemented a four-tier model. Given this rather robust implementation of the three-tier pyramid, that model is the basis for this text.

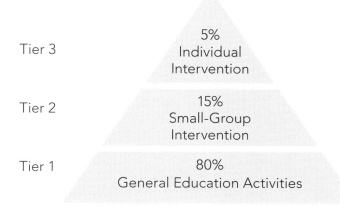

Figure 1.1: The three-tier RTI pyramid.

In the three-tier RTI model, as well as in some of the four-tier RTI models (such as those used in North Carolina and Georgia), the lower tier of the pyramid represents effective instruction provided for all students within the general education classroom (Fuchs & Fuchs, 2005, 2006; Howell et al., 2008; NASDSE, 2006). Instruction delivered in this tier may include whole-class, smaller-group, or tutorial instruction. A wide variety of research-proven instructional procedures are typically implemented as the basis for Tier 1 instruction, such as grouping students for instruction, scaffolding instruction, and using group projects, learning centers, cooperative instruction, or differentiated instruction. The general education teacher is the primary facilitator of instruction for Tier 1.

Tier 1 Instruction

Tier 1 instruction is the foundation for all instructional interventions in mathematics, and it should be considered the single most important tier in the intervention pyramid, since effective instruction at this level greatly reduces the number of students requiring more intensive instruction at other levels of the pyramid. Proponents of the three-tier model suggest that this instructional tier should meet the needs of perhaps 80 percent of the students in a classroom (Boyer, 2008; Bradley, Danielson, & Doolittle, 2007; Fuchs & Fuchs, 2007). Because of the critical importance of effective mathematics instruction in Tier 1, chapter 2 focuses exclusively on effective instructional and performance monitoring procedures in Tier 1 mathematics for primary and elementary classes.

> Tier 1 instruction is the foundation for all instructional interventions in mathematics, and it should be considered the single most important tier in the intervention pyramid.

Tier 2 Interventions

The interventions in Tier 2 of the RTI pyramid have been described as targeted, supplemental, systematic interventions for a small group of students who are struggling in mathematics. Unlike the occasional small-group instruction in Tier 1, Tier 2 supplemental instruction is more targeted, and it takes place over a longer period of time, possibly a grading period or two (Cummings, Atkins, Allison, & Cole, 2008; Fuchs & Fuchs, 2006, 2007). While 20 to 25 percent of the student population may require supplemental instruction in mathematics at this level of intensity, this intervention tier is typically described as meeting the needs of perhaps 15 percent of the school population. Therefore, in a typical class of twenty-four students, one might expect that five or six students will struggle in mathematics and require a level of supplementary instruction that is more intensive than the instruction offered to the entire class in Tier 1. In some school districts, the general education teacher is expected to deliver this supplemental instruction, but there is wide variety as to how to deliver instruction in the higher tiers of the pyramid (Berkeley et al., 2009). Subsequent chapters explore a variety of options concerning who delivers instruction in various intervention tiers.

> Tier 2 interventions are targeted, supplemental, systematic interventions for a small group of students who are struggling in mathematics.

Tier 3 Interventions

Tier 3 interventions are described within the three-tier RTI model as highly intensive educational interventions targeted at either one student or a very small group of students (Boyer, 2008; Bradley et al., 2007; Fuchs & Fuchs, 2007). These interventions have become the basis of some confusion as districts move to implement RTI. Proponents of RTI generally agree that if the instruction during Tier 2 intervention does not result in a student moving forward academically, that student will require a more intensive intervention within the framework of general education in order for his or her needs to be addressed.

> Tier 3 interventions are highly intensive educational interventions targeted at either one student or a very small group of students.

In contrast, some suggest that Tier 3 interventions should take place only after a student has been declared eligible for special education or other specialized services (Fuchs & Fuchs, 2006). Those other services might include programs for English learners or programs for migrant students. Fuchs and Fuchs (2006, 2007), for example, suggest that Tier 3 interventions take place after eligibility for specialized services has been documented.

There is no right or wrong standard of practice; however, most state models of RTI indicate that Tier 3 interventions will be provided prior to actual eligibility decisions, or as a component of the eligibility decision-making process (Berkeley et al., 2009; NASDSE, 2006). This level of intensive intervention is frequently described as one-to-one instruction and is designed to meet the needs of the remaining 3 to 5 percent of the school population (Fuchs & Fuchs, 2005; Howell et al., 2008). Therefore, in our example of the classroom with twenty-four students, perhaps one or two students would require supplemental instruction in mathematics at this level of intensity.

Given the wide variety of RTI models and implementation procedures in use throughout the United States (Berkeley et al., 2009), it is somewhat difficult to discuss generally interventions in mathematics from the RTI pyramid. For purposes of this book, we define and describe the tiers in the same way as the majority of U.S. educators—a three-tier model in which all three of the intervention tiers take place as a function of general education and prior to special education eligibility decisions (Berkeley et al., 2009; NASDSE, 2006).

Of course, educators working in districts that employ models other than this should interpret our suggestions and guidelines appropriately within the context of their own district policy. Most state departments of education present some type of RTI model on their state department website, and in many cases, the information on RTI applications for reading and mathematics is quite extensive. Educators should check that source to see the type of model their state uses, as well as any guidelines on implementation of RTI in mathematics versus implementation in reading.

Foundations of the RTI Process

In almost all state models for RTI, five foundational principles undergird the RTI process, as shown in the following feature box (Bender, 2009a; Boyer, 2008; Buffum et al., 2009). First, almost all models are rooted in the concept of universal screening to identify students struggling in various subjects. This concept suggests that given the critical importance of both reading and mathematics, all students should be screened frequently (usually three times each year) to ensure that they are meeting their benchmark goals in each area. To date, this principle has been more widely applied in the primary and elementary grades, since benchmarking basic skills is more directly related to the content in those grades. However, universal screening is likely to gain emphasis across all grade levels as middle and high schools gear up to implement RTI procedures.

Foundational Principles of the RTI Process

1. Universal screening to identify students struggling in mathematics

2. A multitier model of increasingly intensive educational interventions

3. Research-based curriculum in each tier

4. Frequent monitoring of each child's performance related to benchmarks

5. Data-based decision making involving a collaborative team effort

Almost all RTI models depict different educational interventions in various levels or tiers (Boyer, 2008; Buffum et al., 2009) and at increasing levels of intensity, with an array of options for providing targeted, explicit instruction to struggling students in their areas of difficulty.

Most RTI models specifically emphasize the use of research-based curriculum, and in that sense, RTI is similar to other national initiatives such as No Child Left Behind (Kame'enui, 2007). Also, frequent monitoring of each individual student's progress within that curriculum based on benchmarks is required in the RTI process. In addition to the universal screening three times each year, most districts require more frequent benchmarking (or progress monitoring) assessments during Tier 2 and Tier 3 interventions (Bender, 2009a).

Finally, all RTI models emphasize data-based decision making involving a collaborative team in order to accurately interpret a student's progress relative to curricular standards in mathematics. Using actual data about the student's performance allows educators to make time-critical decisions about an individual student's educational planning.

RTI Implementation in Schools

In 2004, federal legislation was enacted that allowed the use of RTI progress-monitoring data to become the basis for learning disability diagnosis (Kame'enui, 2007; NASDSE, 2006). For that reason, some educators have associated RTI with special education. While information from the RTI process can help determine eligibility for students with learning disabilities and can be used in other eligibility procedures for students with other disabilities (such as behavioral disorders), that is not the primary purpose of RTI. Rather, RTI is a support network of universal assessments in critical areas, paired with increasingly intensive interventions in those areas, for students having difficulty in any academic or behavioral area (NASDSE, 2006). Furthermore, in all states, RTI interventions take place primarily within the context of general education and not special education. Thus, the RTI initiative will significantly impact general education teachers in profound ways, and it should not be viewed as a special education initiative. This makes a school's RTI implementation process an extremely appropriate topic for consideration by the school PLC (DuFour, DuFour, & Eaker, 2008; DuFour, DuFour, Eaker, & Karhanek, 2004) or school leadership teams.

> In all states, RTI interventions take place primarily within the context of general education and not special education. Thus, the RTI initiative will significantly impact general education teachers in profound ways, and it should not be viewed as a special education initiative.

To date, discussions of RTI implementation have focused primarily on reading assessments and interventions in the primary and elementary grades, and only recently have proponents of RTI begun to provide information on how this procedure might work in the area of mathematics (Ardoin, Witt, Connell, & Koenig, 2005; Fuchs,

Fuchs, Compton, et al., 2007; Jordan, Kaplan, Locuniak, & Ramineni, 2007). With little guidance available on how to conduct RTI procedures in mathematics, school districts have been somewhat slower in implementing RTI in mathematics as compared to reading. In a March 2008 nationwide survey of special education administrators, 84 percent indicated that their school district had begun implementation of RTI procedures in reading, whereas only 53 percent indicated RTI implementation had begun in mathematics (Spectrum K12 School Solutions/CASE, 2008).

In fact, some school districts have decided to implement RTI exclusively in reading initially and concentrate on implementation of RTI in mathematics and other areas later. West Virginia, for example, initiated RTI procedures in reading in thirty-six pilot schools in 2005, but it took a few years for those schools to implement RTI in mathematics (Boyer, 2008). With that noted, all schools in the nation will eventually implement some version of RTI for a wide variety of academic subjects, and one of the first will probably be mathematics. Teachers will require an understanding of the RTI process as well as how that process applies in mathematics.

Why Is RTI in Mathematics Necessary?

Researchers have begun to advocate for RTI procedures in mathematics for two specific reasons: (1) many students need help in mathematics, and they can benefit from RTI procedures, and (2) RTI-based instruction works. Some research suggests that as many as 25 percent of primary- and elementary-level students may experience some difficulty in mathematics (Baskette, Ulmer, & Bender, 2006; Fuchs, Compton, Fuchs, Paulsen, Bryant, & Hamlett, 2005). In addition, between 6 and 10 percent of young children experience challenges that are severe enough to be identified as mathematics disabilities.

> Researchers have begun to advocate for RTI procedures in mathematics for two specific reasons: (1) many students need help in mathematics, and they can benefit from RTI procedures in mathematics, and (2) RTI-based instruction works.

Student difficulty in mathematics can manifest in a variety of ways. For example, Jordan and her colleagues have documented that young students with difficulties understanding basic number relationships perform less well on timed mathematics achievement calculation exercises (Jordan et al., 2007; Locuniak & Jordan, 2008). Other students encounter problems at certain points in the curriculum in the early years of school when specific new mathematics content is introduced. These times can be thought of as "choke points" within the curriculum; students may do quite well in mathematics until these points, but they then fail to succeed in specific skill areas. In some cases, a bit of extra instructional time at these critical choke points can make the difference between success and failure in mathematics overall.

For example, some students have success with early mathematics facts, such as addition and subtraction problems—even with two-digits—but once the concept of regrouping is introduced, they seem to choke. Other students do well through the primary grades, but demonstrate extreme difficulty once fractions are introduced, usually in grade 3. Fractions are critically important in mathematics since success with fractions of all types (fractional parts, percentages, decimals) provides the basis for many aspects of the mathematics curriculum in later years (NMAP, 2008). Students who fail to master the content are severely handicapped in the higher grades. As struggling students get older, many of their problems in mathematics continue. Mabbott and Bisanz (2008) indicate that many students in the middle grades demonstrate serious mathematics disabilities in various operations or in solving mathematical problems.

This body of research indicates that difficulties in mathematics are fairly common and that these difficulties must be addressed in some fashion if students are to succeed in the higher-grade mathematics curriculum. Clearly, RTI interventions in mathematics will be necessary for many students (Spectrum K12 School Solutions/CASE, 2008). As the United States moves to implementation of RTI as the primary way to support struggling students in general education, we cannot simply implement RTI in literacy and overlook students with mathematics disabilities; that would be tantamount to denial of necessary services for those students.

> As the United States moves to implementation of RTI as the primary way to support struggling students in general education, we cannot simply implement RTI in literacy and overlook students with mathematics disabilities; that would be tantamount to denial of necessary services for those students.

Why Students Struggle in Mathematics

There are several reasons that struggling students have not built a strong academic foundation in mathematics. First, the traditional instructional models in both reading and mathematics have relied on pull-out services to meet the needs of struggling students, such as with Title I instruction and special education services. Some educators have questioned the efficacy of pull-out programs, which tend to de-emphasize the general education teacher's role in mathematics instruction (Bender, 2009a; Boyer, 2008). A rigorous system of differentiated, supplemental instruction in mathematics within the context of the general education class reduces reliance on this pull-out instructional model.

In addition, No Child Left Behind's focus on the achievement of individual subgroups of students (such as English learners, students with special needs, and minority students) has heightened our awareness of the increasing discrepancy of achievement among students in mathematics (NMAP, 2008). This focus on specific subgroups has left some general education teachers feeling inadequate about their own instructional skills in mathematics. Recent research has indicated that many elementary educators feel less confident with mathematics instruction than reading instruction (Burns, 2006; Enochs, Smith, & Huinker, 2000; Minton, 2007). Obviously, teacher knowledge of content and personal comfort in teaching mathematics will both impact the quality of instruction teachers provide.

The inclusion instructional model has also contributed to students' struggles. The intention of inclusion is to re-engage students with exceptionalities and other learning difficulties in the general education environment in order to provide them with access to grade-level content. But inclusion models often leave general educators questioning their preparation for meeting student needs. In contrast, well-designed RTI models depend on high-quality general education instruction in mathematics coupled with a supplemental intervention support network, and thus RTI models empower general education teachers to better address the needs of diverse learners (Bender, 2009b).

A strong facultywide emphasis on quality Tier 1 instruction as part of the RTI model, with appropriate support for RTI efforts in mathematics, has given many students the opportunity to participate in and benefit from the richness of the general education classroom. As educators become proficient with differentiated instruction and research-based instructional strategies of RTI, increasing numbers of struggling students have gained viable access to mathematics content.

RTI and Standards-Based Instruction

Since the presidency of Bill Clinton, our national educational policy has focused on standards that would allow students in our schools to compete with students internationally in all academic areas, including mathematics (Kame'enui, 2007; NMAP, 2008). For this reason, any discussion of a curricular or instructional modification such as RTI must take place in the context of these curricular standards. The NCTM identified instructional standards and content standards for the public school mathematics curriculum in a document titled *Principles and Standards for School Mathematics* (2000). These standards are critically important because of the emphasis on high standards set forth in the political initiatives of the past several presidential administrations. Therefore, almost every state uses the NCTM standards to set curricular expectations in mathematics for all students. They include specific standards in ten broad areas across all grade levels, from kindergarten through grade 12 (Kemp, Eaton, & Poole, 2009). Those broad content areas are subdivided according to specific skills in each grade level. The ten areas of emphasis are as follows:

1. Numbers and operations
2. Algebra
3. Geometry
4. Measurement
5. Data analysis and probability
6. Problem solving
7. Reasoning and proof
8. Communication
9. Connections

10. Representation

The NCTM modified the standards in 2006 when it published a document to identify the curriculum focal points within mathematics for each grade level (NCTM, 2006). Those curriculum focal points for grade levels range from preK through grade 8 (table 1.1). The complete description of each focal point can be found at the NCTM website (www.nctm.org).

Table 1.1: The National Council of Teachers of Mathematics Curriculum Focal Points in Mathematics

Grade 1	*Number and operations and algebra:* Developing understandings of addition and subtraction and strategies for basic addition facts and related subtraction facts
	Number and operations: Developing an understanding of whole number relationships, including grouping in tens and ones
	Geometry: Composing and decomposing geometric shapes
Grade 2	*Number and operations:* Developing an understanding of the base-10 numeration system and place-value concepts
	Number and operations and algebra: Developing quick recall of addition facts and related subtraction facts and fluency with multidigit addition and subtraction
	Measurement: Developing an understanding of linear measurement and facility in measuring lengths
Grade 3	*Number and operations and algebra:* Developing understandings of multiplication and division and strategies for basic multiplication facts and related division facts
	Number and operations: Developing an understanding of fractions and fraction equivalence
	Geometry: Describing and analyzing properties of two-dimensional shapes
Grade 4	*Number and operations and algebra:* Developing quick recall of multiplication facts and related division facts and fluency with whole-number multiplication
	Number and operations: Developing an understanding of decimals, including the connections between fractions and decimals
	Measurement: Developing an understanding of area and determining the areas of two-dimensional shapes
Grade 5	*Number and operations and algebra:* Developing an understanding of and fluency with division of whole numbers

Grade 5	*Numbers and operations:* Developing an understanding of and fluency with addition and subtraction of fractions and decimals
	Geometry and measurement and algebra: Describing three-dimensional shapes and analyzing their properties, including volume and surface area
Grade 6	*Number and operations:* Developing an understanding of and fluency with multiplication and division of fractions and decimals
	Number and operations: Connecting ratio and rate to multiplication and division
	Algebra: Writing, interpreting, and using mathematical expressions and equations
Grade 7	*Number and operations, algebra, and geometry:* Developing an understanding of and applying proportionality, including similarity
	Measurement, geometry, and algebra: Developing an understanding of and using formulas to determine surface areas and volumes of three-dimensional shapes
	Number and operations and algebra: Developing an understanding of operations on all rational numbers and solving linear equations
Grade 8	*Algebra:* Analyzing and representing linear functions and solving linear equations and systems of linear equations
	Geometry and measurement: Analyzing two- and three-dimensional space and figures by using distance and angle
	Data analysis, number and operations, and algebra: Analyzing and summarizing data sets

Source: NCTM, 2006

In 2008, NMAP issued a report that focused on mathematics instruction across the public school grades. The report began with the overall recommendation that all students should be required to pass algebra I and algebra II in order for the United States to continue to be a world leader in science and technology. The report called for more rigorous standards in mathematics, since most states and school districts require completion of algebra I only in their general education curriculum for high school graduation, coupled of course with one or two additional mathematics courses such as geometry, applied mathematics, or general mathematics.

The report made recommendations for restructuring the mathematics curriculum from kindergarten up through high school, noting that preparation in the lower grades provides the groundwork for success in algebra I and algebra II (NMAP, 2008). It made more than forty distinct recommendations in virtually every area of mathematics instruction, such as textbook preparation and teacher preparation, and summarized critically important information on mathematics instruction for teachers in the primary, elementary, and middle school grades. Table 1.2 presents a synopsis of the recommendations that are most relevant to public school educators.

Table 1.2: Selected Recommendations of the 2008 Report of the National Mathematics Advisory Panel

1.	The mathematics curriculum in grades 1 through 8 should be streamlined and recreated to emphasize critical topics in early grades that directly enhance learning and mastery of algebra in the high school grades. This emphasis is consistent with the *Critical Focal Points* report of the National Council of Teachers of Mathematics (2006). The Panel recommends use of benchmarks for mathematics in the elementary grades, and specifically stresses automaticity in mathematics facts and whole-number operations. This parallels the suggestions in the educational literature to focus instruction on the "power standards" that are essential for future success in the subject.
2.	Fractions (including decimals, percents, and negative fractions) are critical for subsequent mathematics and algebra achievement. Thus, this mathematics content, including representation of fractions on a number line, should be stressed much more. Research suggests that this will have the broadest single impact on subsequent achievement in problem-solving performance.
3.	The performance of groups that have been traditionally underrepresented in mathematics fields may be greatly enhanced by stressing social, affective, and motivational factors, as well as by providing explicit instruction in mathematics.
4.	Schools should consider hiring full-time mathematics teachers in elementary grades as one option to enhance mathematics performance. If implemented, this recommendation may provide a mechanism for provision of Tier 2 or Tier 3 interventions, as well as Tier 1 instruction.
5.	Research on instruction suggests that instruction should be based on both teacher-directed and student-centered activities; the research does not support the use of either one exclusive of the other.
6.	Teachers should use various forms of tutoring and/or cooperative learning. Specifically, team-assisted instruction has been shown to increase students' computation skills. This is a highly structured strategy, employing heterogeneous groups of students helping each other through tutoring and/or other cooperative learning formats.
7.	Teachers should regularly use formative assessment, and such assessment is likely to improve students' learning. While RTI is not mentioned in the Panel report, this recommendation may serve as a basis for emphasizing universal screening and repeated performance assessment in a multitiered intervention format for students struggling in mathematics.
8.	Explicit instruction has been shown to work consistently for students struggling in mathematics, including students with learning disabilities and other disabilities. Explicit instruction employs teacher-directed instruction, many practice examples, encouragement for students to "talk aloud" during problem solving, and extensive feedback.

9.	Research on instructional software in mathematics has shown positive results on student achievement. Technology-based drill-and-practice examples can improve student learning in an array of areas.
10.	The use of calculators has limited or no impact on computation skills, problem solving, or conceptual development; however, the Panel cautions that use of calculators may impede development of automaticity, and it suggests that calculators should not be used on assessment items that measure computational fluency.

Source: NMAP, 2008

In addition to these selected recommendations, NMAP (2008) identified a series of eleven critical benchmarks that should guide instruction in elementary mathematics. Table 1.3 presents these benchmarks. A quick review of these benchmarks provides some insight into how instructional practices for mathematics may develop in the future. For example, none of these benchmarks deal with measurement topics; rather, they emphasize automaticity in mathematics facts, fractions, decimals, and problem solving. While it is too soon to tell the impact of this national report, it may lead to some modifications of the current mathematics curricula throughout the elementary grades.

Table 1.3: National Mathematics Advisory Panel Benchmarks

Fluency With Whole Numbers
1. By the end of grade 3, students should be proficient with the addition and subtraction of whole numbers.
2. By the end of grade 5, students should be proficient with the multiplication and division of whole numbers.
Fluency With Fractions
3. By the end of grade 4, students should be able to identify and represent fractions and decimals and compare them on a number line or with other common representations of fractions and decimals.
4. By the end of grade 5, students should be proficient with comparing fractions and decimals and common percents and with the addition and subtraction of fractions and decimals.
5. By the end of grade 6, students should be proficient with multiplication and division of fractions and decimals.
6. By the end of grade 6, students should be proficient with all operations involving positive and negative integers.
7. By the end of grade 7, students should be proficient with all operations involving positive and negative fractions.

continued on next page →

8.	By the end of grade 7, students should be able to solve problems involving percent, ratio, and rate and extend this work to proportionality.

<table>
<tr><td colspan="2" align="center">Geometry and Measurement</td></tr>
</table>

9.	By the end of grade 5, students should be able to solve problems involving perimeter and area of triangles and all quadriaterals having at least one pair of parallel sides (such as trapezoids).
10.	By the end of grade 6, students should be able to analyze the properties of two-dimensional shapes and solve problems involving perimeter and area, and analyze the properties of three-dimensional shapes and solve problems involving surface, area, and volume.
11.	By the end of grade 7, students should be familiar with the relationship between similar triangles and the concept of the slope of a line.

Source: NMAP, 2008

These standards, recommendations, and benchmarks, along with NCTM's ten curricular focal points, must provide the framework for our discussions of curricular or instructional modifications such as RTI. These standards, recommendations, and benchmarks are used as the basis for discussion of mathematics instruction through-out this text; however, we should note that additional changes in state mathematics standards are likely within the next five years (Clark, 2010).

In July 2009, President Obama launched his Race to the Top education initiative, an initiative that promises additional funding to foster school reform and an increased emphasis on educational standards (Clark, 2010). In addition, in order to move toward a set of national curriculum standards that presumably would apply across state lines, the National Governors Association Center for Best Practices and the Council of Chief State School Officers from forty-eight states are working together to develop a set of core standards (Clark, 2010; see also www.corestandards.org). The curricular standards for kindergarten through grade 12 were released in February of 2010, and at this point, no one can predict the impact that these revised standards might have in mathematics instruction. Furthermore, even the NMAP recommendations of 2008 are quite recent and may have yet to be implemented in some states or school districts. Again, educators should check their state department of education website for the specific instructional standards and guidelines for mathematics instruction mandated by their state.

Given the national emphasis on standards-based instruction and the identification of effective instructional practices, schools around the nation have focused consider-able energy on making adequate yearly progress (AYP) toward meeting high educa-tional standards. Schools across the United States have heard the demands from their communities to meet mandated curricular goals. In fact, AYP has been so heavily emphasized that teachers have begun to focus their instructional planning on specific AYP goals within their school.

Efficacy of RTI for Addressing Educational Standards

One way schools have begun to address the issue of meeting high standards is through the implementation of RTI in various subject areas. If implementation of RTI results in schools meeting AYP goals toward higher standards, then RTI will enhance the overall school program and can be considered—and we argue should be considered—as a school-improvement technique. Research on the effectiveness of the RTI process indicates that implementation of RTI does assist schools in meeting AYP, and for that reason, we present some preliminary research in the following sections. Educators involved in RTI implementation should not only become aware of this growing research, but they should share this research with colleagues concerned with meaningful and substantive school reform efforts.

Using RTI to Meet AYP in Mathematics

Research on RTI is fairly recent, and is certainly much more extensive in the areas of reading and literacy than in mathematics (Bender, 2009a). Still, the existing research indicates that RTI procedures help many students struggling in mathematics overcome their difficulties and may actually enable them to catch up with their peers in overall mathematics achievement (Bender, 2009b; Bryant et al., 2008; Chard et al., 2008; Fuchs et al., 2005; Fuchs et al., 2006; Fuchs, Fuchs, & Hollenbeck, 2007). For example, Bryant and her colleagues (2008) documented the impact of a Tier 2 supplementary intervention on first-grade students struggling in mathematics. Of the 161 students in the study, 42 were identified as needing a Tier 2 intervention. That group was provided with a supplemental intervention in mathematics by two trained tutors that involved explicit instruction for twenty minutes per day, four days per week, for twenty-three weeks. Data at the end of that time suggested that this level of intervention resulted in improvements in mathematics that were greater than would have been predicted by pretest scores for those forty-two struggling students.

The research shows that the RTI process does alleviate mathematics difficulties for many struggling students (Bender, 2009b; Bryant et al., 2008; Chard et al., 2008; Fuchs et al., 2005). It is important to note that in the studies mentioned in this section, someone other than the general education teacher delivered the Tier 2 intervention. More research is needed before we can conclude that general education teachers, given their time constraints, would be as effective as support personnel who are able to focus completely on supporting mathematics instruction.

However, these results do look quite promising. RTI procedures do help students meet standards in math, and meeting AYP in mathematics is often a concern for educators. This research collectively suggests that a Tier 2 intervention alleviated the problems in mathematics for between 30 and 60 percent of the students, and that a more intensive intervention may alleviate mathematics problems for the other students as well. Thus, many students who are struggling in mathematics show significant progress towards AYP when provided with supplemental instructional interventions in mathematics within the multitier RTI process. Based on these data, it is fair to say research supports the implementation of the RTI process in mathematics and shows that RTI works for many struggling kids. This is how schools should address the demands of meeting AYP in mathematics.

> It is fair to say research supports the implementation of the RTI process in mathematics and shows that RTI works for many struggling kids. This is how schools should address the demands of meeting AYP in mathematics.

RTI Works for Students Struggling in Reading

While our focus here is RTI in mathematics, educators at all levels will need to understand the positive research that undergirds the national RTI effort, and much of that is in the area of reading and literacy. Research has shown that the provision of intensive supplemental reading instruction can alleviate reading problems and put students back on track towards long-term reading success (Torgesen, 2007; Vellutino, Scanlon, Small, & Fanuele, 2006). In particular, the research demonstrates convincingly that students struggling in reading will benefit from supplemental, phonemically based, explicit reading instruction, and that the academic growth resulting from those interventions is maintained over time (Denton, Fletcher, Anthony, & Francis, 2006; Simmons et al., 2008; Torgesen, 2007).

While some of these early studies investigated efficacy of specific Tier 2 interventions directly, others documented the efficacy of multitiered interventions in a complete RTI process. Hughes and Dexter (2008) reviewed the research on the efficacy of the entire RTI process and found that the process assists struggling students in improving their academic performance. While results vary significantly, the broad body of available research suggests that Tier 2 intensive supplemental intervention alleviates or eliminates between 40 and 60 percent of academic problems for students who are struggling in either reading or math (Hughes & Dexter, 2008; O'Connor, Fulmer, Harty, & Bell, 2005; Simmons et al., 2008; Torgesen, 2007).

RTI Works for English Learners

Several specific subgroups of children face more challenges in school. One persistent concern among educators is provision of effective instruction for students with a primary language other than English. Research has shown that RTI is a very effective way to address the educational needs of these students (Kamps et al., 2007; Linan-Thompson, Cirino, & Vaughn, 2007; Lovett et al., 2008). The data show that within the broader RTI process, even these students will perform much better on various measures of academic achievement (Linan-Thompson, Vaughn, Prater, & Cirino, 2006; Rinaldi & Samson, 2008; Torgesen, 2007).

Other Evidence That Supports RTI

There are a number of other benefits of implementation of the RTI process. First, RTI empowers general education teachers (Bender, 2009a). Virtually every general education teacher has felt pressured to spend a little more time helping a student with his or her mathematics. With RTI, teachers can now expect to have a wider variety of supports available to them. These supports allow them to advocate for and spend more time with students who are struggling (Bender, 2009a).

In addition, evidence shows that initiation of the RTI process does tend to reduce the number of students referred for special education services (Abernathy, 2008; Torgesen, 2007). One nationwide survey of public school administrators indicated that 39 percent of respondents believe that RTI implementation has reduced referrals for special education by at least 10 percent; however, 53 percent indicated data were insufficient to make a determination on that question in April of 2009 (Spectrum K12 School Solutions, 2009). Torgesen (2007) summarized data from a multitier Reading First initiative in Florida and indicated that the percentage of the school population in grades kindergarten through 3 diagnosed as learning disabled fell from 10.4 percent to 6 percent during the three years of that reading initiative. With fewer students requiring special educational assistance, the intensive resources required for those students can be applied elsewhere, and many districts are redirecting those resources into general education classes to support elements of tiered instruction.

Some interesting anecdotal evidence has emerged on the efficacy of RTI in addressing another persistent concern among educators: disproportionality. *Disproportionality* is the long-standing concern for the overrepresentation of minority students in special education. Disproportionality might suggest some inadvertent racial or social bias in the current eligibility procedures, and educators have long sought a remedy for this problem.

At least one preliminary report from the districts that have implemented RTI suggests that disproportionality might be significantly reduced using the RTI process. For example, during the 2004/2005 academic year in New Hanover County, North Carolina, African American students were 1.7 times as likely to be placed in special education as were white students. However, after implementing RTI in 2006/2007, the African American students were only 1.2 times as likely to be placed in special education (Abernathy, 2008). This suggests a significant reduction in disproportionality.

> Early anecdotal evidence suggests that implementation of RTI has reduced disproportionality in some school districts.

RTI and School Improvement

As the evidence suggests, the RTI process should be understood as a powerful, research-proven school improvement effort to enhance education for all students. As the United States increasingly sets high standards in mathematics, educators will need bold new approaches to teaching to meet those standards, and as the research demonstrates, RTI is an effective instructional process for meeting those demands. Furthermore, this process works for many of the students that are most challenged by the high-standards curriculum, including English learners, students already diagnosed with disabilities, students from impoverished homes, and other groups that face educational challenges (Bender, 2009a; Torgesen, 2007). Meeting and exceeding AYP within these specific subgroups has proven to be highly challenging for schools. Initial evidence does suggest that the RTI process can be one of the most effective ways to meet the challenge of making adequate yearly progress toward high educational standards for all students—even those facing special challenges.

> The RTI process should be understood as a powerful, research-proven school improvement effort to enhance education for all students.

We should note that RTI fits very well with other nationally recognized school improvement strategies, such as the PLC model (DuFour et al., 2004). Formative evaluation is recommended as a progress-monitoring tool within PLCs, and that emphasis is certainly characteristic of RTI efforts. PLCs emphasize creation of a schoolwide system of intervention supports, which is virtually synonymous with the RTI model. PLCs within the school are one vehicle for implementation of RTI.

Advocacy for RTI

Educational leaders must serve as advocates for RTI. Strong support from school leaders can greatly enhance the willingness of faculty to undertake the process. Leaders should make sure various supports for RTI are available within the school, including instructional coaches or tutors to lead Tier 2 or Tier 3 interventions, or paraprofessionals to assist in general education classes when teachers are working with small groups of students in Tier 2 intervention.

Overall, however, the most powerful advocacy for RTI typically involves teachers' sense of their own role in the academic lives of their students. RTI is a process that empowers teachers, and it should be presented to educators as effective teaching for the 21st century—an instructional paradigm that works for all students.

> RTI should be presented to educators as effective teaching for the 21st century, an instructional paradigm that works for all students.

Teacher Understanding of the RTI Process

Many educators have begun using RTI in reading and are familiar with the process. Even so, it may be advantageous to have teachers complete a self-assessment on RTI to gauge their understanding. A sample Response to Intervention Self-Report Needs-Assessment for Teachers of Elementary Math is shown in table 1.4. (See pages 168–169 for a reproducible of this table. Visit **go.solution-tree.com/rti** for downloadable versions of all reproducibles found in this book.). A self-assessment survey such as this provides lead teachers, administrators, and RTI facilitators with a snapshot of exactly where educators in their building are in relation to RTI implementation in mathematics and reading.

> A self-assessment survey provides lead teachers, administrators, and RTI facilitators with a snapshot of exactly where educators in their building are in relation to RTI implementation in mathematics and reading.

Table 1.4: Response to Intervention Self-Report Needs-Assessment for Teachers of Elementary Math

Circle one numeral for each descriptive indicator.					
1 = I have little knowledge and want additional in-service on this. 2 = I have some knowledge, but some additional in-service will be helpful. 3 = I have a good understanding of this, but I need to put this into practice this year. 4 = I have complete understanding and have reached proficiency at this practice. N/A = Not applicable for our state, school, or school district					
General Understanding of RTI					
1. The pyramid of intervention in our state and district	1	2	3	4	N/A
2. The problem-solving model for our state or district	1	2	3	4	N/A
3. The tiers of intervention in our school	1	2	3	4	N/A
4. The intervention timelines for each intervention tier	1	2	3	4	N/A
5. How RTI applies to all students	1	2	3	4	N/A
6. RTI in mathematics	1	2	3	4	N/A
General Knowledge of Universal Screening and Progress-Monitoring Procedures					
1. The mathematics screening tests used in our school	1	2	3	4	N/A
2. The early mathematics standards	1	2	3	4	N/A
3. The individual mathematics assessments used in our school	1	2	3	4	N/A
4. Progress monitoring in mathematics during Tier 2 and Tier 3 interventions	1	2	3	4	N/A

continued on next page →

		1	2	3	4	N/A
5.	Data-gathering procedures (weekly or daily) for RTI	1	2	3	4	N/A
6.	The benchmark scores in mathematics across the grade levels	1	2	3	4	N/A
7.	The data-management system for RTI	1	2	3	4	N/A
Knowledge of Interventions to Facilitate Student Progress						
1.	The supplemental mathematics RTI programs used in our school	1	2	3	4	N/A
2.	Frequency and intensity of mathematics interventions	1	2	3	4	N/A
3.	How to use flexible grouping for Tiers 1, 2, and 3	1	2	3	4	N/A
4.	The technology-based mathematics programs used in our school	1	2	3	4	N/A
5.	How to use creative staffing to make time for interventions	1	2	3	4	N/A
My Contributions and Suggestions for RTI in Our School						
1.	In what RTI areas should we plan further staff development?					
2.	What suggestions can you offer for making RTI work better for students in our school?					

Source: Adapted from Bender, 2009a, pp. 13–14.

Implementation Issues

A number of concerns have surfaced as educators have started implementing RTI in reading and math; some of these concerns have become serious problems that need to be addressed during the implementation process (Bender, 2009a; Berkeley et al., 2009; Boyer, 2008; Spectrum K12 School Solutions/CASE, 2008). This section identifies the most pressing implementation concerns and provides guidance on how to deal with problems.

Protecting the General Education Teacher's Time

When general education teachers are introduced to the concept of RTI, their biggest concern is finding the time to do the necessary interventions (Bender, 2009a). Initially, the RTI intervention process was implemented for reading in Reading First schools across the United States (Bender, 2009a; Boyer, 2008). In those schools, the general education teacher was expected to implement Tier 1 instruction for all students, provide Tier 2 intervention in reading, *and* provide Tier 3 intervention for a limited number of students facing severe difficulty. Of course, this raised a critical question: what were the remaining members of the class doing when the general education teacher was conducting a Tier 2 intervention with four to six students, not to mention a Tier 3 intervention with one or two students with significant needs? Resources of some type had to be made available for those general education teachers to make the interventions possible, such as paraprofessional assistance and computer-based instructional interventions.

As RTI has been expanded to include areas such as mathematics, behavioral interventions, and writing, this issue of teacher time becomes even more critical. It is not realistic to think that general education teachers can make the time to do a wide variety of interventions in reading, mathematics, and other subject areas without the resources to assist them (Bender, 2009a). This section presents some options for allowing general education teachers the time they need for these interventions.

Co-Teachers for RTI Interventions

One option many districts have used to assist general education teachers is arranging for someone other than the teacher to do the Tier 3 intervention, and perhaps the Tier 2 intervention (Bender, 2009a). For example, in a co-teaching instructional model, a general education teacher and a special education teacher are teaching in the same classroom at the same time for a portion of the school day. This provides an opportunity for either of those teachers to conduct a Tier 2 intervention while the other teacher is instructing the remaining students in the class. This strategy has the added benefit of allowing special education teachers to become acquainted with struggling students, a few of whom may one day require special education services.

Other Professionals for RTI Interventions

Another option is redefinition of roles for current educators. Various schools have redefined the roles of instructional coaches, lead teachers, or even speech-language pathologists to allow those persons to conduct some of the required interventions. While it seems more common to modify the roles of these individuals and subsequently make them available for conducting the more intensive interventions in Tier 3, some districts may consider using these persons for Tier 2 interventions under certain conditions (Bender, 2009a). For example, when a speech-language pathologist is implementing a curriculum on language production, stressing letter/sound formation or articulation, that intervention might be very appropriate as an early reading intervention for some young children (Bender, 2009a).

Another option may soon exist that involves using certified personnel for RTI interventions. The 2008 report of the NMAP specifically recommends that certified mathematics teachers take over most mathematics instruction in all public school grades. While it is too early to tell if this recommendation will be implemented, doing so would provide another certified teacher who could greatly assist with not only Tier 1 instruction, but also with Tier 2 and Tier 3 interventions. Again, this is merely a recommendation at this point, but with a new presidential administration in office since January of 2009, implementation is a possibility.

Paraprofessionals for RTI Interventions or for Supporting the General Education Teacher

In some districts, paraprofessionals have been hired specifically to make RTI interventions possible (Bender, 2009a). Depending on the expertise of these paraprofessionals and the curriculum selected for the Tier 2 or Tier 3 interventions, the paraprofessional may either conduct the daily intervention activities under the supervision of the general education teacher (while that teacher conducts activities for other class members), or the paraprofessional can monitor classwide activities while the general education teacher works on Tier 2 intervention with a small group. This option holds some financial advantage, since paraprofessionals can be employed for a smaller salary than certified teachers or other certified personnel.

Technology for RTI Interventions

There are now many scientifically validated computer-based curricula in both reading and mathematics available that offer highly targeted, intensive instruction that would be quite appropriate for Tier 2 or Tier 3 interventions (Bender, 2009a, 2009b). Using a computer-based mathematics intervention, for example, a teacher could place a number of Tier 2 intervention students on different computers in the class while continuing to conduct activities for the other class members. Specific examples of these programs are included in chapters 2, 3, and 4 of this text.

Class Sharing

In some districts, none of the previously mentioned options may be feasible. Those schools should explore a simple class-sharing concept. In this arrangement, teachers with similar classes share the responsibility for Tier 2 and Tier 3 interventions (Bender, 2009a). For example, if two third-grade teachers in classrooms across the hall from each other each need to provide a Tier 2 mathematics intervention to five students, the teachers could share their classes such that one teacher leads a Tier 2 intervention for all ten students who need that level of intensive intervention, while the other teacher teaches the remaining class members from both classes (Bender,

2009a). This option has been employed in various districts in Texas with some success, and all of the students requiring Tier 2 intervention received it. Furthermore, this option involves no additional costs to the school district, although it may require some creative scheduling on the part of teachers and administrators.

An Intervention Class

Finally, many districts have devised various schedules that allow for offering Tier 2 and Tier 3 interventions during a separate intervention period (Bender, 2009a). While this is more common in middle and high schools, support intervention classes are also offered in some elementary schools as well. For example, semester-long intervention classes in some elementary schools allow students struggling with particular aspects of the mathematics curriculum to switch to an intervention class for a semester or two. In most cases, the intervention classes are somewhat smaller than the other general education classes, so students will be receiving more individual attention.

Availability of Appropriate Assessments and Curricula in Early-Level Mathematics

While assessment tools and supplemental intervention materials have long been available in both reading and math, the more recent research on early reading interventions has documented specific benchmarks within the kindergarten through grade 3 curriculum. In many ways, this body of research made RTI possible in early-level reading and literacy. For example, by the first month of kindergarten, prior to any formal training at all, students who can accurately detect phoneme similarities can be identified, and they are likely to progress normally in their reading skills. However, students who cannot hear those differences or similarities in sound have much more difficulty in the next set of early literacy skills, the association of sounds and specific letters. In short, that benchmark—recognition of initial consonant sounds—will identify students who need a more intensive supplemental reading program. If students hit such benchmarks throughout the early grades, they will progress normally in reading; whereas if they do not, long-term reading progress is much less likely (Bender & Shores, 2007).

The research on early mathematics literacy is not as advanced as it is in reading. For example, research on benchmarks in early mathematics for preK and kindergarten students is limited. In fact, educators have differing perspectives on the most basic terminology in this area of early mathematics. For example, to many psychoneurologists, the term *number sense* means exclusively the most basic numeration skills (the brain's recognition of the numbers 1, 2, or 3, for instance), whereas many teachers identify number sense as a higher-level skill, even in the context of determining the relative size of improper fractions (Bender, 2009b; Sousa, 2008). In that sense, it is accurate to say that educators do not really agree on what early mathematics skills are, and thus they do not agree what curricula should include for the youngest students.

This lack of agreement on what constitutes appropriate number-sense curriculum is not an issue beyond the beginning of school. As discussed previously, the NCTM (2006) specified appropriate curricular content from the beginning of kindergarten through grade 8; however, that organization did not present a blueprint of the types of mathematics readiness skills that a child entering kindergarten should have previously mastered, so benchmarking mathematics readiness in the early months of kindergarten, as we are currently doing in reading, remains highly problematic. Chapter 3 focuses on implementation of RTI procedures in mathematics during the early school years and addresses this issue on early mathematics readiness assessment and curricula in more depth.

Each of these issues presents some concern when conceptualizing how the RTI process might be implemented in mathematics. While educators have dealt with these issues successfully in the elementary grades, lingering questions about early mathematics assessment may hamper RTI efforts at the very early elementary level (Bender, 2009b). While there are a very limited amount of number sense and early mathematics skills assessments available, none have yet to receive wide acceptance (Bender, 2009a).

Conclusion

This chapter presented the basics of the RTI process in mathematics within the context of the three-tier RTI pyramid along with a synopsis of research supporting RTI in both mathematics and reading. We presented material to assist school leaders in their advocacy for RTI procedures, as well as identified issues of concern for educators to consider as they implement the RTI process in mathematics.

The foundation of the RTI process in mathematics is the quality of mathematics instruction in the general education classroom. The next chapter focuses on Tier 1 instruction specifically. Subsequent chapters will focus on interventions at the Tier 2 and Tier 3 levels in various areas of primary and elementary mathematics. Finally, chapter 6 presents an array of guidelines for schoolwide planning for implementation of RTI in mathematics.

Tier 1 Mathematics Instruction: A Critical Component of RTI

In the most commonly adopted RTI models, Tier 1 instruction is provided in the general education environment across all grade levels, and this instruction is, for the most part, delivered in a self-contained classroom setting (Buffum et al., 2009; Fuchs & Fuchs, 2005, 2006). While some educators use the term *intervention* to describe the first level of the RTI pyramid, we find that it is more accurate and less confusing to describe it as Tier 1 *instruction*, since it does not involve small-group or individual intervention. Rather, Tier 1 instruction typically involves high-quality whole-group instruction, universal screening, and classroom assessments, coupled with some small-group instruction, differentiated instruction, and limited individual assistance in mathematics as needed (Bender, 2009a). Thus, the general education teacher has a number of diverse responsibilities for Tier 1 instruction—the first, and arguably the most critical, component of RTI.

While the tiered instructional models used most frequently in reading and literacy rely on instructional teams collaborating to deliver data-driven instruction—teams including, for example, reading coaches, a reading specialist, general educators, and special educators—this is somewhat less likely in mathematics (Bender, 2009a). Of course, some districts have begun to employ certified mathematics coaches and specialists similar to reading coaches, but it is reasonable to assume that such support might be less likely to be available in mathematics, given the United States' priority on reading. In the current RTI models, elementary general education teachers will be expected to do the majority of mathematics Tier 1 work alone.

As noted in chapter 1, Tier 1 instruction is the basis for all subsequent success in mathematics, so the necessity for high-quality, research-based instruction at this level is undeniable. Simply stated, Tier 1 instruction is the first mathematics intervention students receive, and thus, it is a critical concern for RTI implementation in mathematics.

Challenges to Effective Tier 1 Mathematics Instruction

While reading instruction has long been a national priority, mathematics instruction has only recently received comparable attention. Consequently, a number of factors have been identified that may have hampered our efforts in supporting students' mathematical achievement up to this point.

The Need for Improved Teacher Training

One critical aspect of designing high-quality Tier 1 mathematics instruction is empowering general educators with knowledge and expertise in mathematics. Teachers need high-quality professional development to obtain this expertise. Slavin and Lake (2007) reviewed research on a variety of programs for improving student achievement in mathematics. Their findings can be categorized into various broad strategies for improving student mathematics achievement, including changing the curriculum, supplementing the curriculum with computer-assisted instruction, and modifying classroom practices. The most striking conclusion from the review was the evidence that supported changing classroom instructional practices to align with best practices within the field (Slavin & Lake, 2007), a goal that highlights the need for ongoing, high-quality professional development for teachers. Additionally, a cooperative report from the Colorado, Iowa, and Nebraska Departments of Education (1996) identified several priorities in professional development if teachers are to improve their mathematics instruction. Specifically, the report identified the need to increase teachers' level of knowledge of mathematical content as well as their ability to integrate critical thinking into instructional activities in mathematics. To support quality Tier 1 mathematics instruction, all stakeholders, from school districts to teacher preparation programs in higher education, will need to invest in quality professional development opportunities to increase teacher effectiveness in mathematics instruction.

As we discussed in chapter 1, the NMAP's report (2008) recommends that research be conducted on the use of full-time elementary mathematics teachers who would teach mathematics to several general education classes, and it is too early to tell if this recommendation will be realized. While middle schools and high schools have traditionally used teachers certified in mathematics, use of teachers certified in mathematics to conduct all mathematics instruction in primary and elementary schools would represent a significant change in the delivery of mathematics instruction. Implementation of this recommendation might be more efficient than providing the necessary training to increase all elementary teachers' mathematical knowledge and comfort level to optimize student achievement. However, research would have to be conducted to protect students from any potentially adverse effects of an overly departmentalized approach for our youngest students.

Should schools begin to employ teachers in the primary and elementary grades to teach mathematics exclusively, then those teachers, rather than the general education teacher, would be responsible for Tier 1 mathematics instruction. Until then, however, general education teachers will have these responsibilities, and research suggests that many of these teachers require more extensive professional development support than they have been given in the past.

The Need for Improved Instructional Materials

Instructional materials may also prove problematic in our RTI efforts in mathematics, and this may best be discussed in terms of explicit instruction versus inquiry-based instruction. The NMAP's report (2008) addressed this issue. Specifically, some school curricula have interchanged explicit, standards-based mathematics instruction with discovery learning, or inquiry-based mathematics instruction. While inquiry-based mathematics activities are beneficial as one aspect of standards-based learning (NMAP, 2008), and are supported by research related to constructivist learning theories, some textbooks and core curricula in mathematics may have moved to an overreliance on inquiry-based activities. Instructional materials that exclude explicit instruction may contribute to the neglect of important aspects of mathematical skill development, and in that sense, some modern mathematics curricula may in fact become a barrier to effective mathematics instruction. The NMAP report (2008) states the goal of integrating both teacher-directed explicit instruction and inquiry-based, student-centered learning activities, specifically because research does not support the use of one of these instructional strategies to the exclusion of the other. Well-designed direct instruction that engages students and is integrated with inquiry-based, student-centered learning activities that provide adequate opportunity for students to internalize and develop ownership of mathematical concepts is mutually beneficial.

This ongoing debate between direct instruction in mathematics and inquiry-based approaches has left many teachers feeling somewhat frustrated with mathematics instruction in general. One thirty-year veteran of the classroom summarized the sentiment of many teachers relative to the inquiry-based approach: "We need to be careful not to do to mathematics what we did to reading with whole language" (J. Parker, personal communication, September 15, 2008). Reviews from the national What Works Clearinghouse (2007) support this teacher's sentiments: current mathematics curricula are generally insufficient in engaging practice activities to support student acquisition of mathematical skills in many areas. In fact, upon reviewing the research associated with over seventy mathematics curricula, the What Works Clearinghouse found only one curriculum that had an adequate research support overall—the *Everyday Mathematics* curriculum by Wright Group/McGraw-Hill.

Many teachers and teacher preparation programs have recognized that in order to develop more rigorous and engaging mathematics learning experiences, instruction needs to shift from an overdependence on pencil-and-paper, drill-and-practice instruction to the integration of direct instruction with student-directed discovery learning techniques that are supported by constructivist theories. In fact, constructivist instructional procedures have been shown to be effective in developing deep understanding of mathematical content (see Bender, 2009b, for a review of constructivist theory in mathematics). The goal of developing deep conceptual understanding seems to necessitate this integration (NMAP, 2008). Still, few curricula do this effectively, and this causes concern when one considers the need for high-quality Tier 1 instruction in mathematics.

> Instruction needs to shift from an overdependence on pencil-and-paper, drill-and-practice instruction to the integration of direct instruction with student-directed discovery learning techniques.

The remainder of this chapter discusses the Tier 1 responsibilities of general education teachers in mathematics. We begin with a brief discussion of the need for universal screening and benchmarking in mathematics. We then present several published universal screening instruments that schools and districts can use to identify students in need of intervention, as well as for progress monitoring during subsequent Tier 2 and Tier 3 interventions. Next, we outline several instructional approaches—differentiated instruction and scaffolded instruction—as the basis for effective mathematics instruction in the general education class (Bender, 2009b). We then identify a variety of instructional tactics to help educators link instructional activities with research-based strategies to assist them in providing quality Tier 1 instruction for students in the general education mathematics program.

Universal Screening in Tier 1 Mathematics

As we mentioned in chapter 1, a critical aspect of RTI involves screening all students in certain subject areas, a process referred to as *universal screening*. Universal screening in mathematics will probably be the responsibility of general education teachers (Fuchs & Fuchs, 2007; Fuchs, Fuchs, Compton, et al., 2007); this chapter presents information on how to accomplish this universal screening. First, we must note that universal screening assessment in mathematics is already ongoing in most states. For example, in many state testing programs, all students at various grade levels receive a screening assessment that includes an assessment of mathematics, and data from those universal screening instruments can assist in targeting students who are struggling in mathematics in the primary and elementary grades (Bender, 2009a). While state screening assessments typically do not assist in identifying highly specific strengths and weaknesses for individual students, these assessments can identify students who are experiencing overall difficulties in mathematics. In many cases, students who fall below a certain percentile in mathematics (for example, 20 or 25 percent) may be given additional assessments to identify skill deficits and then given the necessary instructional support within the tiered structure. While this approach works well after a student has received some mathematics instruction, it may not work well during the earliest months of kindergarten. An example from the area of reading illustrates this concern.

Research on reading readiness has progressed to a point where we now recognize the literacy skills that students typically master prior to entering kindergarten, and we can use these benchmarks to identify students who are not ready for early reading instruction (Bender, 2009a). Knowing that a child has a demonstrated need in the first or second month of kindergarten for additional supplemental work on various reading tasks empowers teachers to focus their instructional efforts for those struggling students on their exact weaknesses. Thus, universal screening in reading and literacy is now taking place across the United States, beginning during the first weeks of kindergarten (Bender, 2009a). This task is facilitated by an array of reading/literacy screening instruments that evaluate phonological awareness and phonemic skills even prior to formal reading instruction in kindergarten.

The proponents of RTI advocate this same type of early universal screening in mathematics (Fuchs, Fuchs, Compton, et al., 2007; Griffin, 1998; Hughes & Dexter, 2006), and many U.S. school districts have begun implementation of RTI in mathematics based on statewide assessment scores. Thus, universal screening is already underway in mathematics, though much of the current screening efforts using state assessment tools involve screening only once per year.

However, universal screening in mathematics is problematic if a teacher wishes to assess students who have just begun the kindergarten school year, or if a teacher wishes to conduct universal screening three times per year or more. For example, what skills in mathematics should a child develop prior to entry into school, and can a universal screening during the early months of kindergarten detect weaknesses in those skills? The issue concerning what skills comprise early learning in mathematics is discussed in more detail in chapter 3, but in the context of this discussion of Tier 1 instruction in mathematics, we must note that general education teachers will be expected to conduct universal screening in mathematics, even in kindergarten, and while they can use statewide assessment to some degree, finding an appropriate universal screening device for early kindergarten is more problematic.

One goal of the universal screening process is identification of students who need more intensive intervention in mathematics, and there is a question as to how to evaluate data from the universal screening process to make that determination (Hughes & Dexter, 2006). For example, some states use percentage scores to determine if a student should receive a Tier 2 intervention based on a universal screening assessment. This might take the form of a principal stating, "All students scoring below the 20th percentile on assessment X must receive a supplementary mathematics intervention at the Tier 2 level."

In this case, students who received a score of 20 percent or below on the universal screening assessment would receive Tier 2 mathematics intervention. Other states might use comparisons of a student's performance with selected and highly specific behavioral criteria, which may be mandated in the state or district curricular standards. An example here would be the mandate that "at the end of second grade, all students should be able to add and subtract whole numbers using regrouping where necessary."

Using that standard, students who could not perform that operation (and presumably others that might also be identified) would receive Tier 2 intervention. At present, procedures on determining when a child needs Tier 2 intervention in mathematics range dramatically from state to state (Hughes & Dexter, 2006), and educators should check with their own states and districts to determine what guidelines may be in place for using universal screening data. However, if these curricular "cut off" guidelines have not been established at the state or district levels, school leadership teams or professional learning communities dedicated to RTI implementation should determine such screening guidelines that would allow schools to effectively decide when they should implement Tier 2 intervention.

Test of Early Mathematics Ability

One assessment that is currently available for early mathematics universal screening assessment is the *Test of Early Mathematics Ability* or *TEMA-3* (Ginsburg & Baroody, 2003). This assessment is normed for children ages 2 through 8. It is one of the only assessments available for use with children of such a young age. The *TEMA-3* assesses students on both school-based mathematics skills (such as reading and writing numbers), as well as intuitive mathematics and related early mathematics concepts such as counting, quantity, and magnitude judgments. Some research has reported high reliability for this instrument (Murphy, Mazzocco, Hanich, & Early, 2007), and, given the impending implementation of RTI in mathematics, this assessment will probably become more widely used for universal screening in the immediate future.

Even with state assessments used for year-to-year screening and other universal screening instruments such as the *TEMA-3,* many teachers in the elementary grades will probably have to rely on assessments included in the core mathematics curriculum. Many publishers are developing assessment tools to support the RTI model as part of their curriculum adoption packages. Therefore, it will be imperative for school districts to carefully scrutinize future textbook adoptions for application in their district's RTI model. School districts must also carefully scrutinize the research base from publishers for claims of effectiveness in regard to providing educators and students with quality mathematics instructional strategies and resources.

Benchmarking for Tier 1 Mathematics

In addition to universal screening, some assessments facilitate benchmarking students in mathematics. Sometimes referred to as *progress monitoring*, these frequent assessments are more common at the Tier 2 and Tier 3 levels in the RTI process, though such benchmarking may also be done at Tier 1. *Benchmarking* generally compares student performance to certain standards of performance. In most states, benchmarking assessments in early reading and early literacy are required at least three times per year, and we believe that three benchmark assessments per year is a reasonable approach in early mathematics as well.

> In most states, benchmarking assessments in early reading and early literacy are required at least three times per year, and we believe that three benchmark assessments per year is a reasonable approach in early mathematics as well.

AIMSweb

One early number assessment that may be used for benchmarking is available through AIMSweb®, a technology-based progress monitoring system that addresses mathematics and reading literacy (see www.AIMSweb.com.) The Test of Early Numeracy™ is one component of AIMSweb. It provides some indications of a child's early mathematics knowledge. This progress-monitoring tool assesses number sense by measuring a child's ability to perform a variety of mathematics skills, including counting orally, identifying numbers, identifying bigger numbers from a pair, and identifying missing numbers from a number line.

Number Knowledge Test

For districts that may not be able to afford a commercial benchmarking system such as AIMSweb, Sharon Griffin developed an informal assessment for early mathematics readiness, referred to as the Number Knowledge Test. This test was created as one component of her early mathematics readiness curriculum *Number Worlds* (1998). The Number Knowledge Test can be utilized as either a universal screening assessment or a benchmarking tool, since this informal assessment provides information on the mathematics readiness skills for children as young as three years old. This assessment is presented within levels of developmentally based mathematics skills—Level 0 through Level 3. Each level represents a cognitive development period roughly equivalent to a two-year age span from ages 3 or 4 up through age 10 (Level 0 = ages 3 to 5; Level 1 = ages 5/6 to 7; and so forth). Skills stressed on Level 0 of this assessment include the following items (Griffin, 1998; Sousa, 2008):

- Counting from one to ten (for example, place three counting chips before a child and ask, "Can you count these chips and tell me how many there are?")

- Counting various quantities of manipulatives; viewing two sets of counters for more-or-less comparisons (for example, show a stack of eight chips and a stack of three chips of the same color and ask, "Which pile has less?")

- Discriminating among manipulatives for counting activities (for example, show stacks of three red and four yellow chips organized by color—red, yellow, red, yellow, red, yellow, yellow—and ask, "Count just the yellow chips.")

Level 1 of this assessment, cognitively appropriate for ages 5 through 7, addresses items dealing with simple one-step word problems, questions concerning bigger/ smaller numbers, and simple math facts in addition and subtraction. However, no norms are available for this assessment—a problem that is generally characteristic of early number sense. Still, scoring instructions for the instrument are provided on the author's website (http://clarku.edu/numberworlds), as are recommendations for remedial instructional activities associated with various indicators on the assessment. This assessment can be used three times during a single academic year as a rough benchmark assessment from kindergarten through the primary grades. While the lack of published norms is a concern, we believe that this instrument can serve as a benchmarking tool for many kindergarten and primary classes, at least until appropriately normed benchmarking assessments become available. The assessment is not lengthy and is available free from the author's website.

EasyCBM

Curriculum-based measurement, which is often abbreviated as CBM, provides individual teachers with curriculum-based assessment options for RTI in mathematics, and teachers are generally familiar with CBM procedures. EasyCBM is a free progress-monitoring system that initially provided only reading assessments in kindergarten through grade 8, but now provides mathematics assessments as well. It was designed by researchers at the University of Oregon and is available from www .easycbm.com.

The system's assessment in mathematics is associated with the NCTM focal points (2006), which are described in chapter 1 (pages 10–11). The reading benchmarks available from this source allow teachers to benchmark students three times each year. Unfortunately, while mathematics CBMs are currently available from the website, the norms for those assessments and the benchmark indicators are not yet available. While this information will probably become available in the near future, this lack of adequate norms is representative of a common problem in mathematics benchmarking assessment. Still, teachers should become familiar with this system as it will prove to be quite useful in mathematics assessment for benchmarking.

Other Assessment Resources

Educators can anticipate that additional assessments for either universal screening or benchmarking will become available. For example, the publisher of the *Dynamic Indicators of Basic Early Literacy Skills (DIBELS)* by Good and Kaminski (2002), a frequently implemented assessment for universal screening in reading, has also developed a universal screening instrument for early mathematics.

Additional online resources can provide teachers with increased assistance for progress monitoring, and a variety of progress monitoring tools are demonstrated online. These include www.progressmonitoring.org, www.rti4success.org, and www.studentprogress.org/chart/chart.asp. Teachers concerned with monitoring student performance in mathematics should carefully review and monitor these resources so they can remain informed of mathematics assessments that become available.

A universal screening or benchmarking assessment process is only as effective as the screening instrument *and* teachers' interpretation of the data generated by that instrument. Teachers may benefit from forming a task force to investigate various screening instruments in mathematics, by comparing those assessments with their state standards on a grade-level by grade-level basis, by comparing the screening assessment tool and the focal points identified by the NCTM (2006) discussed in chapter 1, or by considering how their faculty might use data from the various instruments to plan effective interventions. More information on universal screening is provided in each of the case studies in subsequent chapters, and in almost every case, teams of educators work together on data interpretation from universal screening assessments.

> Teachers may benefit from forming a task force to investigate various screening instruments in mathematics.

High-Quality Instructional Approaches for Tier 1

In addition to universal screening and benchmarking assessments, Tier 1 also involves providing highly effective instruction in mathematics, and as we've discussed previously, Tier 1 instruction is critically important. This section provides some instructional suggestions for primary and elementary school teachers implementing RTI in mathematics as they consider the types of Tier 1 instruction their students require. While the variety of instructional options are almost endless, two instructional practices stand out: differentiated instruction and scaffolding. A brief description of each follows, with suggestions for ways these practices may facilitate the RTI process in primary and elementary mathematics.

Differentiated Instruction: Critical Teaching for Tier 1

In *differentiated instruction*, curricular content is presented via a variety of instructional activities that are consistent with current understandings of student learning styles and the emerging research on brain functioning in different learning environments (Bender, 2009b; Sousa, 2008). The methods that characterize a differentiated instructional model can be as varied as providing small-group instruction aimed at particular learning styles, creating focused short- or long-term group projects, or implementing cooperative learning strategies. Effective differentiation can provide an excellent opportunity for learning mathematics in the general education classroom, and it should be considered absolutely critical for Tier 1 instruction (Bender, 2009a). In fact, several state RTI models—Georgia, Texas, and West Virginia, to name a few—specifically stipulate differentiated instruction as one of the fundamental aspects of Tier 1 instructional interventions.

In her book *The Differentiated Classroom: Responding to the Needs of All Learners* (1999), Carol Ann Tomlinson describes differentiation as variations in the learning content, the learning process, and the learning products that are intended to accommodate the learning differences presented by both gifted and exceptional students in classrooms today. Differentiating by learning content requires careful consideration of the content students are expected to master. Differentiation in content should not result in a "watered down" curriculum for struggling students, but rather in variations in the specific mathematics content mastered by students at different stages, depending upon such things as ability level and previous mathematics experiences. The curriculum goals, broad conceptual understandings, and essential questions within the content should remain consistent for all students (Tomlinson & McTighe, 2006).

> Effective differentiation can provide an excellent opportunity for learning mathematics in the general education classroom, and it should be considered absolutely critical for Tier 1 instruction.

Differentiating by learning process acknowledges that students learn in a variety of ways, based on normally occurring learning styles that differ from child to child. For example, some children seem to learn most effectively when information is discussed and implemented in the context of small groups, and those students would seem to have an interpersonal learning style. Small-group instruction encourages social interaction, student questioning, and peer support, and it fosters understanding among students with an interpersonal learning style. Other learners acquire knowledge when it is presented in a movement-based context, and thus a bodily/kinesthetic instructional approach may be most effective for them. Still other students excel when content is represented graphically (the spatial learners), whereas others benefit from content presented musically (musical learners). In the differentiated classroom, teachers should plan mathematics activities that address a wide variety of learning styles and preference for every instructional unit; this is likely to increase students' content retention overall.

Teachers in kindergarten and the lower grades have typically used a wide array of instructional tactics, often including music, spatial displays, and movement to teach content. However, this type of instruction is more rare in the higher elementary grades, even though the recent research on brain functioning suggests that movement is a critically important learning tool for students of all ages (Sousa, 2005). An example of a movement coupled with a chant to teach components of a circle in an elementary mathematics class is presented in the following feature box. This type of activity is recommended for students with strengths in musical intelligence, bodily/kinesthetic intelligence, and spatial intelligence. As this example illustrates, differentiated instructional activities can benefit many students with differing strengths and intelligences.

Movement and Chanting to Teach Components of a Circle

This is both a movement-based and a rhythm-based tactic to teach terms associated with a circle—circumference, radius, and diameter (Bender, 2009b). First, teach the chant below using the rhythm for the song, "We Will Rock You." Chant the timing for the line, "We will, we will rock you!" one time for each of the following lines:

"This is circumference, all around the side."

"Next comes radius, middle to the side."

"Next is diameter, all the way through!"

"All of that's a circle, I'll show it to you."

After the class has learned the chant, ask students to do the chant while some members move through the components of a circle. Begin the movement by having students stand in three lines, with six to eight students in one line, three students in a second line, and five students in a third line. The first line of students (six to eight students) should move into a circle formation as soon as the chant begins, to represent the circumference of a circle. They should complete the formation of that circle during the first line of the chant.

The second line (three students) should begin to move into the center of the circle at the beginning of the second line of the chant to represent the radius. The first person in this line of students should be instructed to stop in the middle of the circle.

The third line (five students) should begin to move through the circle in a fashion perpendicular to the radius, and they should cross the circle entirely, representing the diameter. They should begin to move when the third line of the chant begins.

Differentiation by learning product allows variations in the products that indicate mastery of knowledge (Tomlinson & McTighe, 2006). Mathematics teachers have long realized that class projects allow students to demonstrate knowledge while challenging them with increased cognitive demands for application of mathematics concepts. Furthermore, a wide variety of assessments can also be used to illustrate a student's understanding of critical mathematics content. Some types of assessments provide richer opportunities for some students than for others. For example, students who learn best by moving through the mathematical concepts (bodily/kinesthetic learners) may be at a significant disadvantage when confronted with a written unit test. Those students should be given the opportunity to demonstrate their knowledge in ways other than pencil-and-paper tasks.

Most proponents of differentiated instruction recommend an array of assessment options that emphasize authentic learning experiences, such as rubric-based performance tasks, product demonstrations and explanations, and portfolio-based assessments (Bender, 2009b). The more choices, the more likely it becomes that all students can adequately demonstrate their knowledge of newly mastered concepts. Of course, many of these assessments fit easily within the RTI paradigm, though longer term assessments (such as portfolio-based assessment) might be somewhat more difficult to use in an RTI framework.

Differentiation, brain-compatible instruction, and the RTI process are, to a large degree, mutually supportive at the Tier 1 level. First, the RTI process is absolutely dependent on provision of effective instruction in mathematics at every tier in the pyramid. To emphasize the critical importance of effective mathematics instruction in Tier 1, many RTI models stipulate using a wide variety of instructional activities to address all the specific needs of students. Clearly, addressing the unique needs of individual learners and their learning styles is highly effective as a Tier 1 instructional model, and for that reason, teachers have begun to adopt this instructional approach in conjunction with the RTI process.

One last benefit of differentiation is that it alleviates many of the teacher time concerns with RTI implementation discussed in chapter 1. For example, in differentiated classes, it is a bit easier for a teacher to make time for the type of small-group instruction in mathematics that is required for Tier 2 intervention, since differentiated classes tend to feature small-group instruction very frequently anyway (Bender, 2009b). For example, if Ms. Smith is teaching word problems in her fourth-grade mathematics class within a differentiated framework, she might have one group of seven students working together on a class project that integrates science and math content, while another six students work individually on the computer creating math stories that reflect recently learned mathematical concepts. In that context, Ms. Smith would find it relatively easy to provide a Tier 2 mathematics intervention for eight other students in her class who are struggling in mathematics, since the differentiated nature of the class allows for different groups of students to be working on different activities at the same time. This would not be possible if all instruction in Ms. Smith's class was delivered in the more traditional whole-group fashion.

Scaffolding: Mathematics Success Through Targeted Support

The art of teaching requires an insightful balance between engaging students in activities that challenge them while not frustrating them with unmanageable tasks. Effective instructional activities should encourage and provide for success, but they should not be so easy as to result in boredom. Educators should strive to deliver instruction that balances the need for engaging challenge while preventing the frustration that may trigger students to shut down.

A key element in designing such instructional settings is *scaffolded instruction*—the provision of the exact level of cognitive support a student needs to master a mathematical task, and the systematic withdrawal of that support as the student masters the task. Mathematics theorists have long stated that the creation of mathematical knowledge requires that educators are actively forcing the rebuilding of cognitive structures to accommodate new information. For example, Asiala et al. (1996) state that learning mathematics content requires cognitive structures to adapt to disturbances from novel situations and reflective abstraction to construct new mathematical knowledge. The challenge for educators is to utilize professional knowledge to present such "disturbances" in a controlled fashion, while providing each student with instructional assistance and addressing the learning differences among students.

Scaffolding is one instructional approach that facilitates that learning process. While research on scaffolding has generally emphasized reading and literacy activities, application of this instructional strategy in mathematics has also been recommended (Rosenshine & Meister, 1991). Scaffolding is, in this sense, an essential element of effective data-driven instruction for the general education mathematics classroom. It allows teachers to accommodate individual student learning needs and provide exceptional students access to grade-level content.

> Scaffolded instruction is an essential element of effective data-driven instruction for the general education mathematics classroom.

Vygotsky (1978) contributed to the theoretical development of scaffolding instruction through his development of the concept of the *zone of proximal development*, which generally refers to the range of skills a child can comfortably perform while being supported to increase those skills. In explaining this concept, Fournier and Graves (2002) provide the analogy of training wheels. As a child learns to ride a two-wheeled bike, the training wheels provide enough support to prevent frustration or injury and are adjusted to challenge the child's zone of proximal development. As the child becomes more independent with the skill of riding the bike, the training wheels continue to be raised to provide less support by touching the ground less frequently. They are finally removed altogether. Through the scaffolded learning process in the classroom, the responsibility of the task moves increasingly from the teacher to the student until the student is functioning independently in the mathematical task at hand.

When using scaffolded instruction to teach a particular mathematics concept, teachers must be thoroughly familiar with both the mathematics skills required and the skills specific students possess. Scaffolding begins by identifying essential prerequisite skills a student has mastered and then identifying his or her individual learning style. Task analysis can help educators identify these essential prerequisite skills as they apply to an overall skill.

For example, in order for a student to learn rounding to the nearest hundred, what prerequisite skills must the student master? Will the student need to be able to count? How far does he or she need to be able to count? Will the student need to be able to identify or understand place value? What elements of number sense are needed? Several purposes are served as the teacher analyzes the foundational skills necessary for acquisition of this new skill. First, this depth of knowledge facilitates the teacher's delivery of explicit instruction on the skill to be mastered—in this case, rounding numbers. In addition, the process helps identify what structures or supports the teacher can put in place that will allow the student access to grade-level content. If a particular student has some difficulty understanding place value, he or she can be given a visual graphic as a reference on that concept during rounding numbers activities. If another student struggles with counting or with number sense, a color-coded number chart could be the scaffold that supports his or her learning. A student who benefits from kinesthetic or tactile approaches could utilize small manipulatives that might be placed on a number chart to identify the nearest hundred. All of these strategies are examples of scaffolded instruction.

Quantile scores measure how well a student understands concepts across the scope of mathematics skills. Quantiles indicate areas in which some students may need additional support to be ready to approach the new task.

One resource to assist teachers in their identification of prerequisite skills and knowledge is the concept of quantile scores. *Quantile scores* are measurements of a student's mathematical skill within a global taxonomy of mathematics skills, concepts, and applications. These quantile scores measure how well a student understands concepts across the scope of mathematics skills. Quantiles indicate areas in which some students may need additional support to be ready to approach the new task.

Many state assessments link student scores to quantile scores to provide teachers with data that can help guide instruction overall. Textbook publishers also link materials to quantiles so that educators can utilize student quantile scores to identify prerequisite skills that students have not previously mastered. Many districts now opt to formally train staff members on the use of quantiles. The Quantile® (www .quantiles.com) website offers free resources to educators and parents and identifies partner companies that have developed mathematics materials, including assessments reflecting quantile scores, that can be used throughout the RTI process.

There are several other benefits of scaffolded instruction. First, the process of moving the responsibility of learning from the teacher to the learner aligns completely with recommendations of the NMAP (2008). Next, scaffolding enhances student self-esteem as the learner takes increasing levels of ownership of the skills (NMAP, 2008). Scaffolding also contributes to students applying mathematics skills beyond traditional rote learning practices to solve new problems. Scaffolded learning experiences increase the application of higher-order thinking skills, as recommended by the NMAP (2008). Table 2.1 presents guidelines for implementing scaffolded instruction in elementary mathematics.

Table 2.1: Guidelines for Scaffolding Mathematics Instruction in Elementary Mathematics

1.	Use pre-engagement by identifying prerequisite skills that are necessary for student understanding of the skill to be introduced.
2.	Use informal assessments (for example, pretests, observation, and concrete objects) to ascertain student levels of functioning.
3.	Consider student learning preference (visual, auditory, kinesthetic, and so on), and link support materials to these preferences. For example, if a student is highly responsive to kinesthetic opportunities, provide concrete models of concepts and allow the use of manipulatives until the student has transitioned to conceptual understanding.
4.	Design and implement preteaching opportunities to build students' confidence.
5.	Identify and set a common goal; establish *with* students the goal or outcome. One tool to use is the Test Talk strategy. During Test Talk, teachers and students, either in small groups or individually, meet to discuss what skills students mastered on recent assessments and what skills need additional practice. Teachers guide this conversation to help students set learning goals.
6.	Monitor student understanding throughout the instruction. Ask students to restate concepts, prompt them with the first half of the answer, provide them with opportunities to model the concept, and provide them with immediate error correction.
7.	Provide explicit feedback that identifies student behaviors necessary for successful ownership of a skill. For example, as students practice using manipulatives to conceptualize counting on as an addition strategy, a teacher's comment might be, "I like how you touched each block as you counted." Then, to scaffold application of the skill, the teacher should model saying the larger number and counting on by touching each additional block that represents the addition problem being solved.

continued on next page →

8.	Chunk practice activities to provide more consistent reinforcement.
9.	Provide mathematics aides (such as calculators, tables, and color coding) to focus student attention. Support student development of automaticity through supplemental activities.
10.	Provide a classroom environment that fosters risk taking. As teachers remove scaffolded supports, students must feel comfortable taking the risks associated with independent application of the mathematics skill (not to mention a willingness to try new approaches). For example, make comments such as, "Something exciting just happened! Sara used tally marks instead of the blocks to help her add two-digit numbers!" Teachers should also use mistakes to clarify mathematical thinking and encourage risk taking by celebrating students' willingness to take risk.

As educators seek ways to enhance Tier 1 mathematics instruction in general education, approaches such as differentiated instruction and scaffolded instruction will become more critical. Every teacher in the primary and elementary grades should develop his or her understanding and application of these instructional approaches for mathematics.

Ten Explicit Tactics for Tier 1 Instruction

In addition to the broader instructional strategies of differentiated and scaffolded instruction, the NMAP (2008) emphasizes implementation of explicit instructional tactics in mathematics that foster high levels of student engagement with the mathematics content. There are an almost infinite number of instructional tactics that can be implemented to facilitate mathematics instruction at the Tier 1 level, and teachers are already quite familiar with many of them. With that noted, the following section describes several relatively new ideas to expand teachers' repertoire.

Bell Ringers

For many years, educators have recognized the importance of introducing lessons and activities in a way that hooks students' attention. Teachers who bring meaning to mathematics during the introduction of a lesson move the learning beyond passive discussion of a skill to active exploration of real-world application; this engages students with the content much more powerfully. "Bell ringer" activities are used extensively in different content areas to facilitate this shift to active learning. Bell ringers are introductory activities designed to immediately engage students in brief tasks that review previously learned concepts and preview new conceptual ideas in mathematics. These bell ringers elicit high levels of student involvement with the task and strengthen Tier 1 mathematics instruction by linking concepts to real-world learning and assessments.

Because of the emphasis on goal setting in recent years, many teachers have been prompted to post the instructional goals or objectives for each class daily, and this can, on occasion, engage students' attention. But while this practice can also be a useful forerunner to assessment activities, the act of posting daily goals does little overall to actively engage students in the learning process. Of more significance to student learning is the posing of mathematics stories, mathematics riddles, mathematics challenges, or problem-based learning scenarios that are modern, interesting, and relevant to the students, as indicated in the following example:

You have a $20.00 music download card! How many songs can you download if each one costs $1.49? How much money would be left on your card?

Doesn't almost every student today download music from one source or another?

Of course, instructors must create these bell-ringer introductions in a manner that is reflective of their students' background knowledge and interests. Differentiated instructional approaches that reflect individual learning styles should also be embedded within the bell-ringer scenarios.

For example, to begin an instructional unit on rounding to the nearest ten, small groups of students could be confronted with word problems requiring the addition of five to ten two-digit numbers. The story content could vary from group to group to include story elements such as soccer scores, age of grandparents, number of members in a marching band, or number of raisins in snack bags. For some students, the conceptual understanding of the story will be sufficient, while other students may benefit from manipulatives (such as counters to represent the members of the marching band), and still others may be best served by a concrete, real-world example (such as raisins in snack bags). In general, abstract representations such as pictorial representations and generic manipulatives require more complex understanding of concepts than do concrete examples. Educators can use that knowledge to engage students at a variety of skill levels and embed scaffolding and differentiated instruction even at the earliest points in the introduction of lessons.

To introduce the concept of rounding numbers to the nearest ten, a teacher might present the mathematics challenge of adding groups of numbers in a very short amount of time. As students discover the impossibility of the task, the teacher prompts them to brainstorm what strategies they could use to complete the task; as the last step, the teacher provides explicit modeling. Another possible introduction to the same concept could use a story that centers on adding the cost of items less than ninety-five cents.

The Fishbowl

Another simple strategy for engaging students is the "fishbowl" in which students are taught to join the teacher on a small carpeted area of the floor in a circular formation. The fishbowl analogy refers to the ability to see in from all sides (as one can in a fishbowl), and represents the arrangement of students on the carpet so that students can view the modeled mathematics activity from all sides and angles. Initially, when using the fishbowl, the teacher should explain the comparison between a fishbowl and the circular arrangement. This idea is especially powerful in the lower elementary grades if a real glass fishbowl is brought to the classroom the first time this strategy is used. If a real fishbowl is not available, a quick online search produces many real-life video and animated examples. As students become familiar with the fishbowl concept, the teacher continues to emphasize that students can investigate the mathematics concept "from all sides." In the center of the fishbowl, the teacher then presents a model of the new instructional content to be mastered. If the content lends itself to manipulatives or other types of hands-on examples, materials should be available to the teacher seated in the circle for those demonstration activities.

After initial introduction of the fishbowl concept, it becomes a quick routine for students to use; they will soon learn to physically arrange themselves to be able to view the introductory lessons. Teachers can select some students to sit in the fishbowl to help model and practice the new activity as others watch. After initially introducing the activity, the teacher can embed a scaffolding component by moving outside the fishbowl and helping students repeat the targeted activity with guidance and support from other members of the class.

> As students become familiar with the fishbowl concept, the teacher continues to emphasize that students can investigate the mathematics concept "from all sides." In the center of the fishbowl, the teacher then presents a model of the new instructional content to be mastered.

Teachers should choose students for inside the fishbowl carefully. Some students may have particular strengths in verbalizing their thoughts and choices as they model a game or activity. Other students may need the opportunity to practice in a supportive environment with verbal or visual prompts prior to doing an activity in front of other class members.

Mini-Fishbowls

The fishbowl strategy can easily be adapted to mini-fishbowls to differentiate the activity for students. After the introduction and modeling of the new skill or activity, many students may be ready to work with small groups of peers to continue practice of the newly acquired skill. However, a small group of students may continue to need a more supportive experience in order to be able to participate in the activity. To differentiate for these students, a teacher may consider a few options depending on class make up and capacity. During small-group practice, the teacher may select a mini-fishbowl group to continue the supportive engagement in the task on the carpeted area, while other students initiate more independent work on the concept at their seats. The teacher could then work with this smaller group to provide embedded scaffolding and differentiation based on student needs, making this mini-fishbowl an important opportunity to increase student understanding. In the mini-fishbowl, teachers also have increased opportunity to monitor student understanding through further discussion of the concept and increased student involvement.

"I Can" Statements

Student engagement with the mathematics curriculum is critical for learning, and using "I can" statements fosters increased engagement. Having students practice the use of "I can" statements encourages them to undertake some formative assessment of their own abilities and skills. Rick Stiggins (2007) has convincingly identified periodic formative assessment—assessment *for* learning—as a critical component of instruction.

Historically in education, we have relied heavily on the value of *summative assessments*—the performance assessments on which students demonstrate the level of knowledge they have acquired from classroom instruction. Summative assessments include the high-stakes testing that the majority of districts use to judge, at least to some degree, the effectiveness of schools and, hence, educators. Stiggins (2007) explains that engaging students in the process of assessing their own learning holds tremendous value for increasing student progress and acquisition of skills. Thus, *formative assessment*—assessments that allow students and teachers to periodically take stock of student skills and to formulate learning activities for mastering the next skills—is critically important in learning overall.

> Having students practice the use of "I can" statements encourages them to undertake some formative assessment of their own abilities and skills.

One element of such formative assessment for learning is the use of student-friendly language related to the concept or instructional goal being introduced. The creation of "I can" statements links the skill focus to the student's sense of empowerment and can be quite effective for helping students identify the relationships between skills to be mastered. For example, when introducing a mathematical skill such as graphing the results of a survey, the teacher would model the following statement:

> *For this lesson, our "I can" statement will say, "I can graph what we learned from the survey." This means I can draw a graph that shows our data so that someone else will understand it.*

At that point, the teacher would then model the "I can" statement and the task, using explicit direct instruction, to demonstrate the skill of graphing of data.

"I can" statements facilitate motivation, and creative teachers can explore various uses of these statements. One example is the creation of an "I can" wall. "I can add two-digit numbers," "I can measure the length of items with centimeters," and "I can add fractions with like denominators" are examples of sentences that could be posted on the "I can" wall. Students who demonstrate mastery of the skill can get further reinforcement from the entire class by being encouraged to autograph their "I can" statements. Thus, the wall will foster extensive peer support for learning new skills. Table 2.2 presents additional ideas that build from the "I can" statements. All of these ideas can foster student self-examination of their skill development, as well as highly positive peer support for learning mathematics. (See page 170 for a reproducible of this table. Visit **go.solution-tree.com/rti** for downloadable versions of all reproducibles found in this book.)

Table 2.2: Ideas for Using "I Can" Statements

The "I Can" Wall	Post a series of "I can" statements on a bulletin board, and allow students to autograph below the statements once they demonstrate that particular skill.
Peer Reinforcement for "I Can" Statements	Some teachers have a class celebration each time a student demonstrates a skill. The celebration can range from mere applause to a pizza party any time a student accomplishes a particular skill and documents it with an "I can" statement.
"I Can" PowerPoint Presentations	Teachers may encourage students to work either individually or as a team to develop a PowerPoint presentation. The PowerPoint may begin with explicit instructions on how to do a task and should culminate with the "I can" statement.
"I Can" Video	Again, this is a celebration opportunity for students once they accomplish their goal. Students can be videotaped demonstrating use of the mastered skill. The class should watch videos together to celebrate with the student his or her newly learned skill. An additional option is to post the video on a safe site that would allow families to access the learning celebrations.
"I Can" Teams	For certain skills, teachers may have students work in teams to foster differentiation and encourage students to support each other in development of the skill. They should work on the skill until each team member can say, "I can!"
"I Can" T-Shirts	Celebration for accomplishing particularly difficult skills should involve more reinforcement. Some teachers have actually printed "I can" t-shirts as rewards for the class accomplishing difficult mathematics objectives.

Mathematics Journals

Encouraging students to summarize their understanding in a mathematics journal can be a very effective strategy, in particular for students with strength in intrapersonal intelligence, because it involves deep self-reflection. The mathematics journal has several potential uses. First, the NMAP (2008) identifies the ability to express mathematics concepts as one important goal of mathematics acquisition, and journaling daily or several times per week about new mathematics concepts can build student understanding. Second, a student's ability to articulate mathematics knowledge is directly linked to his or her ownership of vocabulary related to the concepts. Hence, rich, explicit vocabulary development should be integrated throughout mathematics instruction, and journaling activities will foster the use of such vocabulary.

Mathematics journals are effective tools to use in the introduction of skills, the promotion of vocabulary acquisition, the link between school and home, the generalization of mathematics skills, and student engagement in the assessment process. Teachers can utilize these math writing opportunities to monitor student learning. What skills or concepts does the student demonstrate? Does the student draw connections to other skills or real-life applications? Does the student have a literal, basic level of understanding, or has the student deepened his or her understanding to an application level? A teacher's comments can validate student work or challenge a student to think more deeply about the mathematics.

Figure 2.1 shows sample entries in a mathematics journal. Note that in these examples, the teacher provides an initial question to facilitate student reflection. One differentiated instructional strategy is to use such preliminary questions only for selected students who need those supports, and not provide such questions for students with higher levels of linguistic skill.

Math Journal for Grade 4 Preassessment

I can compare fractions with unlike denominators. This means . . .

> I can tell which is bigger.

I already know . . .

> Fractions are equal parts and that the denominator is the number on the bottom. It tells how many pieces in all.

I need to know this so . . .

> I can tell if I order a pizza and they don't give me enough.

Math Journal for Grade 4 Formative Assessment

I can compare fractions with unlike denominators. This means . . .

> I can draw a picture of the fractional parts and see which fraction is the biggest and smallest part of the whole. I look to see which one covers the most area.

Figure 2.1: Sample mathematics journal entries.

continued on next page →

I know now . . .

That when the denominators are different, each of the wholes was cut into different numbers of equal parts. I discovered that bigger denominators mean the pieces are smaller!

I need to know this because . . .

If I have to pick $\frac{4}{6}$ or $\frac{4}{8}$ of a pizza to take home, I want to know which is more! Also, I saw in a Christmas ad some things were on sale for $\frac{1}{2}$ off, and some things were $\frac{1}{3}$ off. I will need to know which is more so I can save money!

Teacher's Summary of Student Learning:

Mark, your writing shows that you understand the unlike denominators, and you can use what you know about the denominators in different ways. I'm glad you'll be able to save money when you shop!

Math Journal for Grade 5 Preassessment

I will be able to solve multidigit whole-number division problems using different strategies and be able to explain my answer. This means . . .

I will be able to divide large numbers and tell someone how I got the answer.

Some math skills I have that will help me with this problem are . . .

I can multiply, I know my multiplication tables, and I can already divide smaller numbers.

I need to be able to divide multidigit numbers . . .

So I can put things into groups and share equally with my friends, and so I'll know how many things are left over.

Math Journal for Grade 5 Formative Assessment

I will be able to solve multidigit whole-number division problems using different strategies and be able to explain my answer. This means . . .

I am able to estimate an answer and use the division algorithm to find my final answer. I multiply my estimate by the divisor and subtract the answer from the dividend. If the number left is bigger than the dividend, I have to try a bigger number.

Some math skills I have that will help me with this problem are . . .

I can multiply, I know my multiplication tables, and I can already divide smaller numbers. Also, I can round numbers to the nearest ten and hundred, and I can estimate answers to multiplication problems. I can also use a calculator to check my thinking. We worked on this kind of problem in class this week, and today, I got all eight problems correct!

I need to be able to divide multidigit numbers . . .

So I can figure out how much money I will have left if I buy more than one of something—like when I wanted to buy four games. Each one cost $17.95, and I had $45.00. My Mom made me use my math to find out how many I could buy, and she wouldn't let me use the calculator until I estimated the answer!

Teacher's Summary of Student Learning:

Marshall, you thought about how to use the math you've already learned to solve this problem and broke the problem into smaller steps. By estimating, you can think about whether or not your answer makes sense. Would it make sense to estimate that you could buy ten games with your $45.00?

Mathematics journals can also be used as a preassessment tool for teachers and students through two additional strategies. In the journal-entry samples in figure 2.1, the first journal entry asks students to predict what the skill means and what applications it might have. In the primary grades, the use of "I can" statements can serve as the catalyst for journal entries. Younger students might also be asked to draw a picture of what they think the skill could be related to, or to rate their prior knowledge of the skill or prerequisite skills. For example, kindergarten students could draw a picture showing how they may put toys in different groups. Of course, teachers should not become overly dependent on the journal, since it is, in some measure, a relatively unsupervised activity. Still, these journal entries can provide teachers with effective alternatives to the traditional pretest in order to identify students' level of background knowledge.

As the skill is introduced and students begin to formulate an understanding of the new skill, journaling can continue to serve as an ongoing assessment opportunity. Asking students to write a simple three-minute summary of what they have learned once or twice each week provides a rich opportunity to monitor student understanding. Teachers may wish to follow up this activity by asking students to share their understanding with a peer, which will foster the social understanding that is so important to mathematical learning. In addition, with minimal planning, teachers can embed elements of scaffolding by strategically partnering specific students together who may share learning style preferences.

Mathematics journaling continues to be a powerful learning tool throughout the acquisition and generalization of new skills. Periodically throughout the instructional unit, students can revisit graphic organizers or other preassessment entries. As students have the opportunity to add or clarify their knowledge of the skills in their mathematics journal, they can be encouraged to use different-colored writing pens or pencils to visually highlight the new knowledge. In addition, students can add sample problems or explanations that exemplify the target skill. Many of the more skilled students may be encouraged to create written problems, including story or word problems, that exemplify target skills. This supports the generalization of skills, and these problems, in turn, may be used for instruction with other students in the class.

Research has shown that students who are deeply dedicated to understanding content, using instructional strategies appropriately, and linking new knowledge to previous experiences are more likely to master the content than other students (Guthrie, 2001). Journal writing does often foster high levels of engagement with the learning content. Thus, journaling is likely to enhance mastery of many mathematics concepts.

Graphic Organizers

Graphic organizers represent content in some graphic fashion, and they typically assist students in remembering the content. As every teacher will realize, graphic organizers are quite common in a variety of subject areas (such as language arts, history, and science), but such organizers tend to be used less frequently in mathematics. Still, even in the area of math, graphic organizers are frequently recommended for summarizing concepts as well as for introducing new mathematics content (Bender, 2009b). During the introduction of a new skill, teachers should present various graphic organizers that will help students organize their thoughts related to the new concepts. Graphic organizers can also be used to highlight student-friendly definitions and for brainstorming possible applications of the skill. The use of graphic organizers in mathematics as an element of skill introduction can easily be adapted across the primary and elementary grade levels.

For example, second-grade students might be learning to estimate the number of marbles in a jar merely by looking at the jar, whereas fifth-grade students might use a graphic organizer that illustrates the concept of using estimates of subgroups (in this case groups of five people) to estimate the total number of people. Figures 2.2 and 2.3 show these graphic organizers.

Graphic organizers give students increased ownership of learning and provide a source for cumulative review. They can also help teachers manage instruction when a student misses classes or needs further assistance on a particular topic; the student can look at a classmate's graphic organizer and catch up after a short partner time with the

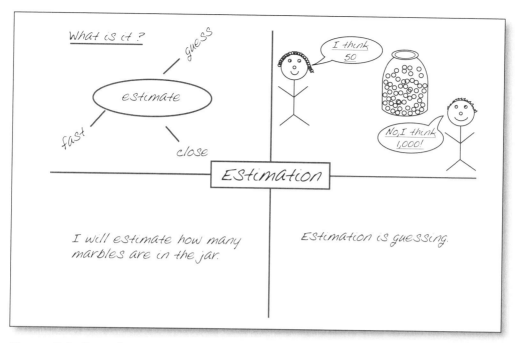

Figure 2.2: Sample second-grade graphic organizer.

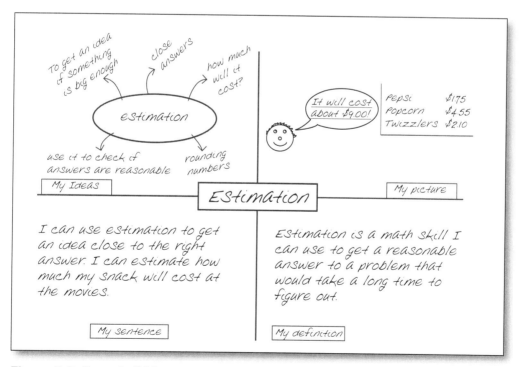

Figure 2.3: Sample fifth-grade graphic organizer.

peer. The subsequent discussions of the graphic organizer will serve as a high-quality learning experience for both students who have missed class and those who haven't.

Another excellent opportunity to scaffold students during this activity is to pull the most challenged students into a small group for teacher-directed instruction centered around the graphic organizer. For other students with strengths in visual learning, the effectiveness of the activity is increased by drawing or modeling the graphic organizer on a dry erase board or with a document camera (ELMO camera). Finally, it is easy to differentiate instruction using graphic organizers, as some can be more complete in content coverage than others, with the requirement that students must fill in all of the content on the organizer as instruction progresses.

Technology-Based Instructional Tools

One instructional avenue that is showing great promise in research is the use of technology, which capitalizes on students' seemingly insatiable appetite for digital information (NMAP, 2008). Technology can enhance almost any of the instructional ideas presented thus far in this chapter. For example, the quality learning experiences of mathematics journals are enhanced through the use of technology when the journaling moves from pencil and paper to the digital world. Through the use of laptops and even iPods and some cell phones, students can complete mathematics activities such as journaling with simple word-processing tools.

Students can create graphic organizers through SmartArt drawing programs or certain programs designed to assist in the development of graphic organizers, such as Kidspiration® (see www.inspiration.com). The process of students creating graphic organizers forces the increased internalization of skills and links concept learning to a higher-order thinking-skill activity. Many tech-savvy teachers create class wikis or use Google Docs tools to share and assess student learning, and students can use these tools to create products as well.

Given the availability of technology and student interest in the use of technology, projects such as video diaries can be a powerful learning experience for students and can serve as a culminating activity to generalize mathematics knowledge. Students can work in teams, which might be proactively designed by teachers to facilitate scaffolding and support of students, to document their understanding and application of mathematical learning. Often grant funding can be used to purchase video equipment, including digital cameras or the new student-friendly Flip recorders.

Creating video diaries integrates technology and teamwork into mathematics learning experiences, and sharing video diaries with parents during parent meetings is an excellent way to engage parents in their child's learning and show student progress.

Podcasting is the audio recording of students through the use of a computer with Internet access and a simple microphone. For example, students work individually or in pairs to draft a manuscript summarizing the activities and skills from a specific unit or target skill and record that summary. Many websites offer free podcasting opportunities, including Hipcast (www.audioblog.com), ClickCaster (www.clickcaster .com), and Podcast.com (http://podcast.com).

Because technology can be captivating for some students, it is easy for students to "get lost" in the various technology-based projects described here. Many teachers have chosen to use rubrics to guide students. For example, teachers can present a rubric clearly outlining the fundamental expectations for podcasts and video diaries to students prior to the project (see the sample rubric in table 2.3, page 52). Follow-up activities might involve having peers review the podcasts using the predesigned rubric to assist with grading. Since podcasts are accessible on the Internet with appropriate log-in information, they can also serve to connect the school and home.

Student Think-Alouds

The NMAP (2008) recommends the use of think-aloud instructional strategies to foster conceptual understanding. Student "think-alouds"—conversational explorations of the tasks required to complete a mathematics problem—serve as a springboard to inquiry that can redefine misconceptions about mathematics concepts. In this tactic, students are encouraged to think aloud during their mathematics activities, either individually or in groups, and teachers are encouraged to frequently model thinking aloud to illustrate the process for students. The tactic also allows teachers to conduct immediate analyses to identify faulty understanding. In this sense, think-alouds can easily be coupled with error analysis by the teacher.

Ball (1991) emphasizes that elementary general education teachers teaching mathematics must move beyond the identification of right and wrong to error analysis, which offers insights into student thinking. Think-alouds can facilitate this type of error analysis, and may even lead to more in-depth, one-to-one interviews between the teacher and struggling students.

Think-alouds may be more effective, or at least more comfortable for students, in the context of small-group activities such as the mini-fishbowl. Webb and Mastergeorge (2003) describe how small-group environments support students' ability and their willingness to express themselves. They identify the benefits of students being able to help each other through their mistakes and note that students learn by asking peers for explanations. In small-group environments, students receive high-order thinking skill help from their peers and practice what they have learned.

Table 2.3: Sample Rubric for Fifth-Grade Mathematics Podcast

	5	4	3	2	1	0
Use of Vocabulary Essential vocabulary: *x axis, y axis, plot, data table, title, Cartesian coordinate plane, and slope*	All critical vocabulary from current unit is integrated into podcast with clear explanation.	Six to seven of the identified vocabulary terms are presented with clear explanation.	Four to five of the identified vocabulary terms are presented with clear explanation.	Two to three of the identified vocabulary terms are presented with clear explanation.	One identified unit vocabulary term is presented with clear explanation.	No vocabulary terms from the current unit are presented.
Real-World Examples	Three real-world applications that appropriately utilize three graphing formats are presented.	Three real-world applications that appropriately utilize two graphing formats are presented.	Two real-world applications that appropriately utilize two graphing formats are presented.	Two real-world applications that appropriately utilize one graphing format are presented.	One real-world application that appropriately utilizes one graphing format is presented.	No real-world examples are presented.
Collaboration/Overall Quality	Partners worked together respectfully with no redirection needed, *and* sound quality is clear.	Partners worked together respectfully with one redirection, *and* sound quality is clear.	Partners worked together respectfully with one or two redirections, *or* sound quality is average.	Partners worked together respectfully with one or two redirections, *and* sound quality is average.	Partners needed to be redirected more than twice, *or* sound quality is poor.	Partners needed to be redirected more than twice, *and* sound quality is poor.

One important element of this instructional strategy includes a focus on the skills students have already mastered. The teacher may use a model think-aloud to help students reflect on their own prerequisite skills, as in the following example:

Hmmmm . . . I can round numbers to the nearest ten. What do I need to do to round the number 84 to the nearest ten? Well, I know that the digit 8 is in the tens place and the digit 4 is in the ones place. So to round 84 to the nearest ten, I have to look at the number to the right of the tens place—that's the number 4. Now I have to remember that the numbers 1, 2, 3, and 4 signal to me to round down. I remember coloring the hundreds chart, and the numbers 1, 2, 3, and 4 were closest to the lower set of ten.

In modeling this reflective think-aloud, the teacher can further differentiate the lesson by breaking it down into several think-alouds for students who may be struggling with this particular aspect of the content. Thus, that teacher could use this think-aloud initially and then provide some of the students with problems on which to work; then, he or she could use the same think-aloud, breaking it down task by task into sequenced steps for the students who need that level of explicit instruction.

This tactic allows teachers to monitor students' conceptual understanding. While providing all students the opportunity to think aloud mathematically is important, for struggling learners, it is imperative that their thinking is monitored to prevent the development of mathematical misconceptions, which can erode understanding and skill development.

In some grades, teachers may use various cues to help students distinguish between instructional conversations and instruction using think-alouds. For example, primary teachers can support students' development of think-aloud skills by using a "think-aloud cloud"—a cloud shape cut out from white poster paper and used to indicate which student has the floor for thinking aloud. The teacher might hold the think-aloud cloud as he or she presents a think-aloud explanation to students and then pass the think–aloud cloud to students when they have think-aloud ideas to share.

With this strategy, teachers must develop questioning skills to really dig into student thinking and provide prompts that empower students to clarify their misconceptions. After prompting and encouraging students to clarify their own thoughts, teachers should intervene with explicit, direct instruction that presents the mathematics concept in a clear and understandable manner for students who continue to have difficulty.

> While providing all students the opportunity to think aloud mathematically is important, for struggling learners, it is imperative that their thinking is monitored to prevent the development of mathematical misconceptions, which can erode understanding and skill development.

Workstations

Strategies to facilitate small-group work (such as the mini-fishbowl described previously) increase student engagement in the mathematics content and are one of the key factors contributing to increased student achievement in the differentiated class (Bender, 2009b). Classrooms that rely on teach/test instructional methods that meet the needs of average learners must be replaced with classrooms in which students are creatively engaged and challenged so that all students remain competitive with their peers around the globe.

Another grouping strategy that allows teachers to provide differentiated instruction is the use of quality workstations. Historically, the term *workstation*, or *learning center*, has been used to describe small-group learning activities that give students the opportunity to practice skills individually or in small groups. Teachers must consider some key factors when developing small-group activities that will help students internalize the mathematics skills being practiced.

First, teachers should consider what types of grouped activities are appropriate at various points in the instructional unit. Fishbowls, mini-fishbowls, and bell-ringer activities are primarily introductory strategies used not just to introduce skills, but also to introduce activities that will be used later by students independently in workstations. Activities such as those done at workstations (and other activities, such as journaling and mathematical game playing) become richer experiences when performed later in the instructional unit, though almost all can be used at various points during instruction.

Next, teachers should consider class management issues when determining how to group students. They must put into place careful, proactive classroom management practices, such as class-rule systems or class-respect policies. Furthermore, students must clearly understand the expectations and routines that accompany the use of workstations and other types of grouped activities.

Teachers should also consider social issues and how they might impact behavior in the various groups. Teachers should consider questions such as the following: Which students work well together? Which students will challenge and support each other in the workstation? How many students will work well together in a group? Some students can socially manage involvement in a group with four or five peers while other students become agitated or distracted in groups with more than one or two other members.

Another factor that impacts the efficacy of small-group work is the role the student serves in small-group projects. Often in workstations and learning projects, teachers proactively assign roles. Awareness of student strengths and learning preferences increases a teacher's ability to create learning experiences that meet student needs and contribute to the positive learning experience and environment. Continuous monitoring of student needs allows teachers to carefully design quality learning options—one-size mathematics instruction no longer fits all.

While adjusting group size and membership provides differentiation, the activity or process students engage in as part of the workstation activity can also serve as differentiation. For example, students exploring number relationships can be assigned a workstation activity in which they discover how many outfits they can design using predetermined articles of clothing. For this activity, differentiation options might include varying the number of clothing articles for a group to consider. Some students will be able to draw pictures of the clothing to solve the challenge, while other students will need concrete models such as doll clothes or paper cutouts of the clothing.

Telling time using digital and analog clocks is a common mathematical concept taught to younger students. To differentiate workstation practice activities for this skill, teachers can provide direction cards that would have some students match a digital clock to an analog clock. For a more complex task, students can be given a digital time and turn the hands on the analog clock to indicate the digital time. While both activities provide practice with an important early skill, the adjustment within the same workstation tailors the challenge level for student learning. Again, adjusting elements of the activity to meet student needs gives them the best access to the instruction and allows educators to provide enriching challenges to expand student thinking.

> Continuous monitoring of student needs allows teachers to carefully design quality learning options—one-size mathematics instruction no longer fits all.

Mathematics Nights

As schools move toward the implementation of standards-based mathematics programs, many have instituted "mathematics nights" to provide parents and other family members with the opportunity to understand standards-based instruction, as well as how mathematics instruction is evolving. Parents are often surprised to learn that mathematics instruction has moved far beyond the drill-and-practice worksheets of yesteryear, and today incorporates many innovative instructional strategies, including extensive use of technology. During such evenings, families can observe and participate in mathematics instruction. Parents often express surprise that they enjoy the activities and make statements such as, "Wow! Mathematics was never this fun when I was in school!" Hosting four to six mathematics nights during each school year can foster increased understanding of mathematics instruction, more parental emphasis on mathematics at home, and more student enjoyment of mathematics overall. Table 2.4 (page 56) presents guidelines for planning and conducting a mathematics night for parents.

Table 2.4: Guidelines for Planning and Conducting a Mathematics Night for Parents

1.	Build a team to support the planning and organization. Involve teachers and parents with scheduling and planning; the success of mathematics nights is contingent on teachers' and parents' engagement in the process. Classroom teachers and parents often have insights into scheduling conflicts in the community and availability of families for planning. In addition, the committee can design activities and provide organizational assistance; teachers need the activity to be easy to implement and not just another "thing to do."
2.	Provide a family-friendly environment. Plan activities that will involve the whole family so that childcare is not a concern for parents. Often parents who work are resistant to leaving their children and missing additional family time. However, parents often embrace opportunities to engage in family activities, especially ones that do not stretch the family budget.
3.	Plan activities that are fun and easy to replicate. Parents generally want to support their children's learning, but they avoid activities that create conflict or tension in their home. Hence, providing drill-and-practice worksheets does not encourage family interactions. Instead, teach mathematics games that parents can play. These activities will build relationships and mathematics skills.
4.	Choose mathematics activities that reflect and enhance the mathematics curriculum in the classroom. As you present the activity to parents, explain the mathematics skills it reinforces and the standard it demonstrates.
5.	Remember communication and consistency in scheduling. As families manage their complex schedules, having a consistent schedule for ongoing mathematics nights helps them plan for participation. It is important to maintain clear communication regarding dates, times, locations, and activities.
6.	Create Make It/Take It activities. These are learning activities teachers, parents, and students create that then go home with students and their families. These activities are exciting and popular with families. For example, a simple Make It/Take It activity for young students is creating a calendar on laminated paper that can be written on with a dry-erase marker and reused. Older students can create board games that allow them to practice various skills.
7.	Provide food! Serving simple refreshments gives families a chance to mingle and build new relationships with other members of your school community. It is a good idea to model good nutrition and provide healthy choices. For a bonus, connect the snack to a mathematics concept. For example, provide two possible snack containers (short and wide versus tall and narrow) and challenge families to choose the one with the greatest capacity. Ask parents and students to discuss their choice, test their choice with manipulatives, and if you want to be nice, let them change their minds based on their discovery. Follow up with students explaining, illustrating, or journaling about what they have learned.

8. Consider funding options. Mathematics nights can be supported financially by grants, Title I parent-training funds, and/or by local business partnerships. The school-based parent-teacher organization might also support the event.

9. Tell the story. Positive public relations activities boost a school's image in the community. Mathematics nights are a wonderful opportunity to share with the community positive experiences occurring in the school. And the publicity will likely increase future involvement.

Conclusion

Effective Tier 1 instruction in mathematics is absolutely critical in the RTI process, since Tier 1 instruction provides the basis for all subsequent mathematics success. As schools continue to elevate the standards for their students, general education teachers must seek ways to enhance their instructional capabilities in mathematics. The broad approaches of differentiation and scaffolding provide a framework for teachers to consider how their own mathematical instructional activities foster increased engagement in students. The specific tactics provide a variety of strategies that can assist teachers in reaching all students in the mathematics classroom.

In the next chapter, we begin with a discussion of early mathematics readiness and number sense, and we address questions on how a complete RTI procedure might look for a very young student.

RTI Procedures for Number Sense and Early Mathematics Skills

As we discussed previously, the RTI process has drastically impacted instruction in early reading and early literacy; much work has been done in those areas to develop benchmarks to allow for universal screening and repeated performance assessment of the skills that undergird successful reading during the preschool and kindergarten years (Bender, 2009a). Based on that large body of research, educators are able to assess early reading skills at the beginning of kindergarten, and thus early intervention can be initiated quickly and targeted to specific problems in literacy (Bender & Shores, 2007). This suggests that the major emphasis on RTI procedures in mathematics may likewise focus on mathematics readiness skills and early mathematics skills at the primary level.

However, the research base for early mathematics assessment and interventions is much smaller than for early reading skills, and therefore, much less is known about what the actual precursors of successful mathematics are, compared to reading during the early years (Bender, 2009a; Fuchs, Fuchs, Compton, et al., 2007). Furthermore, the early research suggests that kindergarten screening in mathematics may be more time consuming than in reading, since mathematical abilities seem to be more multifaceted than the early phoneme skills on which reading is based (Fuchs, Fuchs, Compton, et al., 2007; Jordan, 2007). Today, there are many questions left unanswered on how RTI procedures might apply in early mathematics, which is one reason we chose to devote an entire chapter to what is known about RTI procedures aimed at early mathematics skills.

This chapter discusses early mathematics readiness, early mathematics skills, and an RTI procedure appropriate for a kindergarten or first-grade student. We then present several curricula for early mathematics instruction and intervention. An RTI case study for the first years of schooling shows what Tier 1 instruction and Tier 2 and 3 interventions look like for a very young elementary student. We then present some important issues for RTI in early mathematics and discuss what may happen next if a Tier 3 intervention is not successful.

Let's begin with a discussion of the issues involved in our conceptualization of number sense in preschool and kindergarten. A review of the concept indicates that this concept is not as readily understood as many believe.

What Is Number Sense?

Even a cursory glance at the literature on early mathematics skills will show that the term *number sense* has been widely used whenever educators consider early mathematics readiness and early mathematics skills in young children. However, as often as this term is used today, there is not any solid consensus as to exactly what it is (Chard et al., 2008; Devlin, 2000; Jordan, 2007). Number sense has received much more attention in recent decades as educational research has continued to document the benefits of early learning. Unfortunately, no clear, widely accepted understanding of this concept has emerged despite the increased attention. There are at least two differing perspectives on what the term means. These include a relatively limited psychoneurologically based view and a broader educational view (Sousa, 2008).

> There are at least two differing perspectives on what the term means. These include a relatively limited psychoneurologically based view and a broader educational view.

The View of Neuroscience

Psychoneurologists point to evidence that has emerged from studies on brain functioning and early number recognition in infants (Berger, Tzur, & Posner, 2006; Sousa, 2008) that indicates very young infants display several early mathematics readiness skills. First, infants seem to have a conceptualization of *numerosity*—a general conception of and ability to recognize quantity. Second, young infants seem to recognize differences in the number of objects in two sets, as long as that number is around four or below; this ability is often referred to as *subitizing* (Sousa, 2008).

For example, research on visual fixation time (how long one looks at a series of objects) indicates that even infants can detect changes in the number of items in a set, as long as the total number is lower than three or four (Strauss & Curtis, 1981). Eye scan studies indicate that infants fixate their gaze on three-item sets longer than on two-item sets, indicating additional brain processing time for the larger three-item set. In fact, this initial numeric understanding—even in the absence of a language-based counting or number system—is considered to be a function of our innate visual processing system, a system that seems to work nearly instantly to quantify groups of four or fewer items (Sousa, 2008). Thus, this level of basic numeration seems to be hardwired into the human brain from birth,

> Basic numeration seems to be hardwired into the human brain from birth.

and the numeric value of those lowest numbers is actually processed by a different mental processing system than higher numbers, subsequent number skills such as counting, or other mathematical processes.

Bender (2009b) uses the phrase "one, two, three, many . . ." to describe the fact that number concepts for the lowest numbers are interpreted by a different, nearly instantaneous neural processing system. These lowest numbers seem to be interpreted immediately by the brain because these numbers, under certain conditions, might actually impact survival of the organism and ultimately of the species (Bender, 2009b). That is, running from one predator would be different from running from two or three predators, since the planned escape route would probably be different. Therefore, interpreting the difference between one and three could impact both individual and species survival over the long term, and the brain evolved to immediately interpret numbers of four and below. Running from five, six, or eight predators probably did not result in any realistic survival possibility, therefore numbers higher than four were not immediately critical for survival. In evolutionary terms, this distinction probably resulted in higher numbers not being instantly interpretable by the brain without some instruction, whereas the lower numbers are recognized instantly because they are interpreted by a different neural system.

Given that different systems are involved, neuroscientists generally consider certain basic numeration abilities as hardwired into the brain. These would include only a few basic number interpretative skills, such as the perception of small numeric quantities (for example, subitizing, initial counting skill, and comparison of numeric quantities when the items compared were quite small; Sousa, 2008). In this perspective, these skills are biological in nature, resulting from innate wiring of the human brain over many generations, making these basic number sense skills possible in early infancy. This is one view, admittedly a highly limited view, of what the concept of number sense means.

The View of Mathematics Educators

In contrast, educators who specialize in mathematics tend to have a much broader definition of *number sense* and consider the term to include the skills involved in early numeration (for example, counting up through three or four), as well as a wider variety of lower-level, yet somewhat more complex, mathematics skills (Berch, 2005; Chard et al., 2008; Jordan, 2007; NMAP, 2008). Certainly those skills noted earlier in the neuroscience view would be viewed by educators as basic number sense, but educators would also include more early skills and abilities on their list that are clearly dependent on early learning or formal education, as shown in table 3.1.

Table 3.1: Educators' Additional Indicators of Number Sense

1. The ability to compare sets of items and determine which is larger/smaller
2. Fluency in number reading and interpretation

continued on next page →

3.	The ability to recognize that something in a set has changed when items are removed or added
4.	Ability in initial counting (perhaps 1–5 or 1–10)
5.	The ability to develop strategies for solving complex problems
6.	The ability to use numbers to communicate, process, and interpret information
7.	The ability to understand how operations impact numbers
8.	Recognition of gross numeric errors
9.	The ability to interpret small fractions in various forms

Sources: Bender, 2009b; Berch, 2005; Chard et al., 2008; Jordan, 2007; Sousa, 2008.

The View of Researchers

It is also interesting to compare the various definitions of *number sense* within the literature. For example, Jordan (2007) defines *number sense* as intuitive knowledge of numbers, such as the ability to compare quantities (4 versus 7), the ability to internalize understanding of counting (for example, the last number in a count indicates the quantity of the set), the ability to note that numbers are always counted in the same order, and the ability to estimate quantities. In contrast, Devlin (2000) is more specific, indicating that number sense consists of two components: the ability to compare sizes of two collections seen simultaneously, and the ability to remember numbers of objects presented successively in time. The report of the NMAP (2008) defines *number sense* as an ability to immediately identify the numerical value of small quantities, coupled with basic counting skills and proficiency in approximation of magnitudes of small numbers of objects.

Another way to look at number sense and early mathematics skill is to consider what measures are used to actually define and measure these early mathematics skills in research. Fuchs, Fuchs, Compton, et al. (2007) provide a catalogue of the types of screening measures researchers use to document number sense and early mathematics skills in kindergarten and grade 1. Table 3.2 lists the mathematics readiness skills most frequently defined as components of number sense by researchers. Fuchs and her colleagues (2007) also determined that broader screening measures (measures that included more of these possible indicators rather than any single measure) resulted in better prediction of eventual mathematics success in later years of school.

Table 3.2: Mathematics Readiness Skills Most Frequently Defined in the Mathematics Readiness Research

Repeating digits backward	Reading numbers
Writing dictated numbers	Circling numbers
Comparing magnitudes	Producing numbers

Counting orally	Noting missing numbers
Identifying numbers	Discriminating between quantities
Writing numbers	Knowing basic addition facts
Writing reversible numbers	Counting by twos, fives, or tens
Selecting numbers	

Sources: Berch, 2005; Chard et al., 2008; Devlin, 2000; Fuchs, Fuchs, Compton, et al., 2007; Jordan, 2007; Jordan et al., 2007; Locuniak & Jordan, 2008.

Both basic numeration and early mathematics skills are included in the research as indicators of number sense. Unless one readily accepts the limited view of number sense from the neurosciences, a clear discrimination between number sense and early mathematics skill is not readily apparent. In this text, we use the more expanded view of number sense, which includes early numeration as well as early mathematics skills such as counting, or counting by twos or fives, and so forth. That view is consistent with the standards of the National Council of Teachers of Mathematics (2006) and the NMAP report (2008), as well as with the general perspective of most researchers in the field of early mathematics (Berch, 2005; Chard et al., 2008; Fuchs et al., 2005; Jordan, 2007).

> The more expanded view of number sense is consistent with the standards of the National Council of Teachers of Mathematics (2006) and the National Mathematics Advisory Panel report (2008), as well as with the general perspective of most researchers in the field of early mathematics.

Screening and Assessment of Early Readiness in Mathematics

Since a broader conceptualization of number sense is beginning to receive acceptance, we must now consider screening and assessment. If most children acquire these early mathematics skills prior to kindergarten, then we should be able to develop screening and assessment tools for RTI procedures for use with children kindergarten age and younger. An example from the area of reading illuminates the importance of this issue.

In the early 1990s, teachers began reading instruction with direct instruction in phonics—the pairing of discrete speech sounds (phonemes) with letters written on the page (Bender & Larkin, 2009). That type of reading instruction began in kindergarten and continued during grade 1, and it was assumed at that time that no earlier reading skills deserved instructional attention. However, since then, researchers have discovered that many early reading skills—including phonemic awareness, discrimination, manipulation, and even some concept of symbol pairing—develop much earlier. For example, many parents will tell you that their three-year-old can identify the letter *M* as meaning a favorite fast-food restaurant. Because that particular restaurant's name begins with the letter *M*, children pair that letter with the name of that popular eatery. In one sense, the pairing of the symbol and concept is an approximation of early reading skill (Sousa, 2005).

Other reading readiness skills emerge prior to kindergarten, such as a child's ability to recognize, compare, and manipulate discrete phonemes (for example, telling the difference between the phonemic sounds associated with *B* versus *D*; see Sousa, 2005, for a review). Universal screening procedures on which RTI procedures can be based have been developed for these reading skills (phonemic recognition, letter naming). These universal screening instruments can measure these skills as early as the first several weeks of kindergarten. For example, the popular assessment *Dynamic Indicators of Basic Early Literacy Skills* (*DIBELS*; Good & Kaminski, 2002) became the basis of many RTI procedures in reading.

Additionally, a large body of research (see Bender, 2009a, for a review) indicates that remediation in the particular phonemic skills measured by that instrument (phonemic recognition, initial letter naming) resulted in impressive gains in reading achievement. This research indicates that the skills measured by that assessment (and similar assessments) were measuring the "right" set of early reading skills. That is, this instrument measured the exact skills that should be the target of remediation efforts. On the basis of that research, educators could, with confidence, build RTI progress-monitoring procedures as well as early intervention procedures around those specific skills.

In contrast, research in the area of early mathematics readiness has not proceeded nearly so far (Bender, 2009b; Jordan, 2007). While research has progressed to a point where early mathematics readiness can be assessed to some degree (Jordan et al., 2007), no single assessment has captured the attention of educators in mathematics in the way that *DIBELS* has in early reading. The publishers of *DIBELS* are actively working to develop an early mathematics assessment.

There is much research to be done concerning exactly which mathematics readiness skills should be the main focus of mathematics remediation. Thus, even with the universal screening and benchmarking measures currently available (as described in chapter 2), educators are not certain how actual intervention should proceed, or which specific variables should be the focus of that remediation. At present, schools that have initiated early intervention RTI procedures in mathematics are focusing on the entire set of variables presented in tables 3.1 and 3.2 (pages 61–63) as additional research on how RTI might be implemented in kindergarten and grade 1 mathematics continues to progress.

> At present, schools that have initiated early intervention RTI procedures in mathematics are focusing on the entire set of variables presented in tables 3.1 and 3.2 as additional research on how RTI might be implemented in kindergarten and grade 1 mathematics continues to progress.

Mathematics Curricula for Young Children

Fortunately, even with few universal screening tools available, several early mathematics curricula provide a basis for Tier 2 or Tier 3 mathematics interventions for young children. The research support for these curricula varies considerably, and none have been exhaustively evaluated. However, educators should consider these curricula as intervention options for Tier 2 and Tier 3, and they should select the curricula that best fit with the core mathematics curricula in their district.

Early Learning in Mathematics

David Chard and his coauthors (2008) developed an early mathematics curricula designed specifically to strengthen the number sense and early mathematics readiness skills of young children. *The Early Learning in Mathematics* program includes one hundred thirty-minute lessons, each of which is divided into four distinct quarters with differing activities in each quarter. Activities cut across four different strands: numbers and operations, geometry, measurement, and vocabulary. Rather than focusing on a single skill per lesson, the program includes four to five different activities in a thirty-minute lesson. This accommodates very young children's task orientation. Initially, each lesson reviews familiar skills and introduces new concepts. A lesson might include a counting activity, using a horizontal number line, some practice ordering numerals along the number line, and identification of numerals using finger representations. These early activities might be followed with introduction of a geometric shape, some examples of various measurements, or mathematics practice workshops illustrating the types of activities completed previously in that lesson. Every fifth lesson throughout the curriculum focuses on problem-solving activities, making this curriculum somewhat unique in the introduction of problem-solving activities at such a young age. This is consistent with the overall recommendations of the NMAP (2008) that emphasis on problem solving is needed.

Recent research on this curriculum has tentatively suggested promise for early remediation of students' mathematics difficulties (Chard et al., 2008), but much of that research has been done by the authors of the program—a concern with this and most other curricula in this area. Thus, more research on this program is certainly needed. Nevertheless, it is likely that teachers will see this curriculum used increasingly in preschool and kindergarten programs in the coming years as our schools move into implementation of RTI procedures during the earliest years of schooling.

Number Worlds

The *Number Worlds* curriculum, developed by Sharon Griffin (1998; 2003), assists students in strengthening their number readiness and early number skills. This is an intensive intervention program that provides assistance for young children and elementary school children who are one or more grade levels behind in elementary mathematics. This program includes daily lessons of forty-five to sixty minutes that are compatible with most core mathematics instructional programs. While much of the emphasis during original development of the program was on young children, the range of the program is now quite comprehensive. *Number Worlds* (www.sranumberworlds.com/discover .html) includes a prevention program for grades preK through 1 (program levels A–C) and an elementary school series of programs for grades 1 through 8 (levels D–J).

However, the lessons are tied to specific grade levels only in the broadest sense, and teachers are encouraged to implement lessons based on the specific needs of individual students. Students are placed into the intervention lessons based on either the Number Knowledge Test (described in chapter 2; Griffin, 1998), or a placement test that comes with the program.

Research on the *Number Worlds* program, like other recently developed supplemental curricula, is somewhat limited. However, the research does show positive effects for primary and elementary school students (Griffin, 2003, 2004; University of Cincinnati, 2008). In particular, the University of Cincinnati study demonstrated that this program was effective in an experimental study over a multiyear period, though in that study, the effects of the intervention seemed to dissipate after students were moved back into the general education curriculum. Still, this is a research-proven curriculum that is clearly appropriate for RTI interventions.

Math Recovery

Math Recovery was developed by Bob Wright in 1992 as a combination of a mathematics intervention curriculum and a professional development program in mathematics for teachers (Wright, 1992, 2003, 2009). The program is intended as a supplemental intervention for primary and elementary students and can be implemented in conjunction with almost any core mathematics curriculum. The program was originally developed for students in the primary grades to enable them to form a solid foundation working with whole numbers, but it has now been utilized with students in kindergarten through grade 5, and it may be used with older students at higher grade levels who are struggling in mathematics, including students with disabilities (Wright, 2009; Wright, Stanger, Stafford, & Martland, 2006).

The program provides a quick, intensive intervention before students who are at risk can fall too far behind, making it an excellent fit with the overall RTI paradigm. *Math Recovery* begins with a series of math scenarios designed to assess students' current knowledge and their thought processes. Then lessons are planned out based on each child's individual level of knowledge and understanding. Detailed descriptions of the theory, practice, and research support for *Math Recovery* are available at the company website (www.mathrecovery.org) or from various research publications (Wright, Martland, & Stafford, 2006; Wright, Martland, Stafford, & Stanger, 2006; Wright, 2009). There are also three professional development programs available for *Math Recovery.*

This program is unique in that the collaborative training in implementation is offered by a nonprofit company, the U.S. Math Recovery Council, which is dedicated to overseeing and managing the *Math Recovery* program and its materials, methodology, and related intellectual property (www.mathrecovery.org). Educators are invited to become members or affiliate members of this organization, which allows them to participate in various activities, such as conferences, for a reduced fee and to receive periodic newsletters related to the broad topics of mathematics instruction.

While research is limited for this program, some research has shown positive and impressive improvements in mathematics achievement among first through third graders (MacLean, 2003; University of Cincinnati, 2008). Also, the company website presents several evaluation results from various schools and school districts around the United States that show positive results for this intervention and professional development program. We chose to include *Math Recovery* here because of the uniqueness of the combination of an intervention program with comprehensive professional development. This pairing of program and professional development makes this an ideal choice for educators to consider in the RTI context. Additionally, this program was recommended to us by educators from the Roaring Fork School District in Glenwood Springs, Colorado. They have used this program with great success and consider it to be an excellent intervention program that dovetails nicely with their RTI efforts.

What Does an Early Mathematics RTI Look Like?

General education teachers now have some choices for screening instruments and early mathematics curricula, but they still have questions about the actual mechanics of RTI procedures in mathematics, such as, "What does an RTI procedure in mathematics look like?" and "How is the mathematics RTI procedure documented?"

When RTI was first mentioned in federal legislation in 2004, the federal government provided no guidance on exactly what needed to be included in an RTI procedure in any area (Bender, 2009a; Kame'enui, 2007). In the absence of extensive guidelines, states and school districts have devised forms and procedures to assist teachers in documentation of the RTI process, and these vary widely (Berkeley et al., 2009). During initial implementation of RTI in any subject area, every educator should check with his or her local school board and state department of education website to see specific forms that may be required for RTI. Only those sources can tell teachers explicitly what is required within the RTI process for their specific school or district.

> Every educator should check with his or her local school board and state department of education website to see specific forms that may be required for RTI in mathematics.

Despite the differences from state to state and district to district, we can identify the general requirements by exploring the rather large body of literature on RTI. Based on such a literature review, Bender and Shores (2007) present a general form for documenting RTI procedures in mathematics. An adapted version of that form appears in table 3.3 (page 68). Visit **go.solution-tree.com/rti** to download a reproducible version of the form. Each of the document's sections (separated by the bold headings) is completed as the child moves through the RTI process. The person who completes each task signs and dates the form.

Table 3.3: Response to Intervention Documentation Form

Student:	Age:	Date:
Initiating Teacher:	School:	Grade:
1. Student Difficulty and Summary of Tier 1 Instruction:		
2. Tier 2 Intervention Plan:		
3. Observational Notes of Student in Tier 2 Mathematics Intervention:		
4. Tier 2 Intervention Summary and Recommendations:		
5. Tier 3 Intervention Plan:		
6. Observation of Student in Tier 3 Mathematics Intervention:		
7. Tier 3 Intervention Summary and Recommendations:		

Case Study: An RTI for Early Mathematics Skills

We will use the case study of a student named Tony to illustrate the RTI process for Tier 1 instruction and Tier 2 and 3 interventions for early mathematics skills. His first-grade teacher, Ms. Dawson, recognized that he was having some difficulty in mathematics.

Statement of Student Difficulty and Tier 1 Instruction

Ms. Dawson typically used the Number Knowledge Test (Griffin, 1998; see chapter 2) as a benchmarking assessment three times each year. On the initial administration of that assessment, Tony completed only a few of the Level 0 items, indicating a level of mathematical understanding more closely associated with beginning kindergarten than beginning first grade. Ms. Dawson also noted that Tony didn't seem to "understand numbers," so at that point, she talked with Tony's kindergarten teacher. Ms. Dawson kept fairly extensive notes on her observations of Tony during mathematics exercises and on her discussions with his kindergarten teacher.

The kindergarten teacher reported that Tony was never terribly successful in most early mathematics readiness and number exercises, but that he did manage basic counting by the end of kindergarten. Ms. Dawson then verified, based on her own class work with Tony, that he could count up to approximately twenty-five. However, recognition of patterns within a number sequence was highly problematic for Tony. For example, Ms. Dawson presented several number sequences to Tony that involved either counting or skip–counting by twos (for example, 10, 11, __ or 1, 3, __, 7, 9). While both of these skills were taught in Tony's kindergarten class, he could not complete either sequence. He also had difficulty when visually comparing sets of items to answer questions like, "Which has less or which has more?" When Ms. Dawson checked Tony's assessment scores for the end of the kindergarten year, the data indicated that he was nearly a year behind many of the other students, and he was functioning at a level consistent with early kindergarten mathematics readiness at the end of the kindergarten year. Ms. Dawson also noted that in her own class, Tony was having significant problems in simple addition and did not know his basic addition facts.

At this point, Ms. Dawson felt she had documented a significant problem in mathematics, and she did not want to see Tony fall further behind his classmates. She believed the problem might lie in basic number sense as well as early mathematics skills. From her notes and her experience teaching Tony, she completed item 1, the statement of student difficulty and summary of Tier 1 instruction, on a Response to Intervention Documentation Form for Tony to document his mathematics difficulties and the mathematics instruction he had received so far in her class:

> In October of 2009, I administered the Number Knowledge Test to Tony, and that informal assessment indicated he was functioning at approximately the level of a beginning kindergarten student; he completed only one indicator correctly for Level 0 on that assessment.
>
> In addition, Tony was having difficulty in mathematics in his daily work in my class. Typically, we spent fifteen minutes each day working on early addition mathematics facts and additional time on various counting exercises and number patterns. Tony seems to have consistent problems understanding number sequences and mathematics facts. I talked with Ms. Tucker, Tony's kindergarten teacher, who indicated that Tony had difficulty throughout kindergarten in mathematics readiness skills. Ms. Tucker did indicate that Tony could count from one up into the twenties, and I verified he could count up to twenty-five. Ms. Tucker also confirmed that she had taught skip-counting by twos in that kindergarten program, so Tony should have picked up that skill. However, he still has difficulty in recognition of number patterns of that nature. Specifically, when I presented several number sequences to Tony based on skip-counting by twos (for example, 5, 7, 9, __), he could not complete them. Also, Tony had difficulty when visually comparing sets of items to answer questions such as, "Which has less or which has more?"
>
> His achievement scores at the end of his kindergarten year indicate a one-year deficit in his mathematics readiness skills. Finally, in my class work with Tony, I noticed that he was having significant problems

in simple addition and did not know his addition facts. He could not compute addition facts, even when presented with manipulatives.

During his mathematics instruction in first grade, we have used mathematics facts charts to help remember addition facts. Tony has difficulty using this tool in comparison with his peers. I have also used a peer buddy system in which students call out mathematics facts to each other, and while Tony enjoys this, it has not resulted in his learning his addition facts in a timely fashion.

Ms. Dawson, 10/08/09

In this example, Tony's teacher has adequately documented not only the specific problems Tony has demonstrated, but also previous Tier 1 instructional approaches that have not worked. This type of detailed documentation provides the basis for the need for supplemental intervention for Tony in the areas of mathematics facts and pattern recognition. In this early phase of the RTI intervention process, teachers must meet a two-fold documentation responsibility. First, they should describe in detail the types of mathematics difficulties the student is experiencing. This may include description of the specific types of skills the child is having difficulty with, interview notes with previous teachers who worked with the child and noted similar difficulties, and scores from previous universal screening assessments.

Teachers must also provide a description of the Tier 1 instruction provided. Ms. Dawson describes the specific curricular skills Tony has been exposed to, as well as the instructional methods used with him. This description is critical for several reasons: (1) it documents the Tier 1 instruction a student has received, which is crucial at later stages in the RTI process; (2) members of the student support team or others might recommend modifications of that Tier 1 instruction that will sometimes alleviate the problem and make Tier 2 intervention unnecessary. In this case study, both peer buddy tutoring and a mathematics facts chart have been implemented and have not resulted in significant improvement. Ms. Dawson's description was somewhat limited, since she had only been teaching Tony for a month, but based on this information, it was clear to all that Tony needed some additional intervention.

Tier 2 Intervention

Tony's problems suggested he needed additional work in early mathematics skills. Ms. Dawson decided to provide some additional intensive instruction on basic mathematics skills for Tony and three other students in her class as a Tier 2 intervention. All of these students were having some problems and were falling behind, so Ms. Dawson developed a plan to meet with this group three times each week while the students were in their math workstations. She planned for her paraprofessional to supervise the other class members in other learning activities. Prior to initiating such a supplemental Tier 2 intervention, Ms. Dawson had to make certain that she met several obligations, including the following:

- Planning an intervention that was directly tied to Tony's academic problems—not merely following a supplemental mathematics curriculum

- Identifying how intensive that intervention would be for all of the students involved

- Developing a repeated-assessment, progress-monitoring strategy that would allow her to draw conclusions about the efficacy of the intervention for Tony

- Documenting her plan with some detail to address each of these issues

Figure 3.1 shows a sample Response to Intervention Documentation Form completed for this case study. As you can see, the first section of that form includes the paragraphs that summarize the problems Tony was having. The second section of that form presents complete information on the Tier 2 intervention plan that Ms. Dawson developed for Tony and his classmates. (See pages 171–173 for a blank reproducible of this form. Visit **go.solution-tree.com/rti** for downloadable versions of all reproducibles found in this book.)

| Student: *Tony Martin* | Age: *7* | Date: *10/10/09* |
| Initiating Teacher: *Ms. Dawson* | School: *Clayton Elementary* | Grade: *1* |

1. Student Difficulty and Summary of Tier 1 Instruction:

   In October of 2009, I administered the Number Knowledge Test to Tony, and that informal assessment indicated he was functioning at approximately the level of a beginning kindergarten student; he completed only one indicator correctly for Level 0 on that assessment.

   In addition, Tony was having difficulty in mathematics in his daily work in my class. Typically, we spent fifteen minutes each day working on early addition mathematics facts and additional time on various counting exercises and number patterns. Tony seems to have consistent problems understanding number sequences and mathematics facts. I talked with Ms. Tucker, Tony's kindergarten teacher, who indicated that Tony had difficulty throughout kindergarten in mathematics readiness skills. Ms. Tucker did indicate that Tony could count from one up into the twenties, and I verified he could count up to twenty-five. Ms. Tucker also confirmed that she had taught skip-counting by twos in that kindergarten program, so Tony should have picked up that skill. However, he still has difficulty in recognition of number patterns of that nature. Specifically, when I presented several number sequences to Tony based on skip-counting by twos (for example, 5, 7, 9, ___), he could not complete them. Also, Tony had difficulty when visually comparing sets of items to answer questions such as, "Which has less or which has more?"

Figure 3.1: Response to Intervention Documentation Form for Tony.

continued on next page →

His achievement scores at the end of his kindergarten year indicate a one-year deficit in his mathematics readiness skills. Finally, in my class work with Tony, I noticed that he is having significant problems in simple addition and did not know his addition facts. He could not compute addition facts, even when presented with manipulatives.

During his mathematics instruction in first grade, we have used mathematics facts charts to help remember addition facts. Tony has difficulty using this tool in comparison with his peers. I have also used a peer buddy system in which students call out mathematics facts to each other, and while Tony enjoys this, it has not resulted in his learning his addition facts in a timely fashion.

Ms. Dawson, 10/08/09

2. Tier 2 Intervention Plan:

Tony will work in a small group with three other students who need additional instructional time in early mathematics skills, such as pattern counting, skip-counting, and addition mathematics facts. This instructional group will meet with me three times a week in their math workstations for twenty minutes each session while the class does an activity in an area other than mathematics. Tony will not miss his usual mathematics work with his classmates. I'll continue to work on these supplemental mathematics exercises with them for approximately nine weeks. Tony and the other students will be presented with instruction on pattern number exercises and counting practice (skip-counting by twos initially, and then by fives, and tens).

We will continue our work on addition mathematics facts problems taken from the first-grade mathematics curriculum textbook. Because there is no normed, repeated-measure assessment in mathematics that focuses exclusively on this set of skills, I'll use a twelve-question assessment that presents only these skills. Tony will complete it weekly so I can monitor his progress. The data will be charted to document how well Tony is responding to this extra intervention.

I have developed this plan in conjunction with Mr. Carmichael, our assistant principal and chair of the student support team. He has agreed to observe Tony during this Tier 2 intervention in order to address instructional fidelity.

Ms. Dawson, 10/10/09

3. Observational Notes of Student in Tier 2 Mathematics Intervention:

I observed the Tier 2 instruction in Ms. Dawson's class on 10/17/09. Tony participated in a lively fashion throughout the twenty-five-minute intervention period. Tony and the other students completed number pattern work (such as presenting the next number in the sequence) when a series of five numbers was written down. This exercise came from the mathematics text section on skip-counting, and Ms. Dawson presented the material in a clear, straightforward manner as described in the instructor's manual for that text. I also noted that Tony answered several questions correctly and got only one answer incorrect. While only two indicators of weekly assessment data were available for review, those data indicated some level of success and suggest that this is the right intervention for Tony at this point.

Mr. Carmichael, assistant principal, chair of student support team, 10/18/09

4. Tier 2 Intervention Summary and Recommendations:

    I implemented the Tier 2 intervention described above for Tony and three other students for five weeks. Tony's progress-monitoring data are summarized in the accompanying data chart. During week four, Tony was absent on Friday, so he was assessed twice the following week.

    While Tony seemed to be progressing somewhat, he should have been able to grasp all of these skills (number pattern work in twos and math facts addition problems below five) during this intervention. On the data summary chart [see fig. 3.2 on page 79], I charted the work of one of the other students who did master these skills during the first five weeks of intervention (for comparison purposes). This comparison makes clear that Tony is not moving forward quickly enough to have a realistic opportunity to catch up with the other first-grade students on number patterns or early mathematics skills by the end of the year. He is making most of the progress shown here on number pattern work on skip-counting by twos, but he does not seem to grasp the various strategies for simple math facts addition, such as counting on, even though I have repeatedly demonstrated this tactic for early mathematics addition problems. I believe that a more intensive intervention may be necessary for Tony in order to ensure that he does not fall further behind. After discussion with Mr. Carmichael, he and I have decided to hold a meeting of the entire student support team and talk with Ms. Stukes, the mathematics instructional coach for our school, about the possibility of a more intensive, Tier 3 intervention for Tony.

    Ms. Dawson, 10/22/09

5. Tier 3 Intervention Plan:

    Based on a Tier 2 intervention conducted by Ms. Dawson in September and October of 2009, the student support team met, reviewed the intervention data from the Tier 2 intervention, and considered various options for providing a more intensive intervention for Tony. Team members for this meeting on 10/23/09 included Ms. Dawson; Mr. Carmichael; Ms. Stukes; Mr. Sosebee, the special education teacher; and Ms. Thurston, the school principal.

continued on next page →

After reviewing the Tier 2 data collected by Ms. Dawson, this group concurred that Tony was not making appropriate progress to meet his curriculum goals in mathematics this year. We agreed that a Tier 3 intervention would be necessary.

Mr. Carmichael suggested the possibility of having Tony come and join a small group of students in my class who receive individual software-based instruction in number sense exercises, pattern number prediction exercises, and early mathematics skills such as counting on for addition. This software program generates charted data on each student's daily performance, and that will serve as a running assessment of how Tony is performing daily during this Tier 3 intervention.

Tony will work in my class each day from 10:30 until 11:15. Thus, Tony will receive 45 minutes of supplemental mathematics instruction with me daily, while still participating in mathematics with Ms. Dawson daily. The software selected for Tony results in one-to-one instruction using a research-proven curriculum, and the instructional problems will be specifically targeted to the skills Tony needs in the areas listed above.

Ms. Stukes, mathematics instructional coach, 10/24/09

6. Observation of Student in Tier 3 Mathematics Intervention:

I made certain that I had the chance to observe the Tier 3 instruction offered to Tony by Ms. Stukes from 10/24/09 through 11/30/09. Tony is a happy student, and he seemed to enjoy the computer-based work; he participated in a lively fashion throughout the intervention period, and he never seemed to waver in his attention to the problems presented on the computer. The software program presented problems that were at exactly the correct level for Tony. During this observation, I noted that Tony answered almost all of the questions correctly, but did get four incorrect, and each of those questions dealt with an example of addition skills that involved the counting-on strategy. At the end of Tony's work, Ms. Stukes praised him for a great job, and then she reviewed those four problems.

Mr. Sosebee, special education teacher, 11/05/09

7. Tier 3 Intervention Summary and Recommendations:

On 12/05/09, the student support team met to consider Tony's academic performance on the Tier 3 intervention. That team consisted of Ms. Dawson, Ms. Stukes, Mr. Sosebee, and Ms. Thurston.

Ms. Stukes completed a five-week intervention with Tony, and that intervention resulted in charted performance data. These charted data represent an average percentage correct of all the problems Tony completed in the curriculum during the week. The data and the summary notes generated by the computer software indicate that Tony mastered prediction of the next number in number patterns involving both twos and fives within three weeks. [See fig. 3.3 on page 82.]

While it took a bit longer, the data show that he has now mastered use of the counting-on strategy for computing basic addition facts. Ms. Stukes indicated that his timed performance on basic addition facts does not indicate automaticity with these facts. In short, he is now successfully using the counting-on strategy, which should be viewed as a significant stepping stone for Tony, but clearly automaticity with those facts is essential.

For that reason, Ms. Stukes recommended Tony's continuation in the Tier 3 mathematics intervention for at least one more grading period. The student support team concurs with that recommendation, and the team will review Tony's performance at the end of the next grading period.

Ms. Thurston, principal, 12/05/09

There are a number of issues to consider when initiating a Tier 2 intervention, and many of the same concerns arise when initiating a Tier 3 intervention. In planning a Tier 2 intervention, it is critical that the intervention be targeted at the exact problems the child has demonstrated. In the case study, Ms. Dawson selected a set of instructional activities that focused specifically on pattern recognition activities and mathematics facts from the school's first-grade mathematics curriculum. Ms. Dawson believed that additional instructional time in a small-group setting on those exact, specifically targeted skills would assist those four students in catching up with the rest of the class. This is a much more effective strategy for targeted interventions than merely following a general mathematics curriculum with the Tier 2 instructional group.

Frequent, repeated progress monitoring during the intervention itself is critically important, since those data allow the teacher to determine the efficacy of the intervention, modify the intervention if needed, or move to a more intensive Tier 3 intervention, should that become necessary. In order to monitor Tony's performance, Mrs. Dawson devised a set of twelve assessment questions featuring pattern completion (counting odd numbers, counting by twos) and mathematics facts problems (simple addition problems with sums less than 25). She planned on using that assessment each week to carefully monitor the performance of these four students over a nine-week grading period. This level of detail is critically important in developing an effective repeated assessment for progress monitoring during the RTI process, since this will be immediately interpretable and understandable to other educators should a team of educators ever consider Tony's mathematics performance or the possibility that Tony might have a learning disability in mathematics. Ms. Dawson wanted to make certain that Tony's parents were informed about the Tier 2 intervention, so she wrote a note to the parents. While good, open communication with parents is always recommended in education, there is some question on the issue of exactly when parental notification is required under RTI procedures. Special education legislation

(Public Law 94–142, the first Education for All Handicapped Children Act) has required notification of parents prior to undertaking assessments that document the existence of a disability or help educators determine an appropriate educational placement. Of course, in an RTI procedure, the progress monitoring in Tier 1, 2, or 3 can all conceivably lead to documentation of a disability over time, and this raises the question of should parents be notified prior to any such performance monitoring? However, not all assessments in RTI procedures will lead to eligibility decisions, and in fact, the majority of these do not. Therefore, this question about when parents must be informed is not concrete. With that noted, parental involvement should certainly be encouraged by every educator, suggesting that parental notification early in the RTI process is both desirable and beneficial. For that reason, we recommend complete parental notification prior to initiating any Tier 2 or Tier 3 intervention procedures. A sample parental notification letter to Tony's parents is presented in the following feature box. Note that this recommendation is for parental notification of intervention—it is not to solicit parental permission for these interventions.

> We recommend complete parental notification prior to initiating any Tier 2 or Tier 3 intervention procedures.

Sample Parental Notification Letter for Tier 2 Mathematics Intervention

Dear Mr. and Mrs. Martin:

As we discussed previously, Tony is having some difficulty in mathematics, and I want to provide him with some extra assistance to make sure that he progresses in mathematics. I will be working with Tony and three other students on supplemental practice in early mathematics skills. I plan on pulling this group together three times each week for approximately twenty minutes each session, and I'll continue to work with them for approximately nine weeks. During that time, the students will be presented with patterns of numbers they need to complete; counting practice in counting by twos, fives, or tens; simple addition problems; and other types of problems in mathematics. Each week, I'll use twelve questions on Friday as a progress-monitoring check on how well Tony is doing. I'll share those data with you when we meet again.

Please let me know if you have any questions about this extra work, or call me anytime for any other concerns you may have. I enjoy working with Tony, and I'm looking forward to this opportunity to spend a bit more time with him on mastering his mathematics work.

Sincerely,

Ms. Dawson

Before beginning the intervention, Ms. Dawson shared her plan and the proposed activities with her assistant principal, Mr. Carmichael. While federal policies allow an individual teacher to initiate a Tier 2 intervention without consulting with anyone, the vast majority of schools and school districts require some consultation with an administrator and/or with the student support team prior to initiation of a Tier 2 intervention. We strongly encourage such consultation because having another educator involved in the Tier 2 planning process, even if just for a quick read through of the intervention plan, can often strengthen the plan. In order to foster simplicity in this RTI process, we recommend the type of informal consultation presented here; that is, consultation with perhaps one colleague such as a team leader, a grade-level leader, an administrator, or the chairperson of the student support team. A teacher meeting with one colleague on an intervention plan is typically easier to facilitate and thus more efficient than a meeting of the entire student support team.

In the case study, Mr. Carmichael is a certified teacher, as well as an administrator, and he had earned an additional certification endorsement in mathematics instruction. Note that Ms. Dawson also invited Mr. Carmichael to come and observe when Tony and the other students were receiving the Tier 2 mathematics instruction, and they scheduled a time for that observation. Thus, she had one colleague who knew of Tony's problems in mathematics and approved the proposed plan, and he had observed Tony during that intervention.

In schools with active professional learning communities, teachers are already receiving collegial support of the level needed for consultation and assistance during the RTI process, which is a significant advantage of the PLC model (DuFour et al., 2004). In those schools, PLCs are quite active throughout the RTI process.

In schools with active professional learning communities, teachers are already receiving collegial support of the level needed for consultation and assistance during the RTI process.

When progressing from one intervention to the next in an RTI process, each intervention should be more intensive than the previous intervention (Bender, 2009a). Only through such increasing intensity can teachers hold a realistic hope for success. For example, when a child is having difficulty in early math, merely working with that child for five minutes on one occasion is much less likely to alleviate the problem than working with that child for fifteen or twenty minutes three times per week. In the description of the proposed Tier 2 intervention on the RTI documentation form for Tony (pages 71–75), Ms. Dawson addresses a variety of indicators of the intensity of the Tier 2 intervention for Tony. Teachers initiating a Tier 2 intervention in a general education class should describe and document exactly what types of mathematics problems they intend to use as the intervention exercises. It should be clear from the Tier 2 intervention plan that the intervention is more intensive than the general instruction offered for the whole class.

Teachers should also state explicitly in the plan that the intervention is supplemental instruction and that participating students will not be removed from their other mathematics instruction. Teachers should note the intensity of the instruction by describing exactly how many minutes per day, how many days per week, and how many weeks the intervention will be conducted, as well as the overall size of the instructional group (the pupil–teacher ratio). This information is critical if and when a team of educators has to determine whether or not additional supplemental work might be necessary for Tony.

Should Tony progress all the way through the intervention tiers without success in developing early mathematics skills, it is possible that this Tier 2 intervention plan may provide significant information on which a later eligibility determination might be made. Research suggests that Tier 2 interventions in elementary mathematics are effective in that between 40 and 75 percent of students who begin a Tier 2 supplemental intervention have their mathematics difficulties alleviated to a substantial degree by that intervention (Ardoin et al., 2005; Bryant et al., 2008). Thus, the majority of students who begin a Tier 2 intervention will probably not require a Tier 3 intervention. However, these data also document that some students will need a more intensive intervention, and, among those students, some may eventually be considered for placement in special education based on a learning disability in mathematics. Thus, the documentation of the intensity of each intervention can become critical in later stages of the RTI process.

The level of progress monitoring should be noted, and again, it should reflect a more intensive progress monitoring than had been undertaken previously. In the case study, Ms. Dawson indicated exactly how she would monitor Tony's progress as well as how frequently such monitoring would take place. Documenting this monitoring is critical since teachers initiating a Tier 2 intervention procedure with any student will not know at that time if the RTI procedure for that student will progress all the way to an eligibility determination.

Teachers today are required to implement scientifically valid curricula (Fuchs & Deshler, 2007). Of course, teachers realize that interventions should be based on scientifically proven instructional tactics, and in most cases, teachers will probably use commercially available curricula that have received scientific support, as Ms. Dawson did here. Furthermore, Ms. Dawson solicited and received Mr. Carmichael's affirmation that the activities she selected were appropriate for alleviating the specific mathematics problems Tony and the other students demonstrated.

Teachers involved at every stage of the RTI process should consider an issue referred to in the RTI literature as *instructional fidelity* (Bender & Shores, 2007; Fuchs & Deshler, 2007). Instructional fidelity addresses the question, "Was the instruction offered appropriate for and of sufficiently high quality to provide a student with an appropriate opportunity to learn?"

> Instructional fidelity addresses the question, "Was the instruction offered appropriate for and of sufficiently high quality to provide a student with an appropriate opportunity to learn?"

In the case study, Ms. Dawson chose to implement some instructional activities from a scientifically validated instructional curricula. Use of such validated curricula should be the norm in all RTI procedures. As long as she implemented those activities as described in the instructor's manual, she did so with fidelity, since both the curricula and the specific instructional procedures had previously been shown to be effective in scientific studies.

In this case study, Ms. Dawson addressed instructional fidelity in several additional ways. She first shared her instructional intervention plan with Mr. Carmichael and solicited his suggestions during the planning phase. Next, while she was conducting the instruction for Tony and the other students, Mr. Carmichael came into the class-room and observed her conducting the instruction. Based on that observation, Mr. Carmichael wrote some notes that attested to the fact that Ms. Dawson taught those instructional activities as indicated in the instructor's manual. Observation of the actual instruction in targeted intervention tiers is the single strongest way to alleviate concerns with instructional fidelity. Should this Tier 2 intervention become part of a later eligibility determination, Mr. Carmichael can attest that Ms. Dawson imple-mented the instruction in this tier with fidelity. Note that the form includes a section for observa-tion by a third party for both the Tier 2 and the subsequent Tier 3 intervention so as to document instructional fidelity at each intervention tier.

> Observation of the actual instruction in targeted intervention tiers is the single strongest way to alleviate concerns with instructional fidelity.

Ms. Dawson noted that the other two students in the group were moving toward increased success while Tony was not progressing as quickly as she would like. Ms. Dawson began to believe that Tony would need more intensive instructional assistance.

After five weeks in the intervention, Ms. Dawson wrote some informal notes, and then she summarized her intervention efforts for Tony. She also created a data chart to summarize his progress (fig. 3.2). She then took that summary report and the data chart to Mr. Carmichael to determine the next steps in this RTI process.

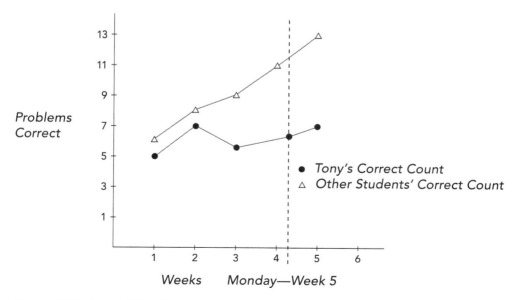

Figure 3.2: Tony's Tier 2 intervention data.

It is important to note the flexibility this RTI procedure gave Ms. Dawson. Note that her original plan for the Tier 2 intervention was to conduct that intervention for nine weeks with Tony and the other students. However, after only five weeks, it was clear (with support from weekly progress-monitoring data) that the intervention was not robust enough for Tony's needs. Thus, Ms. Dawson determined that it was in Tony's best interest to request a more intensive intervention for him prior to allowing the entire nine-week period to pass by. RTI procedures should be flexible in this way by allowing teachers to make instructional decisions as necessary for the students' progress. In this case, Ms. Dawson and Mr. Carmichael decided to bring the matter to the school's student support team for consideration.

In RTI procedures, the student support team, and not a child eligibility team, should take the lead, as indicated in the case study. While different states and districts use different terms for these distinct school-based teams, the team most heavily involved in Tier 1 instruction and Tier 2 interventions is the team at the school level that is dedicated to assisting teachers and students with specific educational struggles. In many states, that team is referred to as the student support team. This is not the team that ultimately makes a recommendation for placement in special education classes (Bender & Shores, 2007). In that sense, RTI is a function, predominately, of the general education faculty at the school, and not the special education faculty or the eligibility team.

> The team most heavily involved in Tier 1 instruction and Tier 2 interventions is the team at the school level that is dedicated to assisting teachers and students with specific educational struggles. In many states, that team is referred to as the student support team. This is not the team that ultimately makes a recommendation for placement in special education classes.

Tier 3 Intervention

Ms. Dawson and Mr. Carmichael met with other members of the student support team including Ms. Stukes, the mathematics instructional coach, and Ms. Thurston, the school principal. Ms. Dawson presented the data summarized in figure 3.2 (page 79) and discussed her Tier 2 instruction with the team. The data suggest that while Tony seemed to be progressing, he was not moving forward quickly enough to have a realistic opportunity to catch up with the other first-grade students, since most of her other students had totally mastered these early number sense and addition facts.

Mr. Carmichael then told the team he had participated in the selection of the instructional activities Ms. Dawson used with Tony. He also stated that he observed one class period when Tony received the Tier 2 supplemental instruction. Finally, Mr. Carmichael indicated that the instructional activities were the correct type of activities for Tony, but that Tony would need more instruction in those early mathematics activities. Therefore, both he and Ms. Dawson recommended that the team consider a Tier 3 intervention that would address the same early mathematics skills, but would offer a more intensive intervention for Tony. After all team members concluded that such a Tier 3 intervention seemed reasonable, Mr. Carmichael suggested implementing an intensive Tier 3 intervention.

Ms. Stukes, the mathematics instructional coach, was typically given a smaller class than the other teachers, and she also had a paraprofessional to facilitate meeting her duties as an instructional coach. These resources allowed her to do extra duties, such as model teaching for other teachers or support struggling students in mathematics. With that extra support, she could also conduct intensive instruction in mathematics for students from other classes. She stated that she was currently teaching an intensive small group of four students for forty-five minutes daily in a computerized mathematics readiness and early mathematics curriculum. That curriculum used the computer to present individually to students a wide variety of tasks in the areas of number sense and early mathematics skills. The curriculum was structured to specifically target individual weaknesses of each student and then emphasize instruction in those areas. The curriculum generated a daily report of progress for each student, which could be used to monitor student performance. Thus, Tony would receive mathematics instruction with Ms. Dawson daily, as well as forty-five minutes of intensive supplementary, Tier 3 instruction on the specific skills he needed. The team decided to go with that recommendation and meet at the end of the next grading period in six weeks to consider Tony's progress.

There are several important points to consider when implementing a Tier 3 intervention. Student support teams should prescribe to the RTI expectation that increasing tiers of intervention provide more intensive instruction, as indicated by factors such as pupil-to-teacher ratio and the time commitment given to the intervention each week. Table 3.4 compares the Tier 2 and Tier 3 interventions provided for Tony and shows how the intensity increased from Tier 2 to Tier 3.

> Student support teams should prescribe to the RTI expectation that increasing tiers of intervention provide more intensive instruction, as indicated by factors such as pupil-to-teacher ratio and the time commitment given to the intervention each week.

As the table shows, Tony's Tier 3 intervention was considerably more intensive than the Tier 2 intervention in every respect. Thus, it was reasonable to believe that Tony's problems in mathematics readiness could realistically be addressed by providing this supplemental program.

Table 3.4: Levels of Intensity of Tier 2 and Tier 3 Interventions

Indicator of Intensity	Tier 2	Tier 3
Time commitment	Twenty minutes, three times per week	Forty-five minutes a day
Performance monitored	Every week	Daily or weekly
Pupil-to-teacher ratio	Four to one	Individual

We should note that implementation of instructional interventions using computerized curricula provides numerous advantages. Many teachers in general education are challenged to find time to implement an intensive intervention while at the same time continuing to teach the other members of the class. Individualized computerized programs offer support for the general education teachers in that regard. In the case study, Tony received his intensive Tier 3 instruction via the computer software while Ms. Stukes instructed the rest of the class. Software-based instruction also addresses the issue of instructional fidelity. Computer software presents the intervention in the same fashion for each student and in the same way as when the program was validated by research. And software programs are typically quite intensive and delivered in one-to-one instructional format. At the Tier 3 intervention level, these characteristics are quite desirable.

> Implementation of instructional interventions using computerized curricula provides numerous advantages.

As the data in figure 3.3 indicate, the weekly progress-monitoring checks for Tony showed impressive progress on these early mathematics skills even before the grading period was over. Thus, Tony was receiving instruction at the exact intensity level he needed in order to make progress and catch up with his classmates over time. At the end of the grading period, when the team reviewed the data in figure 3.3, they decided to keep Tony in the intensive Tier 3 intervention longer to facilitate his continued growth in mathematics.

Important Issues for RTI in Early Math

There are several important issues to consider when providing interventions in early math: support for the general education teacher, the use of multiple interventions, and how long to continue using supplemental interventions.

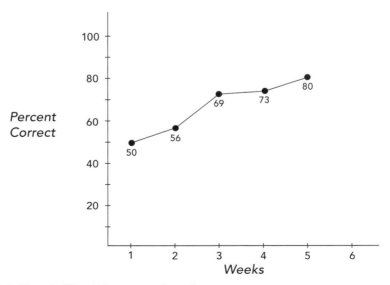

Figure 3.3: Tony's Tier 3 intervention data.

Support for the General Education Teacher

As the case study demonstrates, a general education teacher will typically teach the student in Tier 1 instruction, and, when necessary, initiate the Tier 2 supplemental intervention. In most cases, that teacher will have to undertake these responsibilities without extensive additional support. Thus, finding the time for such interventions may be one of the largest challenges to RTI (Bender, 2009a; Bender & Shores, 2007; Fuchs & Deshler, 2007).

In this case, the Tier 2 intervention from Ms. Dawson, while seemingly appropriate, did not provide Tony with the intensive instruction he needed to progress well in mathematics. Therefore, a Tier 3 intervention was necessary, and it is typically at this point during the RTI process that additional personnel and resources are involved. While schools and school districts vary considerably on what types of additional support they can provide during Tier 3 intervention, we are unaware of any example in which general education teachers are expected to implement interventions at the Tier 3 level without some additional support. While general education teachers will probably implement Tier 1 instruction and the first supplemental intervention—the Tier 2 intervention—for struggling students, they should request and receive some type of support to implement Tier 3 intervention.

What About Multiple Interventions?

The case study brings up an interesting question: should a student participate in more than one supplementary mathematics intervention at any one time? Most of the RTI literature concludes that they should not (see Bender, 2009a, for a review). In the case study, Tony was participating in traditional class instruction with Ms. Dawson and was also receiving a Tier 2 intervention from Ms. Dawson for several weeks. Once the data demonstrated that the Tier 2 intervention was not working as well as necessary, that supplemental intervention ceased, and Tony moved to a Tier 3 intervention in Ms. Stukes's class. Thus, struggling students may be participating in the general education curriculum and a supplemental Tier 2 intervention at the same time, and at a later point, a student may participate in the general education curriculum and a supplemental Tier 3 intervention. However, students should not participate in more than one supplemental intervention at any one time (Bender 2009a), and most state policies stipulate that point, though others do not (Bender, 2009a). A main reason is time; each supplemental intervention will take some time away from the student's other instructional needs, and multiple supplemental interventions simply shortchange other curricular areas. Thus, multiple interventions are not recommended.

> Students should not participate in more than one supplemental intervention at any one time.

How Long Should Supplemental Interventions Continue?

In the case study, the data demonstrated that the Tier 3 intervention succeeded, but that Tony had not completely caught up with his peers after only one grading period in the Tier 3 intervention. Thus, that Tier 3 intervention was continued for the remainder of the year, or until Tony caught up with his classmates on number sense and early mathematics skills. It is quite likely within RTI procedures for students to begin to show success during a Tier 2 or Tier 3 intervention, but then not catch up to their peers during the initial time period for that intervention. In those cases, the intervention, if shown to be successful, should be continued as long as necessary for the student to catch up with his or her peers.

> The intervention, if shown to be successful, should be continued as long as necessary for the student to catch up with his or her peers.

In many schools, this results in a subtle, though fundamental, change. Under RTI, many individual student cases will be "managed" over longer periods of time by the student support team than have been previously. Because most U.S. schools began their student support teams to serve the function of prereferral teams, most cases that reached the student support team were the responsibility of that team for a brief time—perhaps only long enough for the team to review the case file, or in other cases, perhaps for a grading period during which a general education prereferral intervention was attempted. At that point, in most cases, either the intervention was shown to be effective and no further action was required, or the file was turned over to the child eligibility team for consideration of a possible disability. Thus, until recently, it has been fairly rare for the student support team to manage an individual student's case for more than a single grading period.

However, as shown in the case study, under RTI, many students may be monitored for several grading periods by the student support team, particularly if a child is showing progress, but needs to continue in a Tier 2 or Tier 3 intervention. Therefore, within RTI, student support teams will manage the supplemental educational interventions for particular students for longer periods of time. Administrators should plan the team assignments for educators with that additional RTI monitoring responsibility of the student support team in mind.

> Under RTI, many individual student cases will be "managed" over longer periods of time by the student support team than have been previously.

It is important to note that the case study is a first-grade example, while traditionally most students with learning disabilities have been diagnosed in grades 3 or 4. Proponents of RTI expect that that age of onset for learning disability diagnosis will become lower because of implementation of RTI (Bender & Shores, 2007). In fact, given the RTI procedure, it is quite possible to diagnose a learning disability in the first half of the kindergarten year in either reading or mathematics. So students with learning disabilities will probably receive more intensive instruction much sooner than in the past, and this will result in fewer long-term mathematics and reading problems overall.

Diagnosing a Learning Disability in Early Mathematics

In the case study, the RTI procedure indicated that Tony does not have a learning disability in mathematics, since he did respond positively to instruction in the Tier 3 intervention. However, we should consider how the RTI process in mathematics might fit within a diagnosis of learning disability for early mathematics. Had the data in figure 3.3 (page 82) indicated a complete lack of progress for Tony, the student support team would probably have reviewed the Tier 1, Tier 2, and Tier 3 instruction and intervention data, and then concluded that Tony's problems in mathematics had not been adequately remediated. At that point, he would have failed to respond to both Tier 1 instruction, and two separate, targeted interventions (Tier 2 and Tier 3). Based on those data, the student support team would have recommended that the school's child eligibility team convene and consider whether Tony might have a learning disability in mathematics.

Had such a situation occurred, the student support team would not specifically state that Tony definitely had a learning disability. Rather, the team would indicate that the data suggest Tony might have a learning disability in math, based on his failure to respond to high-quality classroom instruction, as well as two separate, highly targeted interventions. At that point, the management of Tony's file would be moved from the student support team to the child eligibility team, and that team would begin the eligibility procedures. In most states, those eligibility procedures are quite similar to non-RTI procedures and include tasks such as conducting a psychological assessment to examine the student's auditory and visual processing skills, his or her memory skills, and other psychological processes that may underlie a learning disability. Also, the team would consider various medical or home factors that might impact a student's performance.

To be specific, after a student has not succeeded in general education classroom instruction and two targeted, intensive interventions (Tier 2 and Tier 3), a learning disability may be suspected, but at that point the learning disability has not been demonstrated. That determination is the responsibility of the eligibility team, and they will use the data from Tier 1, 2, and 3 for their deliberations, coupled with their interpretation of the underlying psychological processes (as demonstrated in a psychological report) as well as other relevant data.

We should point out the increased responsibility that general education teachers have in the eligibility process when documenting a learning disability. Of course, general education teachers have always participated in determining the eligibility of students for services for learning disabilities. Historically, general education teachers have

> Within RTI, general education teachers are responsible for providing one of the two most critical pieces of data in the determination of learning disabilities—the progress-monitoring assessment data charting for Tier 2 intervention.

participated in eligibility meetings, brought in work samples, done error analysis or task analysis of a student's learning skills, and so on, and these responsibilities continue in the RTI framework. However, within RTI, general education teachers are responsible for providing one of the two most critical pieces of data in the determination of learning disabilities—the progress-monitoring assessment data charting for Tier 2 intervention. General education teachers should be made aware of that increased responsibility and provided with support to understand the intricacies of their interventions and progress-monitoring responsibilities under RTI.

Conclusion

This chapter examined number sense and its impact on how RTI procedures in early mathematics are implemented, described some promising curricula for early mathematics, and presented Tony's case study to illustrate an early mathematics RTI procedure in action. It also detailed important issues for RTI in early math, including support for the general education teacher, the question of multiple interventions, and how long supplemental interventions should continue. It ended with a discussion of what happens when Tier 3 interventions are not enough and the role of RTI in diagnosing learning disabilities.

The next chapter will explore several case study interventions for children in the middle elementary grades, including interventions at both the Tier 2 and Tier 3 level.

RTI Procedures in Elementary Mathematics

Most of the limited research available on RTI procedures in mathematics has focused on early mathematics skills in kindergarten or grades 1 and 2 (Ardoin et al., 2005; Bryant et al., 2008; Chard et al., 2008; Fuchs, Fuchs, Compton, et al., 2007; Jordan et al., 2007). This is a concern because more than 50 percent of school districts are currently implementing RTI in mathematics across the grade levels (Spectrum K12 School Solutions, 2009). To ensure the success of these educators gearing up to implement RTI procedures in mathematics across the middle and higher elementary grades, we present in this chapter the information currently available on appropriate mathematics curricula, progress-monitoring tools, and RTI procedures for older elementary students.

We start by sharing some promising data from a study by Ardoin and colleagues (2005). These researchers investigated the impact of multitier interventions of increasing intensity in elementary mathematics. They investigated the effects of a targeted, intensive intervention on fourteen fourth-grade students who were struggling in mathematics. General education teachers were responsible for Tier 1 instruction, and the researchers themselves implemented an intensive tier of supplemental instruction for students showing difficulty in mathematics. Of course, the researcher-administered intervention makes this somewhat less than realistic in terms of how RTI interventions in mathematics are likely to be implemented in the schools. In most classrooms, teachers themselves are likely to have the responsibility for both Tier 1 instruction and Tier 2 interventions. Nevertheless, the data resulting from these interventions are quite promising in demonstrating the efficacy of RTI procedures beyond the primary grades. In the Tier 2 intensive intervention, nine of the fourteen target students made significant improvements. The five students who did not show substantial progress in Tier 2 did show progress with the addition of an increasingly intensive Tier 3 intervention. While this study involved only a limited number of students, and researchers administered the interventions, the results do indicate that a Tier 2 intervention in mathematics can alleviate mathematics difficulties for almost two-thirds of students struggling in mathematics, and even more students can begin to show progress with an increasingly intensive Tier 3 intervention. In short, this study, like studies done in the primary grades, indicates that the RTI procedure works.

Specifically, this chapter presents a brief discussion of several mathematics curricula and assessment tools that may be used in the elementary years, including the middle and upper years. It illustrates how RTI procedures in mathematics might be conducted beyond the primary grade level with several case studies. While almost any mathematics topic could serve as an appropriate example for the case studies presented here, we have chosen to present case studies based on the content and instructional recommendations of the NCTM (2006) and NMAP (2008). Those organizations strongly supported development of deep conceptual understanding in mathematics as well as automaticity with math facts, in particular multiplication and division math facts. The report of the NMAP (2008) also recommends increased emphasis on work with fractions, since students in mathematics in elementary and middle school grades often face challenges in these areas. We end the chapter with a discussion of what happens when Tier 3 interventions are not enough and a learning disability is suspected.

> Tier 2 intervention in mathematics can alleviate mathematics difficulties for almost two-thirds of students struggling in mathematics, and even more students can begin to show progress with an increasingly intensive Tier 3 intervention.

Mathematics Curricula and Progress Monitoring for Elementary Grades

While we could review a number of curricula and progress-monitoring assessment tools, we have instead chosen two mathematics intervention curricula that have progress-monitoring tools built in. When faced with the economic demands inherent in implementation of RTI interventions and progress monitoring, schools are well advised to select curricula that have internal assessment tools. This saves funds that otherwise would be used to purchase separate progress-monitoring assessment systems. Furthermore, it is likely that schools purchasing curricula and materials for RTI may place a higher priority on areas other than elementary mathematics—especially given the current emphasis on reading. Thus, judicious use of funds for mathematics curricula is essential.

Accelerated Math

Accelerated Math™ (www.renlearn.com/am) is published by Renaissance Learning™, the same company that produces the *Accelerated Reader*™ program, which is used frequently for reading and literacy instruction. This software-based mathematics instructional program presents mathematics practice activities ranging from grades 1 through 12 and is intended as either a Tier 1 instructional supplementary program or as an intervention program for Tier 2 or Tier 3 interventions in the RTI context.

Because the program is self-paced and completely individualized, students progress individually through multiple forms of the practice problem for tasks that require extra examples. The program aims for mastery at each level in the mathematics curriculum before allowing the student to proceed to the next level. In that sense, this curriculum ensures that students receive the level of intensity that they need on each mathematics objective, and slower students continue to work on specific objects until they have demonstrated mastery of them. We should also note that according to the company website, this mathematics intervention program has been used successfully for students with learning disabilities.

As in most computerized curricula, teachers can generate a wide variety of reports. For RTI purposes, the *Accelerated Math* TOPS report will be the most useful. This is an individualized student report that identifies specific skills on which the student has worked (such as multiplying money expressions involving whole numbers, estimating products, or rounding one to four digits), and it provides a variety of scores on that skill, including percentage correct and benchmark comparison scores. While this report does not present data in the most commonly used *x/y* axis data chart format found in the RTI literature (Bender, 2009a), the data can be interpreted directly from the TOPS report or transferred by hand to such a data chart in order to monitor progress over time.

Accelerated Math has been positively reviewed by the National Center on Response to Intervention, and has been shown to be an effective way to increase mathematics achievement (Yeh, 2007). Also, because of the relatively widespread use of the related literacy program, *Accelerated Reader*, teachers will feel very comfortable implementing this program in mathematics, and that can be an important consideration at every intervention level in the RTI process.

SuccessMaker Math

SuccessMaker® Math, produced by Pearson Education (www.pearsonschool.com), is one of the most widely used computer-driven mathematics curricula in the United States. This curriculum has been designed and updated to meet state and national content standards across the grade levels from kindergarten through grade 8. At the beginning of the program, individual students complete a placement module that determines their correct starting level. As students complete daily assignments on the computer, the program adapts automatically, presenting more complex work or revisiting skills with which students need extra practice.

The lesson activities are highly engaging and visually stimulating, with full audio support, online manipulatives, and real-world examples of problem solving. Students set their own pace, and teachers can choose to target specific learning objectives. With more than 3,300 hours of instruction available at different levels, this software program can be used with a wide range of learners, including students struggling in mathematics, and that makes the program very appropriate for use in mathematics RTI procedures in the primary and elementary grades.

SuccessMaker Math allows every child to proceed at his or her own pace. The individualized interactive lessons are highly adaptable—they reinforce individual students' weak skill areas as students work to understand basic concepts.

SuccessMaker Math is one of the most widely researched computerized mathematics learning curricula available. Evaluation studies using *SuccessMaker Math* courseware have consistently shown improved student achievement (Kulik & Kulik, 1987; Kulik, 1994). For example, Kulik and Kulik (1987) completed a meta-analysis of twenty-two published evaluation studies of *SuccessMaker Math* and reported that positive effects were especially large and consistent with the program. Average gains of 1.4 years were typical with a yearlong exposure to the program, and high academic gains were reported. Based on this research, we recommend this program for students in the primary and elementary grades, as well as for students who are consistently behind in mathematics.

MathMedia

MathMedia®, produced by MathMedia Educational Software, Inc. (www.mathmedia .com), is a comprehensive mathematics curriculum for students in kindergarten through grade 12 (as well as adults). Topics range from number sense and early operations to algebra, geometry, and GED preparation. The software is available as a site-license program for use on either single computers or local area networks. According to the company website, *MathMedia* is one of the top ten bestsellers in the nation. The curriculum can be used with struggling learners or with students working at an accelerated pace.

Modules are structured into fifteen lessons on specific topics (such as fractions), and each lesson takes approximately thirty minutes to complete. Lessons introduce each topic with multiple screens of information, including various definitions and examples, and then present questions for students to solve. They receive hints coupled with step-by-step explanations as necessary. Beginning students practice facts, and then move on to the task of learning the detailed steps of the mechanics of arithmetic with problem solving. Students do most of their work on the computer, although hard-copy worksheets also accompany the software. More advanced students work the problems using hard-copy worksheets, and then check their work with the computer. At any point in the explanation process, the student may return to the question and enter his or her answer to check its correctness.

Assessment tools are built into the program, as are various reporting options, making this program a good selection for use in RTI procedures. For example, each program contains assessments that can serve as both pretests and posttests. In various components of the curriculum, such as the Arithmetic series and the Basic Math series, student data are automatically recorded for teacher use.

Other Mathematics Curricula

We should note that many other supplemental curricula in mathematics are available commercially, a number of which we presented in chapter 3. We chose to feature these curricula for a variety of reasons, including the availability of assessments within each curriculum, and the focus on the elementary and upper elementary levels. Certainly each of these factors must be considered as schools determine which mathematics curricula may be of assistance for RTI implementation.

Case Study: An RTI for Automaticity in Multiplication Facts

As any veteran teacher in the elementary grades knows, many students in grades 4, 5, and beyond have not developed high levels of automaticity in multiplication or division facts. However, after initial instruction on the times tables, which typically takes place in grade 3, most students do seem to know the multiplication tables that involve pattern responses (or pattern calculation strategies). Table 4.1 shows the times tables and pattern responses that most students understand prior to grades 4 or 5.

Table 4.1: Times Tables and Pattern Calculation Strategies

Times Tables	Pattern Calculation Strategies
Ones	Any number times one is the original number
Twos	Skip-counting by twos
Fives	Counting by fives an exact number of times
Tens	Adding a zero to the end of the number or counting by tens

For many students, automaticity in the other multiplication tables, particularly the higher range of multiplication facts (that is, the threes, fours, and particularly, the sixes, sevens, eights, and nines) may be lacking. Sousa (2008) suggests that while patterns can assist in learning multiplication tables, they may also confuse the novice learner ("Why does $7 \times 3 = 3 \times 7$, and how can that fact help me figure out 3×8?").

Furthermore, both the NCTM focal points (2006) and the NMAP report (2008) emphasize teaching for deep understanding, and conceptually, multiplication and division math facts are frequently taught today as "repeated addition" or "repeated subtraction." Finally, in addition to stressing deep understanding, teachers must emphasize automaticity. In some cases, a lack of automaticity with some of

> Many students in grades 4, 5, and beyond have not developed high levels of automaticity in multiplication or division facts.

these multiplication math facts will lead to great difficulties in many other areas of mathematics. Teachers may well anticipate having to address exactly this type of difficulty in mathematics, and the RTI process provides a mechanism to do so.

In the case study in this chapter, Thomas, a fifth-grade student, is having difficulties in mathematics as a result of his lack of automaticity with multiplication facts. His mathematics teacher, Ms. Gullion, was determined to remediate this problem, so she initiated an RTI process for Thomas. Figure 4.1 documents that RTI process using the Response to Intervention Documentation Form presented in chapter 3.

Student: *Thomas Lovorn*	Age: *10*	Date: *9/14/08*
Initiating Teacher: *Ms. Gullion*	School: *Toccoa Elementary*	Grade: *5*

1. Student Difficulty and Summary of Tier 1 Instruction:

    Thomas is having difficulty in mathematics at the fifth-grade level. His work indicates that he does not know his times tables to a high level of automaticity, and he doesn't know some of the higher times tables at all. This leads to problems in every aspect of math, including working with fractions with unlike denominators, three and four digit multiplication, and word problems. His statewide assessment last year indicated a grade equivalent of 3.2 in mathematics. He will need an intensive intervention, initially aimed at mastering the times tables.

    I have shared a written synopsis of these concerns and the intervention plan below with fifth-grade team leader Mr. Westall.

    Ms. Gullion, 9/14/08

2. Tier 2 Intervention Plan:

    I will provide Thomas with some additional intensive instruction on times tables, along with three other students with similar needs, as a Tier 2 supplemental intervention. I will work with this group of four students three times each week for 15 minutes each time, while my paraprofessional supervises the class in other learning activities. I will use a set of timed instructional activities that focus on automaticity in times tables. At the end of each instructional period, I will chart the number of times tables facts from the six, seven, eight, and nine tables that Thomas can do in one minute. These data collected on Friday each week will be charted as performance-monitoring data. Finally, I will send a letter to the parents of the four students informing them of the intervention. We plan to begin the intervention next Monday.

    Ms. Gullion, 9/22/08

Figure 4.1: Response to Intervention Documentation Form for Thomas.

3. Observational Notes of Student in Tier 2 Mathematics Intervention:

    I observed Ms. Gullion on 10/5/08 as she delivered the Tier 2 supplemental math intervention on times tables to Thomas and several other students. Ms. Gullion used several practice worksheets and did three one-minute timings using a worksheet that included times tables from six through nine. The data from the last timing were used as Thomas's daily score, and he completed nineteen problems correctly.

    Mr. Westall, fifth-grade team leader, 10/05/08

4. Tier 2 Intervention Summary and Recommendations:

    I noticed during this four-week intervention that the other students were moving toward increased mastery on the higher times tables with this supplemental assistance in math. However, Thomas seemed to be making little progress, and based on his weekly assessment data [see fig. 4.2 on page 97], I believe he will need more intensive instruction in mathematics. On 11/15/08, I met with Mr. Westall and Ms. Bullock, two members of our student support team here at Toccoa Elementary School. We jointly decided that the Tier 2 intervention had not been successful and was not likely to have enough impact to help Thomas begin to catch up in mathematics achievement. Therefore, we discussed a third tier of intervention for Thomas.

    Ms. Gullion, 11/15/08

5. Tier 3 Intervention Plan:

    As the instructional coach at Toccoa Elementary School, I typically take responsibility for Tier 3 interventions. In my instructional lab, I have the services of a paraprofessional and various computer-based instructional programs designed to provide remedial intervention support. We conduct very intensive interventions for students working individually using this technology.

    For Thomas, the student support team recommended an intensive intervention of forty-five minutes daily, focusing initially on multiplication tables and problems involving them, such as two- and three-digit multiplication, division, and word problems. The program Academy of MATH by AutoSkill offers initial assessment and instructional intervention in this area, and that is what we will use with Thomas. Therefore, Thomas will receive math instruction with Ms. Gullion each day, as well as forty-five minutes of intensive supplementary instruction on the specific skills he needs in the instructional lab. The student support team will meet at the end of the next grading period in six weeks to reconsider Thomas's progress, and Ms. Gullion and I will work out a time that Thomas can come to the lab each day.

    Ms. Bullock, instructional coach, 11/15/08

continued on next page →

6. Observation of Student in Tier 3 Mathematics Intervention:

    I observed Thomas on 1/6/09 while he worked on a computerized math program led by Ms. Bullock in the instructional lab. Thomas was very engaged, and he completed most of the problems successfully. The program stressed times tables and higher multiplication in the context of various word problems. He followed program directions quickly and correctly, and he seemed to enjoy the work.

    Mr. Westall, fifth-grade team leader, 1/06/09

7. Tier 3 Intervention Summary and Recommendations:

    The student support team met and reviewed Thomas's performance in mathematics. Based on the data generated by the computerized program, Thomas is making good progress in mathematics, but he is not yet at grade level [see fig. 4.3 on page 103]. However, he has responded positively to this level of intensive, computerized instruction. The team determined to continue Thomas's work in the instructional lab, while likewise continuing his work with Ms. Gullion in the general education classroom. The team agreed to review Thomas's progress again at the end of the next grading period.

    Mr. Westall, 1/19/09

Describing the Problem and Tier 1 Instruction

In this case study, Ms. Gullion noted Thomas's difficulty in mathematics shortly after the beginning of the academic year. She postulated that his ongoing difficulties in working with fractions with unlike denominators, as well as his difficulty in long division and three-digit multiplication, stemmed from this lack of instantaneous command of his multiplication math facts. Ms. Gullion noted that Thomas did not know his upper-range times tables. She noted that his mathematics scores from earlier assessments indicated difficulties in mathematics, though those scores did not directly tie those difficulties to deficits in multiplication math facts.

There is additional information that Ms. Gullion could have added to enrich insight into Thomas's mathematics problems. First, she could have done times-table problem assessments to document exactly which math facts were difficult for Thomas. Next, she could have added more information about the types of instruction Thomas had received to date in her fifth-grade class. She did state Thomas's difficulty in various mathematics areas (unlike denominators, three-digit multiplication, word problems, and so on), but more explicit information is always desirable.

Finally, in many cases, general education teachers will be required to consult with other educators in the school prior to initiating a Tier 2 intervention in mathematics. While this is not a requirement in federal legislation, many schools and school districts in which we have consulted have required that general education teachers consult with someone prior to initiating a Tier 2 intervention. This may involve consultation with grade-team leaders, instructional coaches in various subject areas, administrators, or chairpersons of student support teams. If such consultation is required within the school prior to initiating a Tier 2 intervention, that consultation should be noted in the first section of the RTI documentation form. As a general guideline, we prefer to see such consultation required prior to initiation of a Tier 2 intervention, but schools vary considerably in terms of when other support team members or team leaders become involved in the RTI process (Bender, 2009a; Bender & Shores, 2007), and teachers should certainly follow district or state policies concerning when such consultation with other educators is mandatory.

Tier 2 Intervention

In the Tier 2 Intervention Plan section of the form, Ms. Gullion described the plan in terms of the various indicators of intensity, specifically to document that this Tier 2 intervention was more intensive than the Tier 1 instruction Thomas received previously. She notes the following:

- The curricular content of the intervention (six, seven, eight, and nine times tables, which are directly related to the specific mathematics problem noted previously)

- How many students will be in the group (to document pupil-to-teacher ratio)

- The length and timing of the intervention (fifteen minutes, three times per week)

- The instructional focus of the intervention (teaching multiplication facts as repeated addition)

- The progress-monitoring mechanism (one-minute, timed math facts worksheets on each intervention day)

- Frequency of the progress monitoring (data charted at the end of each week)

This level of specificity of the Tier 2 intervention plan is critical for a number of reasons. First, this description, though brief, is a complete blueprint of the planned intervention and should help in providing that intervention for Thomas. Furthermore, such a well-developed plan lets other educators, parents, and the student know what is involved in the Tier 2 intervention. Next, should the Tier 2 intervention not be successful, the child will presumably move into a Tier 3 intervention, and the teacher conducting that intervention will need very specific information on what has been attempted previously. Finally, should this child proceed through both Tier 2 and Tier 3 interventions without mastering the skills, these notes may serve as the basis for an eligibility discussion relative to a learning disability in mathematics. Explicit information on the interventions that were implemented, detailed at least at the level shown here, will be absolutely essential should such an eligibility discussion become necessary.

It is important to note that at the beginning of a Tier 2 intervention, the general education teacher conducting that intervention will not know if such an eligibility discussion will be required in the future. Thus, all Tier 2 interventions must be initiated on the basis of an intervention plan that is complete, well-described, explicit, and that will stand up to later scrutiny during an eligibility process, should one become necessary.

There are several other interesting points relative to this particular description of the Tier 2 intervention. First, when dealing with automaticity, it is important that teachers implement a rate-based intervention (for example, math facts completed correctly per minute), as well as a rate-based measure of performance. Automaticity in math facts does not only deal with accuracy of math facts recall, but also with quickness of math facts recall, so this type of rate-based measure is critically important in this context. Here, Ms. Gullion clearly understood the necessity for a rate-based progress monitoring measure in her planning for this Tier 2 intervention. Given the emphasis on automaticity in the NMAP report (2008), mathematics teachers should anticipate conducting an increasing number of rate-based interventions.

> Given the emphasis on automaticity in the recent NMAP report (2008), mathematics teachers should anticipate conducting an increasing number of rate-based interventions.

Note that in this case study, Ms. Gullion did not specifically identify a particular curriculum that she intended to implement, and for some educators that may raise certain questions. In most of the RTI literature, interventions are most often discussed in terms of implementation of a scientifically validated curriculum. In this example, however, Ms. Gullion stipulated an instructional procedure (timed instructional activities and one-minute timings) that has received research support. This is *precision teaching*, which involves instruction based on timed probes of students' performance in a variety of academic skills, and is based on a significant body of research (Lindsley, 1992; White, 1985). This approach is quite effective, and it has been recommended as a Tier 2 or Tier 3 intervention (Bender & Shores, 2007). While most Tier 2 and Tier 3 interventions will be described in terms of specific curricula, Ms. Gullion and other teachers can certainly implement instructional and progress-monitoring approaches that have received strong research support as components of a broader RTI process.

Documenting the Tier 2 Intervention

Once the supplemental interventions begin, documentation of the steps in the RTI process becomes even more important. The third section on the form for the case study, Observational Notes of Student in Tier 2 Mathematics Intervention, is the first level of documentation of the supplemental instruction provided in Tier 2. This observation is critical for documenting instructional fidelity, as described in earlier chapters. However, when a teacher chooses to use a scientifically validated instructional procedure rather than a curriculum, the documentation of instructional fidelity becomes even more crucial. Notice in this section that the team leader described at some length exactly what she saw Thomas doing during this intervention.

In addition to the instructional fidelity observation, documentation of the impact of the Tier 2 intervention involves two major aspects:

1. The charted data summarizing the Tier 2 intervention (see fig. 4.2)

2. Ms. Gullion's description of the impact of that intervention

Effective and efficient presentation of data is critical for RTI. In almost all of the literature available on RTI procedures, data are summarized in chart form, and in the vast majority of cases, they are summarized in x/y axis charts. In that data-charting format, the x axis represents the measure of performance, and the y axis represents instructional days, weeks, or sessions. This type of charting stems from behavioral charting principles, and is immediately interpretable to most teachers, parents, and students. This has led most proponents of RTI procedures to recommend presentation of data in this format (Bender, 2009a, 2009b; Bender & Shores, 2007; Kemp et al., 2009).

> Effective and efficient presentation of data is critical for RTI. In almost all of the literature available on RTI procedures, data are summarized in chart form, and in the vast majority of cases, they are summarized in *x/y* axis charts. In that data-charting format, the *x* axis represents the measure of performance, and the *y* axis represents instructional days, weeks, or sessions.

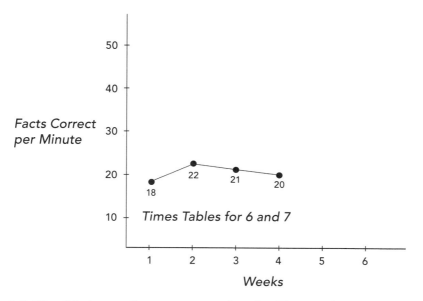

Figure 4.2: Tier 2 intervention summary data for Thomas Lovorn using "one-minute assessment" and precision teaching.

In some cases, curricula or progress-monitoring assessments may provide their own charting formats that use bar graphs or other common charting formats. These charting formats are perfectly acceptable for RTI procedures. The important factor is presentation of progress-monitoring data in an easy-to-use, easy-to-interpret fashion—not the actual charting format used. However, given that most data in the literature on RTI are presented in x/y axis format, should teachers need to develop their own charts to depict data on a student's performance over time during the RTI process as in this case study, we recommend using the x/y axis data chart format as a general practice.

In the case study, the data in the graph in figure 4.2 (page 97) indicate that Thomas was not making a great deal of progress with this level of intensive supplementary instruction. Note that these data involve four data points over a four-week period, with the exact number of problems completed correctly per minute presented under each data point. These data are fairly clear; they indicate virtually no increase in automaticity with the six and seven times tables. Thus, additional supplemental intervention is necessary.

As teachers consider how to interpret data from various RTI interventions, one question that is often asked is, "How much data is enough?" Of course, this is a complex issue, and there are no easy or clear answers to that question. Basically, educators need enough data to make a reasonable decision about the students' educational progress and to gauge whether or not the intervention is assisting the student in catching up to his or her peers over the short and long term.

Another consideration for the question of how much data is enough involves clarity of the data collected. In other words, given a certain data chart, are trends in the data clearly depicted relative to the student's progress, as they are in this case study example? Thomas's data clearly show no increase in automaticity. In cases when the chart of the child's performance data is fairly clear, it is acceptable to use fewer data for interpretive purposes.

However, it is true that the more data available, the more accurate a picture one has of the student's overall performance. Thus, with more data, educators are more likely to make correct decisions for a student's intervention. In that sense, weekly data indicators provide a better basis for educational decisions than data collected every other week, and six to ten weeks of data is better than four or five weeks.

Some state departments of education websites provide more guidance for educators by stipulating specific indicators concerning how much data must be generated from a Tier 2 or Tier 3 intervention. Teachers should check their state websites and their local school district policies for guidance on data collection. These indicators are often presented in different ways, including the following:

- A minimum of six (or eight or twelve) weeks of weekly data
- Daily data compiled for at least four weeks
- A minimum of four (or six or eight) data points over twelve weeks
- Enough data to clearly indicate efficacy of the intervention

Most of the research studies on RTI interventions collected weekly data over a period ranging from four weeks to twelve weeks. To make data collection simplest for educators, we recommend that most Tier 2 and Tier 3 interventions involve data collection at least once a week for a number of weeks equal to the length of a report card grading period at the school.

> We recommend that most Tier 2 and Tier 3 interventions involve data collection at least once a week for a number of weeks equal to the length of a report card grading period at the school.

There are other, more difficult issues with data interpretation beyond how often to collect data. For example, if a student's data chart indicates some increase, but not at a rate that suggests the student can catch up to his or her peers within one or two grading periods, what should be done? In this instance, the data show that the student did respond to an intensive, supplemental intervention, so the data would seem to indicate that the student does not have a learning disability. However, RTI is not primarily focused on merely demonstrating eligibility for special education services—it is intended as an intervention system to assist all struggling students, so the intervention that resulted in some success should be continued (perhaps coupled with even more intensive intervention). For that reason, many student support teams have found that they tend to manage students' instructional cases for longer periods during an RTI procedure. In fact, we have found that when a Tier 2 intervention data chart does show significant progress, the most frequent outcome tends to be continuation of that intervention for additional grading periods, with the student support team reviewing the student's progress periodically throughout the remainder of the year. Other issues concerning determination of eligibility for services in a learning disability program are discussed later in this chapter.

After Tier 2 intervention, educators may choose from a variety of future interventions based on the outcomes of the data collection; the most common are presented in table 4.2 (page 100). This chart is not an exhaustive list of possible future interventions, though most data-based team decisions during the RTI process will involve one of these options.

The teacher's notes on the student's performance are a critical element of the documentation for the Tier 2 intervention (see item 4 in fig. 4.1 on page 93) in conjunction with the data chart. Notes from the teacher who is directly responsible for the daily administration of the intervention provide great insight into the instruction the student has received. The teacher who has ultimate responsibility for daily intervention in each tier should write the notes on the efficacy of the intervention. While this may seem like an obvious point, it is an important one. We have seen paraprofessionals administering Tier 2 interventions in many schools. This is certainly acceptable practice, since many curricula are designed to be implemented in that fashion; however, we strongly recommend that paraprofessionals conducting RTI interventions work under the close supervision of highly qualified, fully

We strongly recommend that paraprofessionals conducting RTI interventions work under the close supervision of highly qualified, fully certified
teachers. We suggest that the teachers who are ultimately responsible for
the intervention prepare the summary
notes on intervention efficacy.

certified teachers. We suggest that the teachers who are ultimately responsible for the intervention prepare the summary notes on intervention efficacy. Should questions arise later in the RTI process, the teacher will be held responsible for that intervention, and thus should contribute the summary notes, even though a paraprofessional working in the class may have done most of the actual daily instruction.

Table 4.2: Options for Future Intervention Based on Possible Data Outcomes

Possible Data Outcomes	Possible Future Interventions
Data chart shows great success, and student is now on grade level or meeting benchmarks.	Discontinue the intervention; student continues participation in general education.
Data chart shows some success, but student is not yet on grade level or meeting benchmarks.	Continue the intervention for an additional grading period; student continues participation in general education. *Or* Modify intensity of the current intervention without otherwise changing it. *Or* Move student to a more intensive intervention and continue participation in general education.
Data chart shows little positive growth on targeted skills.	Move student to a more intensive intervention and continue participation in general education. *Or* Move the student forward toward a child-study team meeting to consider eligibility for special education services.

Planning and Conducting the Tier 3 Intervention

In the case study, the Tier 2 intervention summary and recommendations indicated that the general education teacher, Ms. Gullion, and her team leader, Mr. Westall, chose to meet with the instructional coach for mathematics, Ms. Bullock, at their school when they reviewed the Tier 2 intervention data. In our experiences, almost all Tier 3 interventions are managed by someone other than the general education teacher, simply because of the time requirements for delivering Tier 1 instruction and conducting a number of different Tier 2 interventions (Bender, 2009a). Thus, when Tier 2 intervention data document the need for more intensive instruction, involvement of the educator who might be responsible for delivering that instruction is advisable. In the case study example, notice that the next section of this RTI procedure, the Tier 3 intervention plan, involves planning for a more intensive, Tier 3 intervention for Thomas. In this case, Ms. Bullock, as instructional coach, chose to describe the proposed Tier 3 intervention since she would be responsible for administering that intervention. Again, she describes the intervention in great detail. She describes the number of minutes per day devoted to the intervention, the number of days per week, and the exact curricular focus of the intervention activities.

In this case, the intervention uses a software-based educational curriculum through which Thomas will receive one-on-one instruction based on a research-proven educational curriculum. The *Academy of MATH* curriculum Ms. Bullock selected provides both a computerized intervention and a detailed assessment system. The curriculum has received research support, and it does lead to significant increases in mathematics skill overall (AutoSkill, 2004; see www.autoskill.com). Of course, Ms. Bullock could also have used the *Accelerated Math* curriculum described previously in this chapter, or any other curriculum that included the specific set of skills in which Thomas needed additional intervention and had research support showing its efficacy.

Because Ms. Bullock is using software-based instruction for Thomas, and the software is essentially delivering the Tier 3 intervention, there is somewhat less of a concern for instructional fidelity than if a teacher was delivering an intervention. Software programs will consistently follow the intended curricular design, and they will deliver the intervention in the same fashion each time for each child. Also, most modern software will modify the overall instructional program delivered to the student based on the student's exact responses, as does this curriculum. In that sense, software may be more responsive to student needs than individual instruction from the teacher.

When we discuss software-based interventions in our workshops, several questions inevitably arise. First, teachers sometimes object to software-based instruction as "taking the teacher out of the equation." This is not the case for most software-based instruction. Teachers will always be necessary to select the software, monitor the student's performance, assist the student when he or she gets stuck on particular problems, interpret the student's performance data from the intervention, and perform many other teaching tasks that are not done well by software programs. In short, teachers will never be replaced by software, but well-designed curricular software programs can save teachers vast amounts of time by presenting high-quality, targeted instruction and instructional practice for students at various tiers in the RTI process. In short, we recommend software-based instruction at all tiers of the RTI process, whenever it is feasible and affordable.

Another question involves the attention levels of students during software-based instruction. For example, many students with attention problems seem to attend to high-quality software programs better than they attend to teacher-led instruction. While we are aware of no research to date documenting this phenomenon, many teachers have experienced one or more students with attention deficit disorders who cannot seem to pay attention for more than two or three minutes in class, but will stay totally engrossed in high-quality educational software-based programs for thirty minutes or more. We are not referring to educational games, but rather instructional software in various initial-instruction, nongame formats. In the example of Thomas, when Mr. Westall observed him during the Tier 3 intervention, he noted that Thomas was highly engaged with his software-based work.

Not only does use of high-quality software result in effective instruction, but it also assists with the instructional time concerns inherent in RTI procedures. For these reasons, high-quality software-based instructional programs in mathematics may be the most effective instructional format for some students in the various RTI tiers.

Schools are well advised to consider software-based instruction for struggling students. Not only does use of high-quality software result in effective instruction, but it also assists with the instructional time concerns inherent in RTI procedures. For these reasons, high-quality software-based instructional programs in mathematics may be the most effective instructional format for some students in the various RTI tiers.

As shown in the Tier 3 intervention summary and recommendations for Thomas, the software program used for his intervention resulted in significant educational improvement. This is documented in both the Tier 3 data chart (fig. 4.3) and Ms. Bullock's notes. Note that during the progress monitoring in Tier 3, the times tables were taught using a rate-based format (the assessment measured how many multiplication math facts the student could correctly answer in one minute). The graph also indicates changes in the content taught during the intervention, as the student moved to higher times tables.

In this example, the team chose to continue the Tier 3 intervention for Thomas for at least one more grading period. This will give Thomas more time to make progress on his times tables and allow him to catch up with his peers in the other areas of mathematics that were negatively affected by his lack of automaticity in multiplication facts. In our experience, this type of recommendation is quite common after both Tier 2 and Tier 3 interventions.

Case Study: An RTI for Finding Common Denominators

The report of the NMAP (2008) stresses that much more instructional time should be devoted to teaching students to work with fractions, decimals, and percentages.

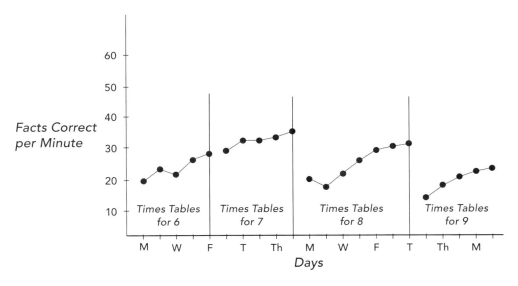

Figure 4.3: Tier 3 intervention summary data for Thomas Lovorn using *Academy of MATH* **curriculum.**

The panel specifically states that skills in this area are critical for continuing academic progress in mathematics through the elementary and middle school years. Furthermore, many students do experience considerable difficulty in mastering the array of sequenced skills involving mathematical operations with fractions.

A Choke Point in Mathematics

Many teachers find that there seem to be specific points in the sequence of skills involving using fractions that are particularly difficult for some students. We have used the term *choke point* to discuss such specific, particularly difficult curricular skills that for some students seem to stifle or halt all forward progress. For example, some students progress nicely in math facts and early addition or subtraction exercises, but seem to lose any forward progress academically once multiplication is introduced. Thus, this may be a mathematics choke point for some students, since this would tend to halt their progress in a variety of subsequent mathematics areas. In working with fractions, most students seem to grasp with no particular difficulty the early concepts involving operations and even understand the initial work on addition and subtraction involving fractions with like denominators. However, these same students seem utterly lost when challenged with the concept of fractions with unlike denominators. This is a choke point that many elementary teachers have noticed in their own teaching experiences.

We must point out that these and other choke points in the school curriculum are based entirely on our personal clinical experience, coupled with repeated confirmations from other teachers that such challenging points exist. This concept of curricular choke points is not based, at least presently, on specific research concerning how students learn. However, veteran teachers typically agree that such difficult areas exist. These choke points seem to be the exact points at which specific Tier 2 interventions in an RTI process can be particularly effective.

The following case study presents a scenario involving development of an RTI process for a grade 4 student, Traci Davis, when she reached a commonly experienced choke point: fractional operations with uncommon denominators. Figure 4.4 shows the Response to Intervention Documentation Form for Traci's case study.

| Student: *Traci Davis* | Age: *11* | Date: *9/14/09* |
| Initiating Teacher: *Mrs. Snyder* | School: *Eastonalle Elementary* | Grade: *4* |

1. Student Difficulty and Summary of Tier 1 Instruction:

In the fourth-grade mathematics class, we have begun to work on operations with fractions involving unlike denominators. While working on several practice sheets involving addition and subtraction operations with fractions, I noticed that Traci completed the problems that had like denominators, but she did not successfully complete a single problem that involved finding a common denominator. I've seen this same problem on three different days while working on operations with fractions. On her last worksheet, which included seven such problems, she merely added the denominators together in the problems involving unlike denominators. This suggests that she does have a grasp of operations with fractions, but is having difficulty finding a common denominator. I inquired to her third-grade teacher about this, and she indicated that she had seen no problem in Traci's work in fractions, but she then pointed out that problems with uncommon denominators were not frequent in the third-grade curriculum. Traci's third-grade state testing data indicated a grade equivalent of 3.4 in mathematics, and, while that is a bit low for an assessment administered at the end of the third-grade year, the overall assessment noted no general problems. I conclude that Traci is having difficulty specifically with finding common denominators, and intend to work with her in that area.

Mrs. Snyder, 9/14/09

2. Tier 2 Intervention Plan:

In my fourth-grade class, seven students in addition to Traci are having difficulty finding the common denominator. I intend to work with this group for twenty minutes, four days a week (Monday through Thursday), while other class members complete a group project in social studies under the direction of my teaching assistant. Thus, these students will not be taken out of their mathematics class, but they will receive supplemental instruction directly dealing with finding common

Figure 4.4: Response to Intervention Documentation Form for Traci.

denominators. We will use the activities in our adopted mathematics curriculum, and during each twenty-minute instructional session, I will reteach the process for finding a common denominator, stressing the concept of equivalence between the fractional components. I anticipate using various manipulatives to assist in reinforcing the equivalence concept for seeking common denominators.

I will teach this group of students for six to eight minutes with the students working on one to three problems in teams of two. I will use the instructional steps described in lesson twenty-three in the teacher's manual from that curriculum. The final twelve to fourteen minutes will be spent on individual practice, and students will complete five problems each day involving both finding the common denominator and then completing either an addition or subtraction operation. Each day, I will chart the total number of times the individual students found the common denominator, as well as the number of times each student got the correct answer. Students who get the highest number correct on that score (ranging from zero to ten) will be rewarded each day.

I presented this intervention plan to Traci's parents (and all of the parents of the other students involved), and I also shared this with Ms. Toomie, who chairs the student support team for Eastonalle Elementary School. She agreed that the plan seemed appropriate, and that she would review the individual progress-monitoring data for all of these students along with me in four weeks.

Mrs. Snyder, 9/15/09

3. Observational Notes of Student in Tier 2 Mathematics Intervention:

Mrs. Snyder, one of the fourth-grade teachers at Eastonalle Elementary School, requested that I visit her class when she was conducting a Tier 2 RTI for several students who needed additional work on finding common denominators. On 10/12/09, I was able to visit and observe her instruction and the students' responses to that instruction. She was working with seven students in a small group (one student was absent). I noticed that she followed the curricular instructor's manual and provided a demonstration example using fraction manipulatives in a subtraction problem involving finding the common denominator. During the final fifteen minutes, Traci attempted five problems and was not able to obtain a single correct common denominator, and as a result, she was not successful in obtaining the correct answer.

Ms. Toomie, chair of the student support team, 10/12/09

continued on next page →

4. Tier 2 Intervention Summary and Recommendations:

    As the mathematics instructional coach for Eastonalle Elementary, I met with Ms. Toomie and Mrs. Snyder to discuss the academic performance of several students, including Traci Davis. While several students responded well to the Tier 2 intervention conducted by Mrs. Snyder on finding common denominators, Traci's daily problems do not show substantial progress, as shown in the data chart [see fig. 4.5 on page 109]. Mrs. Snyder and Ms. Toomie concur with this general conclusion, and they believe that a more intensive intervention will be necessary for Traci. I would note here that both Mrs. Snyder and I were somewhat surprised by these intervention data, as she expected that this intervention would alleviate Traci's difficulties on this particular mathematics task.

    In planning the next course of action, Ms. Toomie indicated that a meeting of the full student support team would not be necessary in this instance, as the data on Traci's performance are fairly clear. We jointly decided to provide a Tier 3, intensive supplemental intervention in mathematics focused specifically on finding the common denominators for Traci. I will develop and present to Ms. Toomie and Mrs. Snyder a plan for that Tier 3 intervention. Pending approval, I will also provide that instruction for Traci.

    Mr. Cheeks, mathematics coach, 10/21/09

5. Tier 3 Intervention Plan:

    Two students are experiencing significant difficulty in learning to identify common denominators and perform mathematical operations in fractions. I will work with these two students as a small group for thirty minutes each day at 10:30 (immediately after recess) on this particular mathematics skill. I will use the curriculum adopted by our school and select lessons specifically on finding common denominators. I will conduct a weekly assessment on this skill and chart the data on each student's ability in finding common denominators and performing addition and subtraction operations with fractions. We will begin this intervention in one week, right after the report cards are disseminated, and the students will work on this intervention for the next nine-week grading period.

    Mr. Cheeks, 10/28/09

6. Observation of Student in Tier 3 Mathematics Intervention:

    (No observation conducted.)

7. Tier 3 Intervention Summary and Recommendations:

Traci participated in the Tier 3 intervention focused on finding common denominators, working with Mr. Cheeks daily for nine weeks. She missed only one day in this timeframe, and Mr. Cheeks indicated that Traci participated actively in the intervention. She still seemed unable to grasp the concept, even with Mr. Cheeks using manipulatives almost daily. While Ms. Toomie was scheduled to observe this intervention for Traci, she became ill during the second week of the grading period, and was unable to do so. While such observation is desirable during each RTI intervention tier, it is not required. In the absence of Ms. Toomie, I, Mr. Kreger, assistant principal, have been serving as chairperson of the student support team. On 11/09/09, I presented Traci's progress-monitoring data to the entire student support team. Mr. Cheeks serves on that team, and for the discussion concerning Traci, Mrs. Snyder was also present.

The data [see fig. 4.6 on page 111] do not indicate significant progress on this discrete skill. While a small level of progress is evident (a slight increase overall), Traci is still missing more problems than she gets correct, and this level of progress will not allow Traci to move forward in her mathematical skill development.

Because working with fractions is so critical to higher success in mathematics, we have spent considerable time in two distinct interventions working with Traci on this skill. Data from both the Tier 2 and Tier 3 interventions indicate a general lack of progress overall.

For this reason, the student support team determined to seek further assistance for Traci by having these interventions reviewed by the child eligibility team to determine if some type of disability may be negatively impacting Traci's performance in math. The team instructed me to summarize these findings and pass these data and this RTI summary report on to the child eligibility team, which I hereby do, on 1/28/10.

Mr. Kreger, assistant principal, 1/28/10

Describing the Problem and Tier 1 Instruction

The RTI process in this case study follows the same general format as RTI procedures previously discussed in this text. In the first section of Traci's Response to Intervention Documentation Form, Mrs. Snyder describes the specific problems Traci demonstrates and relates those to Traci's overall mathematics achievement. In most schools, the skill of finding common denominators is introduced in grade 4, and so this particular difficulty has not resulted in significant academic deficit for Traci up to this point. However, Mrs. Snyder indicates that such a skill deficit will impact Traci's progress during grade 4, and thus, there is a need for supplemental Tier 2 intervention to assist Traci through this curricular choke point.

At the outset, it seems clear that Mrs. Snyder believes that some supplemental instruction will greatly assist Traci in that mathematics choke point, since Mrs. Snyder did not note any other extreme difficulties in Traci's work. Many times, students need only a bit of supplemental assistance to get past particularly difficult subject matter, and a Tier 2 intervention may be all that is required. As discussed previously, research has shown that between 25 percent and 75 percent of students who receive a Tier 2 intervention have their mathematics difficulties alleviated by that intervention and do not experience ongoing difficulties in mathematics (Bender, 2009a; Fuchs et al., 2006; Fuchs, Fuchs, Compton, et al., 2007).

> Research has shown that between 25 percent and 75 percent of students who receive a Tier 2 intervention have their mathematics difficulties alleviated by that intervention and do not experience ongoing difficulties in mathematics.

Tier 2 Intervention

Mrs. Snyder's planned Tier 2 intervention (as noted in the Tier 2 supplemental intervention plan section of the documentation form) is aimed directly at Traci's area of difficulty. She provides appropriate detail to document the exact intervention and how she would use the instruction time. However, Mrs. Snyder had to face one issue in this RTI procedure that was somewhat different from previous RTI procedures described in this text. In the elementary grades, many RTI procedures are likely to involve more complex problems than mathematics facts or simple operations, and complex problems take longer than simple, single-operation problems. Therefore, some consideration needs to be given to time required to adequately monitor performance on complex problems.

In this case study, Traci had to calculate a common denominator and then perform an addition or subtraction operation, and that takes more time than merely performing operations for problems with like denominators. Given the limited time in each daily Tier 2 intervention (twenty minutes in this example), only some of that time could be devoted to progress monitoring (twelve to fifteen minutes per Mrs. Snyder's description). In that limited timeframe, how many multioperation problems can Traci realistically complete?

Requiring Traci to complete fifteen or twenty such problems daily for progress monitoring would not allow her to finish the daily intervention in the limited timeframe. Using the actual practice problems as the daily progress monitoring measure saves Mrs. Snyder some time each day, but this meant Mrs. Snyder had to require completion of a limited number of problems daily in order to complete the intervention each day.

The problem with this solution is that considerable error can be introduced in the assessment data by limiting the number of problems on the daily assessment. If the number of problems on the daily assessment is too few, the measure becomes highly inaccurate. In an extreme example, one might imagine the difference between missing one problem out of a set of two problems, yielding a grade of 50 percent, versus missing one problem out of a set of ten problems, yielding a grade of 90 percent.

Our recommendation is to provide a minimum of five problems on the daily or weekly assessment for complex problems such as multistep fraction problems. Another alternative is to use weekly assessment data and collect such data only on Friday. Furthermore, if the data-charting procedures can be structured to provide some detail on which aspect of the problem was missed (as it does in this case study), that can be of benefit to the teacher in carefully monitoring performance. In this example, the data chart (fig. 4.5) clearly shows the distinction between errors on calculating the common denominator and errors on simple addition or subtraction of the fractions. Again, this will assist Mrs. Snyder in identifying ongoing problems.

> Our recommendation is to provide a minimum of five problems on the daily or weekly assessment for complex problems such as multistep fraction problems.

Mrs. Snyder informed both the parents and the chairperson of the student support team, Ms. Toomie, of her planned Tier 2 intervention. Local schools and school districts typically encourage such notification, even though it is not required by most state regulations. We certainly encourage a free flow of information to parents and other educators.

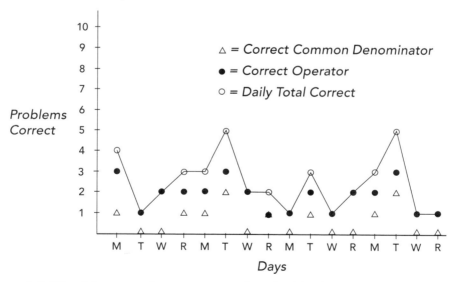

Figure 4.5: Tier 2 intervention summary data for Traci.

When Ms. Toomie observed Mrs. Snyder delivering the Tier 2 intervention to her small group, Ms. Toomie noted that Mrs. Snyder followed the prescribed lesson plan in the instruction manual, and furthermore, she noted that Traci was experiencing little success. Thus, that observation served both as initial documentation of response to intervention and as a check on instructional fidelity in the Tier 2 intervention.

Without question, we live in a time when data-based decision making is an absolute requirement. If data have not been collected and are not displayed in some meaning-ful, interpretable fashion, then an intervention has not been conducted. In this case study, the Tier 2 data chart (see fig. 4.5, page 109) and the written summary of the Tier 2 intervention both supported Ms. Toomie's observation: the Tier 2 interven-tion did not work. While it is rare that data will present such a clear picture of the failure of an intervention—indeed most interventions do seem to work to one degree or another—this type of failure will sometimes happen, and when it does, the team members have some options in terms of how they might proceed.

In this example, because of the clarity of the performance data, Ms. Toomie made the decision that a full meeting of the student support team would not be necessary prior to moving into a Tier 3 intervention for Traci. As discussed in chapter 3, we strongly sup-port team-based decision making and extensive, active involvement of all student support team members as a guiding principle. However, we also strongly support efficiency in decision making; we have been teachers and understand the time burdens on educators in the classroom. In this instance, because of the clarity of the data, three educators, rather than an entire student support team, were involved in the transition from the Tier 2 to the Tier 3 intervention: Mrs. Snyder, the general education teacher, Ms. Toomie, the chair of the student support team, and Mr. Cheeks, the mathematics coach. While we support early involvement of the student support team in general, we recommend that, in most school set-tings, the chair of the student support team and the general education teacher should be free to make some intervention decisions independently about the necessity of a Tier 2 intervention, in the interests of time and efficiency.

> While we support early involvement of the student support team in general, we recommend that, in most school settings, the chair of the student support team and the general education teacher should be free to make some intervention decisions independently, in the interests of time and efficiency.

Tier 3 Intervention

The Tier 3 intervention is almost always conducted by someone other than the general education teacher. In Traci's case, Mr. Cheeks, the mathematics coach, con-ducted the intervention. His description is highly specific and detailed, as is the Tier 3 data chart he includes in his plan (see fig. 4.6). While these data do indicate some improvement in Traci's ability to identify a common denominator, they do not show the type of substantial progress that would allow Traci to move toward grade-level skills in mathematics. In short, a move from 20 percent accuracy to 40 percent accu-racy on a skill that should have been mastered previously is not substantial enough to allow this student to move forward in mathematics overall. It is not uncommon for data to show some progress while still indicating a substantial skill deficit, and in that situation, the educational team will have to make a determination about what is best for the student in question. In some cases, further general education interventions might be in order, whereas in other cases, a referral to the special education eligibility team might be the option of choice.

Note that in this example, no one observed the Tier 3 intervention for Traci; this is explained in Traci's documentation form. The assistant principal, Mr. Kreger, is correct in noting that no observation is required for these interventions, but as we have pointed out repeatedly in this text, these observations are recommended in order to adequately address the instructional fidelity issue.

These interventions, taken together, indicate that Traci did not benefit from two highly intensive interventions that directly addressed her inability to identify common denominators and successfully perform mathematics operations with fractions that require finding common denominators. These results seemed to surprise the educators and suggested to them that Traci may have some undiagnosed disability in mathematics. The following section uses Traci's case study to illustrate the use of RTI procedures for diagnosis of learning disabilities in mathematics.

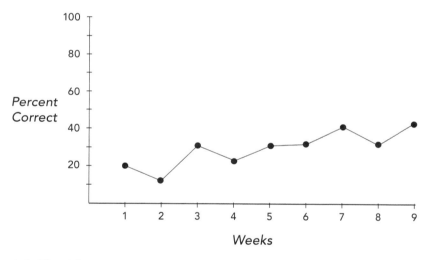

Figure 4.6: Tier 3 intervention summary data for Traci.

Diagnosing a Learning Disability in Elementary Mathematics

After a student has not shown positive response to two separate and increasingly intensive interventions, one may well ask, "What happens next?" As we have discussed previously, the primary focus of RTI procedures is to provide assistance to struggling students. However, 73 percent of school districts now use RTI procedures in the diagnosis of learning disabilities, as reported in one recent survey (Spectrum

K12 School Solutions, 2009), and perhaps 5 percent to 10 percent of those RTI applications will involve diagnosis of a learning disability in mathematics (Fuchs & Fuchs, 2002), as was the case with Traci in this example. Thus, some discussion of using this RTI in diagnosis is in order.

Traci has received two structured interventions, Tier 2 and Tier 3, aimed at alleviating her difficulties in mathematics and neither worked very well. When the student support team reviewed the Tier 2 and Tier 3 intervention data, they concluded that Traci's mathematics difficulties had not been adequately remediated—that is, she failed to respond to two separate tiered interventions, even though there was a slight increase in her performance during the last four weeks of the Tier 3 intervention. The student support team determined that the indication of some slight progress was not sufficient to allow Traci to catch up with her peers, and thus that indication of a slight increase was not deemed significant. Based on their overall review of these data, the student support team recommended that the child eligibility team convene and consider the possibility that Traci might have a learning disability in mathematics.

As discussed briefly in chapter 3, a student's failure to respond to several intensive interventions does not, by itself, indicate a learning disability, though certainly it provides evidence for one. The child eligibility team will meet to consider the evidence provided on how Traci responded to the Tier 2 and 3 interventions, and then they will conduct additional assessments to determine if a disability is indeed present. Educators should check their state or local eligibility policies to determine which assessments for learning disabilities are required and which are optional.

When a school uses RTI procedures to diagnose learning disabilities, staff members must perform a number of tasks: (1) tasks for implementation, support, and monitoring of the RTI procedures and (2) tasks for special education program eligibility. In most states, the student support team, primarily made up of general educators, performs the first role. In contrast, the child eligibility team, made up of general and special educators, psychologists, team leaders, administrators, parents, and others as necessary, is primarily charged with making decisions regarding eligibility for special education services. In most states, two different teams have performed these functions, and that is why we have chosen to discuss these teams as distinct throughout this text.

We have, however, seen some school districts use one committee for both the student support team function and the child eligibility team role. For example, in Toledo, Ohio, the public schools have traditionally had one team, the instructional response team, that performs both of these distinct roles. In schools and districts such as this one, some reorganization of RTI implementation may be necessary to allow one group of educators to monitor progress of students in Tier 1 instruction and Tier 2 and 3 interventions, and another group of educators to be responsible for subsequent eligibility decisions relative to special education placement.

However, we recommend establishing different teams for these two distinct roles—the student support team and the child eligibility team—to allow team members time to fulfill their respective functions. As mentioned in chapter 3, the "business" of the student support team is likely to increase using RTI procedures, as those teams manage students in Tier 2 over longer periods of time than in the past.

Conclusion

RTI procedures in middle and later mathematics are likely to be as varied as the wide array of skills within the mathematics curriculum itself, and educators should be prepared to develop appropriate Tier 2 and Tier 3 interventions in the areas in which students frequently have difficulty. For that reason, this chapter has presented two case studies on how RTI might be implemented in the upper elementary grades. As more and more states emphasize RTI procedures in mathematics, teachers will need to initiate these critical interventions with increasing frequency throughout the middle and upper elementary grades.

The next chapter focuses on problem solving, an area of concern the NMAP report (2008) identifies. In particular, the report stresses the need for problem solving skills in the upper elementary grades. RTI procedures can assist students struggling in this most challenging area of mathematics.

RTI and Problem Solving

Two trains departed Philadelphia at 12:00 pm and were traveling 965 miles to St. Louis, Missouri. Train A was carrying 1,622 passengers and 53 tons of cargo. Train B was carrying 2,612 passengers and 29 tons of cargo. If train A traveled at 53 miles per hour and train B traveled 7 miles per hour faster than train A, what time will each train arrive?

In mathematics, story problems (also known as word problems) have long been used to connect skills and content with student experience, values, and emotion. Story problems tend to strengthen student engagement in the learning experience. Given the vast options for personalization, stories are effective means for introducing mathematics concepts and for enhancing students' understanding of concepts by increasing their motivation to solve problems.

Story problems capitalize on the research-supported concept of building upon students' prior knowledge in order to increase learning (Askew, 2002; Swan, 2002). In addition to engaging students emotionally and cognitively, the best story problems challenge students to connect the skills they learn in the classroom to real-world situations. Story problems can encourage complex problem-solving skills or simply increase the enjoyment and fun of mathematics.

In many ways, story problems represent the fundamental reason to master mathematics—to solve problems. In fact, the NMAP (2008) emphasizes problem solving as one fundamental goal of mathematics. However, problem solving of this nature has proven to be challenging for many students in elementary school mathematics (Barton & Heidema, 2002; Fuchs & Fuchs, 2002). In this chapter, we discuss problem solving in elementary mathematics in terms of both effective instructional tactics for the three RTI tiers, and as a basis for RTI mathematics procedures in the elementary grades.

> In many ways, story problems represent the fundamental reason to master mathematics—to solve problems.

Mental Processing of Story Problems

Most story problems focus on relatively straightforward applications of the mathematics skills taught in our schools. The general intention of story problems is to challenge students to apply mathematics skills in a problem-solving situation. To successfully complete word or story problems, students must engage a wide variety of metacognitive processes that go far beyond either knowledge of mathematics facts or the rote implementation of mathematics in various operations (Bender, 2009b; Sousa, 2008).

Take a few moments to reflect on the story problem at the beginning of the chapter. What metacognitive skills must a student utilize to successfully complete the problem? A task analysis of problem solving suggests that many types of metacognitive activities are involved, including precomputation steps, computation steps, and postcomputation steps (see table 5.1). To successfully solve most story problems, students must undertake these activities in a sequential order. As the steps in table 5.1 indicate, solving story problems is anything but a simple task.

Table 5.1: Metacognitive Activities Frequently Involved in Problem Solving

Precomputation Steps	Computation Steps	Postcomputation Steps
1. Read and comprehend the story problem.	5. Organize mathematical data.	8. Check work for correctness.
2. Identify relevant information.	6. Implement computational strategies.	9. Check work for reasonableness.
3. Identify necessary tasks.	7. Record answers.	
4. Plan steps for completion of the problem; perhaps develop an equation for problem solution.		

These varied demands in problem solving require students to employ different areas of the brain than those involved in simple computational activities (Sousa, 2008). When completing mathematics problems that are based upon readily identifiable computation strategies, such as simple operations with whole numbers, the parietal lobe of the brain is quite involved. However, in developing a sequential plan of steps necessary to complete a story problem, the prefrontal cortex plays a much more significant role, since planning and forethought, as well as monitoring of one's progress in a complex task, take place in that region. The parietal lobe is also heavily involved in problem solving since operational

> These varied cognitive demands in problem solving require students to employ different areas of the brain than those involved in simple computational activities.

computation will, at some point, be required. Solving word problems is clearly a more complex task than solving computational mathematics problems (Bender, 2009b; Sousa, 2008).

While some insight into brain functioning during various mathematical processes is helpful for teachers, it is probably much more helpful for mathematics educators to develop a heightened awareness of the various cognitive aspects of problem-solving activities, such as those listed in table 5.1. Students' skill in problem solving can be highly responsive to instruction (Bender, 2009b; Sousa, 2008), and there is a compelling need for teaching problem solving by combining mathematics computation skills with stronger conceptual understanding and the metacognitive skills involved in problem solving. This type of instruction should allow students to adapt mathematical skill knowledge to novel real-world learning experiences as they prepare to compete with their international peers in mathematics.

The Problem With Story Problems

Interestingly, the traditional story problems posed in American classrooms have earned little respect from educators internationally (Lewin, 2008; Toom, 2007). In fact, in relation to international standards, American students have fallen behind in problem solving and other mathematics application skills. For example, in 2007, fifteen-year-old U.S. students ranked twenty-fifth among thirty developed nations in mathematics literacy and problem solving (Lewin, 2008). Andrei Toom (2007) in part attributes the lower achievement scores of American students to the lack of well-designed, meaningful story problems as compared to story or word problems integrated into the mathematics curricula of Russia and Singapore. Furthermore, the structure of story problems in traditional texts may have been somewhat confusing. A review of story problems in curricula in the United States indicates that the problems posed tend to be one step and focused on direct application of mathematical concepts that have been most recently taught (Toom, 2007). In contrast, the Russian and Singapore models focus on multistep problems that are scaffolded in complexity across grade levels. The following is a paraphrased example of a story problem from a fourth-grade U.S. textbook:

> Chris, Dan, and Will want to buy a $4.00 sandwich. They want to each pay an equal part. How much money will each need to give?

The following is a paraphrased example from a fourth-grade Russian textbook:

> A musician needs to produce 35,000 t-shirts to sell at a concert. Shop A can produce these shirts in 30 days. Shop B can produce these shirts in 45 days. How long will it take to produce these shirts if both shops work at the same time?

The differences between these story problems are extensive. First, the U.S. example is a one-step computation problem. Students must determine that $4.00 must be divided by 3. This simple division problem solves the word problem.

The Russian example, however, not only challenges students to determine how many t-shirts each shop can produce in one day (which they calculate by dividing 35,000 by 30 for Shop A and 35,000 by 45 for Shop B), but they must then add the daily production of each store to determine a combined daily production, and then divide that total into 35,000. While both problems address the skills of problem solving and division, the problem posed to the Russian students is more rigorous and includes more complex problem-solving elements, such as planning the steps in problem solution.

In addition, some researchers have suggested that the very structure of story problems may be confusing to many students (Barton & Heidema, 2002). The following story problem provides an example of this confusion:

> Chris won or placed in several events on the track and field team at his high school. In the most recent competition, he won the 100-yard dash and the pole vault, and he placed second in the high hurdles and the 400-meter run. His team received five points for each first-place victory and three points for second place. How many points did Chris score for his team?

While this problem is relatively straightforward, some students are likely to have difficulty reading it correctly. Specifically, students are generally taught to read by looking for the main idea or topic sentence of the paragraph, and that is frequently presented as the first sentence in the paragraph (Barton & Heidema, 2002). However, in most story problems like this one, the main idea—in this case, the main question, "How many points did Chris score for his team?"—is located in the last sentence of the paragraph. Thus, the paragraph for this story problem is structured in a fundamentally different way, and this can be quite confusing for some students (Barton & Heidema, 2002).

Enhancing Story Problem Instruction

Recent research and educational initiatives have significantly strengthened the overall mathematics curriculum (Thompson, 2009), which has led to improvements in some of the issues with story problems. The focus on standards-based mathematics has moved teachers and students toward learning experiences that combine and balance the need for computational fluency, conceptual understanding, and problem-solving skills that are mutually reinforcing as recommended by the NMAP (2008).

For example, Ted McCain, an internationally recognized speaker on school reform, challenges teachers to begin designing instructional units by presenting students with real-world problems before the actual instructional activities (McCain, 2005). He points out that adults tend to learn new skills, refine their knowledge, and apply previously learned information when they are challenged with a problem that requires a solution. Furthermore, as adults, we do not receive step-by-step directions to solve or discover a solution to a problem, either in personal or professional experiences. Rather, adults must identify the various components of the problem, plan an appropriate solution, and then perform the activities to reach that solution. These activities involve extensive planning and metacognitive thought, rather than simple mathematical operations. Successful adults are adept at integrating various skills, knowledge, and resources to define a problem, develop a plan, predict possible outcomes, evaluate possible solutions, implement a perceived best-choice solution, and evaluate the results to determine any necessary next steps. We present several metacognitively based instructional strategies aimed at strengthening this specific skill set in the learning strategies section later in this chapter.

> Adults must identify the various components of the problem, plan an appropriate solution, and then perform the activities to reach that solution. These activities involve extensive planning and metacognitive thought, rather than simple mathematical operations.

Real-world problem solving often involves predicting outcomes. Even as adults, individuals who neglect to consider possible outcomes of a proposed solution before implementation often experience less-than-ideal outcomes when confronted with complex problems. For example, an employer who agrees to provide pay raises to employees before evaluating long-term costs and impacts on consumers may face some difficult circumstances. This example could be adapted for our students' understanding by simply challenging student groups to consider what effect giving concession-stand employees at the movie theater a raise may have on moviegoers. Instructional activities that begin with the presentation of a problem stemming from that type of real-world situation, including problems in which no predetermined path to a specific solution is apparent, tend to increase student engagement and students' quest for knowledge (McCain, 2005). Sousa (2008) has suggested that students must see the meaning of the story problem in the real-world context, and that by thoroughly establishing a real-world need for the problem's solution, teachers engage students' attention at a higher level.

In addition, students experience the need to integrate a wider variety of skills and resources when problems are presented in this fashion (McCain, 2005). This type of instructional model caters to the changing needs of the 21st century learners in our classrooms, and it aligns nicely with NMAP's (2008) expectations and the standards published by the NCTM (2000, 2006). Instructional opportunities that challenge students to integrate knowledge in order to create solutions will prepare them for the challenges of the 21st century. These learning experiences deepen students' understanding of content-area learning, including mathematical learning, to a level of understanding that allows the use and application of skills, as opposed to merely the surface-level understanding needed for computational exercises. In fact, the entire standards-based mathematics instructional movement is based upon students developing a greater depth of understanding of mathematical problem solving as opposed to merely performing mathematics operations (McLaughlin, Shepard, & O'Day, 1995).

The goal of mathematics instruction must include and foster student acquisition of mathematics literacy that contributes to students' ability to engage in problem-solving experiences throughout their lives. The next section of this chapter presents several instructional approaches that are highly effective for problem-solving instruction in Tier 1, though many of these instructional approaches are also highly effective as Tier 2 or Tier 3 interventions. We also describe several Tier 1 assessment options since general educators in the elementary grades are responsible for universal screening and providing data that demonstrate a child's difficulty in story problems. Also included are strategies we recommend for Tier 2 or Tier 3 interventions. Finally, we present a case study focused on instruction for story problems, since many elementary teachers communicate that they often have difficulty with this specific content area.

> The goal of mathematics instruction must include and foster student acquisition of mathematics literacy that contributes to students' ability to engage in problem solving experiences throughout their lives.

Effective Tier 1 Instruction for Problem Solving

NMAP's final report, *Foundations for Success* (2008), emphasizes the increased need for students to be empowered to utilize mathematics concepts and skills to successfully engage in problem-solving activities as we prepare them to be competitive with their global peers. It is imperative that teachers have a variety of effective strategies to support students who struggle in this critical area within the context of quality classroom instruction and intervention. The following section identifies effective strategies that teachers can utilize to increase student engagement and success.

Strategies to Increase Student Engagement

In spite of the frequent use of story problems at all levels of mathematics, many students do not seem to connect with them, which can lead to a lack of motivation that may decrease the likelihood of learning story-problem skills (Sousa, 2008). Story problems are only effective when students are motivated to actively engage in the challenge of solving them. For that reason, teachers need to know how to enrich the story-problem experience for challenged learners by increasing their level of active cognitive engagement with the story problem. Tactics such as *story retelling*—that is, students rereading the story problem and rephrasing it in their own words—can greatly facilitate students' success. Students may also be challenged to use the think-aloud strategy (as described in chapter 2) as they read a story problem through a second time.

> Story problems are only effective when students are motivated to actively engage in the challenge of solving them.

Another tactic to increase engagement is teacher questioning. With targeted, highly specific questioning, teachers can focus students on relevant aspects of the problem or on the sequencing of various required operations. However, evidence suggests that some teachers are not adept at student questioning. One study compared Chinese teachers to U.S. teachers and documented different use of questioning and different responses to student errors (Schleppenbach, Flevares, Sims, & Perry, 2007). The study compared the frequency and types of questions teachers asked. Results indicate that Chinese educators were more likely than their U.S. counterparts to follow student mistakes with additional questioning. Additionally, the questioning Chinese teachers use requires students to work through their understanding of the story problem, whereas U.S. teachers rely more heavily on direct statements that tell students the correct response or correct procedures. Teachers in the United States are also more likely to merely redirect their question to another student upon receiving an incorrect answer. This study certainly challenges educators to consider the use of their questioning procedures in mathematics.

The following feature box lists additional teaching strategies that can enhance student engagement with story problems and prove to be critical components of effective Tier 1 instruction across the primary and elementary grade levels.

Strategies for Enhancing Student Engagement With Story Problems

- When initially presenting a story problem, don't let students finish reading it completely. Ask them to stop and predict the ending (the question they expect to be asked).

- Challenge students to change the story in some way—perhaps by modifying data within the story problem.

- Ask one team of students to rewrite the story problem as a new challenge for classmates to solve.

- Read the story problem (or ask students to read it) without letting them see the accompanying illustrations. Then ask students to create illustrations.

- Write story problems personalized to specific students in your class. For example, use students' names in a story problem about kids as they travel through a local amusement park and keep track of the money they have spent.

- Ask students to act out the story problem or use manipulatives to model the mathematics elements.

- Establish a "story problem challenge" with another class in the school in which students write mathematics story problems for another class to solve.

Cooperative Learning Strategies

Teachers have used cooperative learning activities in classrooms for some time with positive effects for many students. Research accumulating since the early 1990s provides strong support for the use of cooperative learning instructional practices to increase conceptual understanding in mathematics (Hutchinson, 1987, 1990; NMAP, 2008; Partnership for 21st Century Skills, 2007; Silver & Lane, 1991). Traditional mathematics classrooms have focused on the need for students to complete work independently and have tended to be somewhat competitive in nature. In contrast, the recent shift to standards-focused mathematics classrooms has included the use of cooperative learning experiences that provide students the opportunity to explore, hypothesize, test, and evaluate mathematics strategies with peers, and these tactics have been supported in research literature (Hutchinson, 1987, 1990; Silver & Lane, 1991). These tactics include hands-on experiences resulting in high levels of engagement, active learning that is fostered within cooperative groups, high levels of student engagement in discussion, prediction of outcomes, defending one's solutions, and providing learning connections that move from concrete physical to symbolic language (Hutchinson, 1987, 1990; Silver & Lane, 1991).

The popular saying "Two heads are better than one" has long been used to inspire motivation to work together and to celebrate joint problem solving. In mathematics, this idea has helped students acquire mathematical knowledge they probably would not have mastered individually (Fuchs et al., 1997; Silver & Lane, 1991). For example, Fuchs et al. (1997) document the positive effects of collaborative learning experiences on increasing achievement and conceptual understanding for students both with and without learning disabilities. It is important to note that in order to be most effective, collaborative learning experiences should provide both scaffolded supports and reciprocal instructional responsibilities for students who are struggling with mathematics content. Many cooperative learning approaches use classwide peer tutoring in which one student serves as tutor for another student, and after a bit of time (usually ten minutes or so) the roles are reversed (Greenwood, Delquadri, & Carta, 1997). Thus, every student receives instruction on his or her specific instructional task, and then serves as a tutor for another student in a different instructional area.

> Collaborative learning experiences should provide both scaffolded supports and reciprocal instructional responsibilities for students who are struggling with mathematics content.

Peer-Assisted Learning

Peer-Assisted Learning Strategies (*PALS*; http://kc.vanderbilt.edu/pals) is an instructional curriculum built upon a reciprocal relationship between peers working through mathematics problems (Fuchs et al., 1997; Fuchs et al., 2001). The *PALS* strategy moves beyond the one-way tutoring relationship in which high-achieving students tutor lower achieving students. Many have expressed concern that always using high-achieving students may exasperate both the high achievers (who don't receive the instruction they need), as well as the struggling students (who may face self-esteem issues) (Fuchs et al., 2001; Greenwood et al., 1997). With *PALS*, collaborative reciprocal learning activities enhance students' enthusiasm for learning and their determination to achieve academic success, resulting in increased achievement of students of all ability groups (Lan & Repman, 1995; Stevens & Slavin, 1995).

The *PALS* program uses a version of classwide peer tutoring that combines explicit instruction, clear models, an array of examples, and extensive practice (NCTM, 2006; NMAP, 2008). The authors of *PALS* have developed a series of lessons addressing various mathematical skills in kindergarten through grade six. Other educators have extended the strategy through the creation of additional lessons that follow the same format.

As classes utilize the *PALS* approach as a possible intervention strategy, students support each other in reciprocal roles as "coaches" and "players" using explicit scripts that include step-by-step directions for problem solving. One student serving as the coach reads the script, which includes step-by-step explicit instructions, while another student, the player, follows the coach's directions to solve the problem. The coach's script provides verbal prompts that guide students through the mathematical activity. For example, as students work in pairs, the coach may present verbal prompts such as, "What kind of problem is it? What do you do first? Add the numbers in the ones place. Is your answer less than 10? If yes, then record that number in the ones place."

In this reciprocal relationship, both students are developing a deeper conceptual understanding of the mathematics learning in combination with improved computational skills. In the course of practice activities, partners change regularly and all students serve in both roles. Classroom interactions like those used in the *PALS* program enhance learning with understanding (Hanna & Yackel, 2000), and research supports this approach to mathematics instruction in general education classes (Fuchs et al., 2001; Greenwood et al., 1997).

> Classroom interactions like those used in the *PALS* program enhance learning with understanding, and research supports this approach to mathematics instruction in general education classes.

Student Explanations

Another collaborative approach that has significantly impacted student learning is the practice of students explaining their thinking in relation to problem-solving activities (Chapin, O'Connor, & Canavan, 2003; Fuchs et al., 1997). For example, in using this approach, Sarah, a struggling fifth-grade student, might be paired with Ryan, a student who has mastered general mathematics concepts that are integrated into the problem–solving activity. Each student then has the responsibility to explain a strategy for completing the following story problem:

> Tom's allowance is increasing by 2 percent, and he is saving for a ski trip during winter break. Tom's current allowance is $7.50 per week, and he is saving 25 percent of that for the ski trip. He currently has $102.50 of the $150.00 he needs for the trip. If he continues saving 25 percent of his allowance after the increase, how many more weeks will it take Tom to save enough money?

To scaffold Sarah's success, her teacher might encourage her to use a checklist to help her organize and plan a solution. This checklist might include items such as the following:

- Indicators that identify all relevant information
- Questions that help her determine what additional information she might need
- Suggestions on how to determine that information from the data in the story problem
- Recommendations for pictures that might represent this problem
- Items that remind her of the mathematics operations she might employ
- Blank template that may prompt her to create the appropriate algorithm

Whereas Sarah might need the scaffolded list of reminders, Ryan would presumably not need such a checklist since his performance has been acceptable on story problems. In implementing the student explanation tactic, both Sarah and Ryan would explain their thinking to each other, and then they would come to a consensus regarding a series of sequenced steps for solving the problem. This process of students explaining their thinking forces both students to organize their thoughts, evaluate their reasons, and justify their solutions, all of which greatly enhances their mathematical learning (Chapin et al., 2003; Fuchs et al., 1997).

These few examples highlight the relationship between cooperative learning and the recent emphasis on problem solving in mathematics. Cooperative learning should be implemented in some form in almost every Tier 1 mathematics program, as this research-based strategy results in significant positive effects on students' mathematical conceptual understanding (NMAP, 2008).

Project-Based Learning

As teachers become more skilled with the integration of real-world problems into the learning process in all content areas, the development of project-based learning experiences (PBL) in mathematics is expanding. In *project-based learning* (sometimes referred to as problem-based learning), instructional units reach far beyond mere story problems and more closely resemble problems stemming from tasks that adults might confront in the real world (Fleishner & Manheimer, 1997; Knowlton, 2003).

PBL frequently leads to more involved, longer-term work projects for mathematics problem solving.

While teachers have experienced the value of projects as learning experiences for some time, application of this instructional approach in general education mathematics classes is more recent. Still, the development of PBL has resulted in deeper, more full and rich instruction in mathematics, which in turn, leads to more in-depth understanding and application of mathematics, as well as richer connections between mathematics and other content areas. Table 5.2 is a sample planning guide for a PBL task that involves mathematics at various stages.

Teachers should begin by describing the project and identifying key skills they wish students to acquire. Then they should consider how the project meets various learning standards before describing the activity in specific detail. Teachers should also consider how community members could support the students in their projects, thus bringing even more of a real-life feel to the project. Table 5.3 (page 126) shows a detailed four-week unit plan for the PBL activity with ideas for differentiation.

Table 5.2: Sample Project-Based Learning Planning Guide

Umbrella Topic	This project-based learning unit involves exploration of the costs associated with extra recreational activities, such as soccer, swimming, football, and so on, that promote physical fitness. It explores the need for community support of such activities.
Standards Focus	Mathematics standard: Students should be proficient with the addition and subtraction of whole numbers. Reading/language arts standard: Students can use digital technology to demonstrate their reading, writing, speaking, listening, and language use. Social studies standard: Students will use civic skills, such as using criteria to make judgments and to arrive at and defend positions. Health standard: Students will have the necessary knowledge and skills to establish and maintain physical fitness in order to maintain personal health.
Description of Culminating Project	Groups of four students each will identify a local government or civic group to present information to regarding the cost of recreational activities that promote physical fitness and request supplemental support. The proposal must include sample financial costs of activities and benefits of participation in these recreational activities.
Support Personnel	Other adults in the community that could help support student learning include an accountant, physical fitness teacher, college sports coach, parents, and local elected officials. Consider inviting individuals such as these to participate in the project-based unit.

Table 5.3: Lesson Ideas for Sample Project-Based Learning Activity

Week 1: Teacher introduces "hook" activity (the activity teachers use to gain students' attention and to help motivate learning at the outset of the project), identifies teams, lists expected responsibilities for each team member (students can develop this with some guidance from the teacher), lists needed skills and background information, and completes group planning chart for necessary activities with activities delineated for all subsequent weeks. Teacher may begin some direct instruction on various mathematical operations that might be used in this project (for example, part-whole fractions and operations with fractions). Students working in teams may begin to determine activities necessary to complete the unit project.

Week 2: Student groups review their work plans with the teacher and gather needed research. Direct instruction may include additional procedures that might be necessary in solving this problem (for example, averaging, addition, subtraction, percentages, and budgeting). Teachers or selected students may provide this instruction. Two days of cooperative instruction using student explanation tactics could follow. The Week 2 assessment may involve an individual quiz on the previous mathematics procedures.

Week 3: Student groups prepare multimedia presentation materials including financial report elements. Student teams might review the mathematics procedures taught in week two for various team members who may need assistance. The teacher and students working together develop and review a final rubric for the culminating project. Also, students may begin to develop a PowerPoint presentation of their work, summarizing their activities. The assessment that follows week three may involve the averaging of team grades so that every team member receives that average grade. While the assessment will not be used to influence intervention needs, assessment for learning activities including teacher questioning, quizzes, and independent tasks will provide assessment data that can be a part of consideration for intervention.

Week 4: Students must complete all of their work fairly early this week, as well as complete their PowerPoint presentations. Assessment meetings with teams should begin at this point with the teacher reviewing the team's work and the proposed presentation. These reviews should stress the relationship between what the students have accomplished and the various activities listed on the rubric for the project. At the end of this week, the class should invite their targeted community participants into the class and share their solutions, asking participants to comment on the proposed activities and solutions.

Differentiation Ideas:

Teachers may use differentiation in the PBL unit in many ways, including the following:

- Identify students who may need specific scaffolded support on particular mathematics topics, and work with those groups.
- Use partnering activities to strengthen learning.
- Do some preteaching on mathematics activities for selected students.
- Challenge students to work with students from other teams with similar learning styles and learning preferences.
- Develop a checklist for scaffolded instructional ideas on various topics that students may access and use alone or in small groups.

- Identify and teach different group roles and responsibilities during the problem-solution process. As necessary, preteach those responsibilities by modeling.
- Develop a vocabulary guide for use in the unit.

In PBL experiences like the example in tables 5.2 and 5.3, it is imperative that teachers give careful considerations to the multifaceted application of mathematics skills. For example, in this project, students must utilize various mathematics concepts including percentages, ratios, and addition of decimals. Those mathematics concepts are deeply embedded within the task. Students must also explore and identify financial costs of activities and extend those costs to an annual projected cost. Students must calculate the effect of a tax credit based on a percentage discount for families. Generally speaking, working with percentages and decimals can be somewhat problematic for students in the context of story problems, and showing the relationship between fractions, decimals, and percentages is critical for student understanding.

Furthermore, challenging mathematics activities such as percentages and decimals do not tend to foster high levels of student engagement. However, when presented in the context of a cooperative-learning project, these activities have a higher probability of engaging student interest and enthusiasm—students may even ask to learn more about these mathematics concepts and show other signs of excitement about learning (Partnership for 21st Century Skills, 2007).

While the initial planning of PBL experiences can be somewhat labor intensive, the strategy has demonstrated a long-term impact on student achievement in mathematics (Fleishner & Manheimer, 1997). Good learning experiences result when teachers challenge students to solve problems that arise in real life as opposed to the more predictable story problems of the past (Fleishner & Manheimer, 1997). Thus, PBL provides a strong option for Tier 1 instruction on story problems in mathematics.

> When presented in the context of a cooperative-learning project, these activities have a higher probability of engaging student interest and enthusiasm—students may even ask to learn more about these mathematics concepts and show other signs of excitement about learning.

Project-based learning presents some unique opportunities for differentiation. Teachers can design projects to tap into student interests and talents. They can proactively design groups to maximize learning. This does not mean, however, that the high-achieving students are continuously grouped with low-achieving students. Teachers may group students homogeneously based on skills to allow extension of learning for some and a more supportive experience for others. While a PBL activity may be designed to primarily address mathematical standards, it will likely intertwine with other content areas, a benefit to many educators who face the challenge of teaching a multitude of instructional goals.

> While a PBL activity may be designed to primarily address mathematical standards, it will likely intertwine with other content areas, a benefit to many educators who face the challenge of teaching a multitude of instructional goals.

Another advantage of PBL is that there is not a predetermined solution to the problem or project. Rather, learning stems from the students working collaboratively to discover and create the solution.

Next, skill acquisition is likely to be enhanced in a PBL unit. Careful planning of differentiated instructional needs is essential, especially for students who struggle with related mathematical concepts; some differentiation activities were noted in table 5.3 (page 126). Scaffolding student skill application and progress can support student engagement in a Tier 1 PBL experience for some of the students, while other students may be simultaneously receiving Tier 2 or 3 interventions designed to remediate mathematical skills within the context of the larger project.

In summary, instruction via project-based learning seems to be increasing in schools nationally, and research has generally been supportive of this trend (Fleishner & Manheimer, 1997; Strobel & van Barneveld, 2008). Thus, general education teachers may find themselves implementing this type of instruction for Tier 1 and then planning Tier 2 interventions that are tied with the types of tasks presented within the project-based instruction.

The Explicit Inquiry Routine

One running debate in mathematics education involves the efficacy of inquiry-based learning versus explicit instruction (NMAP, 2008). *Inquiry-based learning* is primarily student directed, is characterized by ties to constructivist cognitive theory, and has been shown to be effective in establishing the conceptual basis for mathematics, at least for some students (Bender, 2009b; NMAP, 2008). Other students who struggle with mathematics, however, seem to benefit more from *explicit instruction*, which is teacher directed (NMAP, 2008). A recent meta-analysis of fifty studies demonstrated that explicit and systematic instruction had a strong positive effect for both students with disabilities and low-achieving mathematics students (NCTM, 2006), but the research does not specifically rule out the use of inquiry-based learning (NMAP, 2008).

With this in mind, the *explicit inquiry routine* (EIR) was designed to combine the benefits of inquiry and dialogue on mathematical problems with intensive, explicit instruction (Scheuermann, Deschler, & Schumaker, 2009). Using this method, teachers directly lead instruction using focused, explicit techniques such as modeling or think-aloud procedures, but they then supplement those techniques with targeted questioning to help students reflectively focus on what might be required for task completion.

In addition to combining these research-based practices, the EIR engages students in one of the most prominent and validated instructional sequences used in education: the *concrete-representational-abstract method*, or C-R-A (Maccini & Ruhl, 2000; Witzel, Mercer, & Miller, 2003). The C-R-A instructional sequence is used primarily in a teacher-directed setting and engages students in a transfer of learning from the use of concrete manipulatives (base-10 blocks, counters, or tiles) to representational models (tally marks, dots, pictures), and finally to abstract cognitive exercises represented by mathematical equations. The EIR presents mathematical concepts with some combination of strategies that are appropriate given the unique needs of each student. For some student groups, teachers can design instruction to use concrete manipulatives, like fraction bars, and then move directly to the abstract mathematical representations. In this case, instruction may begin with illustrations using fraction bars or fraction circles and move directly to students recognizing the numerator/denominator mathematics representation of the fraction. In other situa-

tions, a student may require that the instruction move systematically from concrete to representational before addressing the abstract. With EIR, instructional design is based on student needs as determined by data sources and ongoing formative assessments.

> The explicit inquiry routine (EIR) was designed to combine the benefits of inquiry and dialogue on mathematical problems with intensive, explicit instruction.

The EIR is based on three underlying premises (Scheuermann et al., 2009):

1. Explicit and sequential instruction increases students' ability to perform mathematics procedures.

2. For students to completely understand a mathematics concept, they should discover or experience the concept.

3. Scaffolded experiences with mathematics concepts delivered in a sequential manner establish understanding and proficiency with mathematics procedures.

The EIR design effectively supports student mathematical problem-solving skills while providing an inquiry-based learning experience in the context of the general education class. These instructional practices are supported by research with special education populations, so the EIR would prove quite beneficial in Tier 2 or 3 interventions (Scheuermann et al., 2009).

The first step of EIR requires the teacher to identify the essential concept and then break it down into individual "instructional bites"—that is, the teacher needs to task analyze the concept and identify the individual components (Scheuermann et al., 2009). For example, if the concept is the addition of fractions with unlike denominators that is embedded into a story problem, the task analysis would identify the instructional bites of finding the least common multiple, multiplying the numerator and denominator to create fractions with like denominators, and finally, adding the numerators. In the EIR, the teacher would identify the least-complex elements for which to provide explicit instruction, ensuring that students would master the prerequisite skills, and then he or she would address the next skill required.

The inquiry phase of EIR instruction involves a scaffolded inquiry component (Scheuermann et al., 2009). During this phase of instruction, the teacher provides the interactive learning experience in three stages of inquiry. In the first stage— "Tell me how"—students tell the teacher how to illustrate and manipulate problems.

Students work together to offer suggestions and evaluate results. The teacher is not responsible for telling students how to solve the problem, but rather provides scaffolded instructional assistance to guide their inquiry by highlighting insights critical to the problem. The end result is that the teacher, through his or her questioning, highlighting, and challenges to student thinking, leads the group to the correct model of the problem's solution.

The second stage of the inquiry phase is called "Tell your neighbors how." During this part of the routine, students illustrate and manipulate problems with a peer and then share their perspectives and insights through modeling (Scheuermann et al., 2009). The teacher facilitates these discussions by circulating and asking any necessary questions to probe student thinking and correct any misconceptions.

The third stage of the inquiry phase is called "Tell yourself how." During this stage, students explain using a self-talk dialogue the process they worked through to solve the problem (Scheuermann et al., 2009). This is essentially the same as the think-aloud procedure described in chapter 2. During this stage, just as in the "Tell me how" and the "Tell your neighbors how" stages, the teacher is actively facilitating and supporting student learning.

A vital element to scaffolding student success is teacher monitoring of the dialogue. In order to allow solid comprehension and mastery of the concepts involved in each element of the task, the teacher needs to monitor student thinking, ask probing and clarifying questions, and encourage the think-aloud process.

While the developers of the EIR have just begun to validate their work with a research base, early results are quite encouraging. The initial research project focused on twenty students in grades 6 through 8 who were diagnosed with a mathematics-based learning disability. Data were collected regarding word problems involving single-step problems and one-variable equations. The resulting data showed that all but one student progressed to 80-percent mastery of the task and that student had shown a 50-percent improvement from baseline to the final assessment (Scheuermann et al., 2009). While this work is encouraging, future validation projects may consider measuring the effectiveness in upper elementary settings. The EIR strategy certainly links to the common instructional approach "I do, we do, you do." Thus, this modeling and collaborative approach provide for the gradual transfer of responsibility for task completion from the teacher to the student. Given the promise this strategy has already shown for supporting students with mathematical difficulties, it would be reasonable for upper elementary teachers to consider this approach and monitor ongoing student progress, especially in the work of a school-based professional learning community.

The conceptual base of the EIR has been identified as an effective intervention by Best Evidence Encyclopedia, a federally funded website of effective practices located at Johns Hopkins University (www.bestevidence.org). The site provides educators with reliable, unbiased reviews of research to help them identify proven programs that best meet the needs of their students. Thus, the EIR is certainly an instructional tactic that mathematics teachers should become familiar with for Tier 1, as well as perhaps a Tier 2 or Tier 3 intervention procedure.

Assessment Options for Problem-Solving Skills

As described in chapter 2, general education teachers will be responsible for universal screening in math, as well as for some progress monitoring on the efficacy of Tier 1 instruction and perhaps Tier 2 intervention. While teachers can accomplish such monitoring with worksheets of mathematics facts problems or other simple worksheets for many mathematics skills in lower grades, assessment on complex skills is a bit more challenging. Two assessment strategies that have not been used often in traditional educational settings are now coming to the forefront of instructional research in mathematics (Allsopp et al., 2008; Fleishner & Manheimer, 1997): (1) error analysis and (2) clinical mathematics interviews. Each of these formative assessment options provides an opportunity for teachers to investigate how students solve problems during Tier 1 instruction and generates data that result in effective modification of instruction.

Error Analysis

Error analysis involves an in-depth analysis of a student's errors so the teacher can understand inaccuracies in the student's thinking. Error analysis provides teachers with information that can be directly used to guide instruction, and thus, it supports student achievement more than traditional summative test scores. However, to be effective, error analysis must address key criteria.

Teachers must be sure there are sufficient examples to determine the cause of any errors. Are observed errors caused by inadequate mastery of facts, incorrect operations, or ineffective use of mathematical strategies, such as sequencing the steps for solving the problem?

For example, with story problems, one type of error may be related to simple computation. Other errors may be caused by improper processing of information or incorrectly identifying relevant information. Another common error is referred to as a "smaller from larger error" (Riccomini, 2005). This subtraction error relates to the tendency of some students to reverse the order of numbers in the ones or tens place in order to take the smaller number from the larger number. Here is an example:

> Lori had 35 books and she donated 7 to the local library. How many books does she have now?

In this story problem, the smaller from larger error might result in the answer of 32 if the student subtracts 5 from 7, subtracting the smaller number from the larger number in the ones place. This error represents a misunderstanding of the concept of place value, rather than a computational problem.

While patterns of errors may, in most cases, be easily identified, research conducted by Riccomini (2005) documents that only 59 percent of teachers correctly identify error patterns, and even fewer teachers design instruction that correctly addresses the error patterns they observe. This research suggests that many general education teachers need additional opportunities to identify error patterns in story problems, as well as strategies to plan instruction that aligns with student error patterns.

Teachers should use error analysis for all students demonstrating difficulty on story problems in Tier 1 instruction. Carefully considering and analyzing patterns of student error can lead to meaningful learning experiences for students that may serve as a springboard for inquiry as they begin to examine and critique their own understanding of mathematics processes (Borasi, 1994). Such in-depth error analysis also provides critical information for teachers planning subsequent Tier 2 interventions on story problems.

Clinical Mathematics Interviews

Clinical mathematics interviews are another formative assessment approach general education teachers may wish to utilize for students struggling with story problems (Allsopp et al., 2008; Ball, 1991; Ginsburg, 1987). *Clinical mathematics interviews* are one-to-one, prompted discussions between a teacher and student that focus on what a student did to solve the problem. In the clinical interview, the teacher inquires about how and why the student solved the story problem in a particular way. The teacher also notes his or her observations on what the child was doing while engaged with the story problem. These interviews should be viewed as flexible in that they are undirected, yet highly structured conversations that allow teachers to delve into what concepts a student understands and where the student shows misconceptions or flawed understandings of mathematics concepts.

Lack of conceptual understanding of mathematics is certainly an underlying factor that causes many students to struggle with solving story problems. When the cognitive mathematical challenge is increased to the application level, students' misconceptions or faulty conceptual frameworks impair their ability to solve abstract problems. It is in this academic setting that students must move beyond rote application of skill sets to the identification and selection of relevant mathematics processes for application and synthesis. Hence, the clinical interview is a valid assessment option that allows educators to move beyond right/wrong judgments to discover the hows and whys of a student's answer (Ball, 1991).

The clinical interview is a valid assessment option that allows educators to move beyond right/wrong judgments to discover the hows and whys of a student's answer.

As discussed previously, research has strongly supported the C-R-A sequence of instruction as an effective pedagogical strategy (Witzel et al., 2003). When designing clinical interviewing questions, teachers should probe students to assess their understanding at these various levels to ascertain the appropriate starting points for instruction. Students may be able to use manipulatives (concrete objects) to solve story problems that require repeated addition, but they may have no understanding of how to use manipulatives or representations of manipulative counters in multiplication.

Error analysis and the clinical interview technique also work very well together. Often educators use information identified from error pattern analysis to identify starting points for structuring the clinical interview. Following is an example.

Students are involved in a project-based learning experience in which they are expected to calculate funds received over a two-week period from a local shoe store. Rachel, a fifth-grade student, has calculated the amount from the first week:

$$
\begin{array}{r}
1175 \\
673 \\
415 \\
+285 \\
\hline
1438
\end{array}
$$

After analyzing Rachel's errors from this sample plus additional work samples, Mr. Morris noted a lack of understanding of place value and regrouping in addition, an error pattern that could easily impact Rachel's work on story problems or PBL experiences. Because Rachel's fall benchmark and ongoing formative assessments have concurrently indicated scores below grade level, Mr. Morris decided to conduct a clinical interview using the instructional format included in his core mathematics series. He began this assessment process with place-value probes and then moved into questions on regrouping. Thus, the clinical interview Mr. Morris conducted allowed him to probe into Rachel's thinking in several areas in sequence (Ginsburg, 1987).

Three models for clinical mathematical interview questions are presented in table 5.4 (page 134), including "Tell me how," "You be the teacher," and think aloud (Ball, 1991; Ginsburg, 1987). Educators can adapt these clinical interview formats to form probing questions that assess the concepts the student understands and identify areas for further instruction. Mr. Morris prompted Rachel to think aloud as he solved a word problem that required the addition of three five-digit numbers, and he then discovered that Rachel did not have a conceptual understanding of place value or regrouping. While Rachel explained that she had to carry to the tens place because the answer was more than ones, her explanation of her actions in the hundreds place was "1300 plus one more makes 1438." Despite an additional prompt from Mr. Morris (such as "Is there something different we could do?"), it was evident that Rachel did not grasp the concept of hundreds place or thousands place. Her conceptual understanding was limited to sets of tens. However, Rachel's work did indicate that her conceptual understanding of the story problem and the concept of addition was appropriate. This information, gleaned from a clinical interview, can ultimately provide a starting point for Tier 2 intervention.

Table 5.4: Clinical Interviewing Question Formats

Interview Prompt	Verbal Sample	Concrete-Representational-Abstract Examples
Tell me how	"Would you tell me how you found your answer? What did you do first?"	"Use the blocks to show me how you found your answer. Tell me what you're doing."
You be the teacher	"Now you're the teacher. Teach me how to find the answer to this word problem. What do I do first?"	"Draw a picture on the dry erase board to show me how to find the answer."
Think aloud	"Let's pretend to think aloud. Tell me everything you're thinking while you're working."	"When you teach me, show me the equation I'll need to use."

Source: Adapted from Allsopp et al., 2008, pp. 6–16.

Teachers must be sensitive when using the clinical interview format to reflectively detect the cause or causes of students' mathematics problems, particularly when interviewing students who may have underlying expressive language difficulties. Students who struggle to express thoughts and ideas may not be able to accurately demonstrate their mathematical understanding, even when their conceptual understanding is sound. For students with expressive language challenges, teachers may offer differentiated assessment options in the context of the clinical interview. For example, a particular student may be able to build a concrete or digital representation of a problem while offering supporting explanations or providing written summaries of his or her work, and teachers would then analyze those pieces of information. As in all assessment data, teachers using a clinical interview must reflect on the knowledge of each individual student in conjunction with a compilation of various other data sources, such as data from end-of-unit tests or state assessment data.

Generally, no single assessment tool will provide the needed composite picture of student learning to drive quality differentiated instruction. However, error analysis and clinical interviews used together provide deep insights into students' thinking and reasoning and are supported by research as appropriate assessment practices (Allsopp et al., 2008). Because of limitations on teachers' time in general education classrooms, it may seem a daunting task to conduct an in-depth mathematical clinical interview for every student. Fortunately, such in-depth information may not be necessary for all students. While teachers will often interview students on particular solutions to various mathematics problems, only students who are struggling in Tier 1 mathematics are likely to receive a full clinical mathematics interview.

In fact, teachers may use "mini-interviews" as one option for informal assessment during Tier 1 instruction. The mini-interview strategy is similar to the clinical interview, involving the same interview models in a less-developed format. For example, as students work in small groups to collaboratively solve real-world story problems, proactive teachers might visit each group and, using several think-aloud interview questions, probe into the thinking process of students within the group. By periodically challenging students to explain or justify their thinking, teachers can make sure that conceptual misunderstandings are not being masked by group efforts (Allsopp et al., 2008). Webb and Mastergeorge (2003) note that the discussion that occurs in well-designed small groups facilitates student recognition of misunderstandings as students express their thinking to the group. Thus, mini-interview questioning also fosters students' ability to critique the thinking of others.

The questioning/interviewing concept has applications for each tier in the RTI process. Quality mathematics instruction involving effective questioning goes far beyond limited pencil-and-paper computational practices and has evolved into a very dynamic, socially and verbally rich learning experience. Assessments that provide data from error analysis and interviewing move beyond the traditional unit test approach to support learning for struggling students.

Effective Tier 2 and 3 Interventions for Problem Solving

While there is much emphasis in mathematics on project-based unit instruction for problem solving, we believe that interventions using traditional story problems are probably a more appropriate focus in Tier 2 and Tier 3 than PBL units. Project-based learning units are complex, abstract, completed over longer periods of time, and intertwine a large variety of skills. Given that structure, it would be difficult to design a Tier 2 intervention based on a PBL experience. Story problems are somewhat simpler, and they allow the teacher to monitor performance more frequently and focus explicitly on student skill deficits or conceptual misunderstandings. It certainly would be quite reasonable to break down elements of the mathematics expectations within a PBL unit to design Tier 2 interventions that help students master specific missing skills.

For that reason, we recommend the following strategies for Tier 2 and Tier 3 interventions for problem solving. Of course, these strategies are likewise very appropriate for Tier 1 instruction, but because of a strong research base and the ease of progress monitoring associated with these strategies, they seem to be the best interventions to assist students with problem solving in Tier 2 and Tier 3.

Learning Strategy Instruction

The transfer of learning from rote application of mathematics operations to the application of mathematics concepts involved in problem solving can be difficult for students with learning challenges, and many students may require a Tier 2 intervention for story problems (Bender, 2009b). Some students have great difficulty with the organization and planning tasks required of story problems, while other students seem to "get lost" in the steps of solving complex story problems. It is imperative that these struggling students get support in the critical problem-solving skills they lack.

> Some students have great difficulty with the organization and planning tasks required of story problems, while others seem to "get lost" in the steps of solving complex story problems.

Learning strategy instruction guides students through the planning, organizational, and self-monitoring elements involved in solving story problems. *Learning strategies* are sets of step-by-step directions students can learn to guide them through the problem-solving process. For example, Alan and Mackenzie each experience frustration when working through story problems. Their teacher, Mrs. Owens, used clinical interviews to recognize that while Mackenzie easily identified the essential information in the story problem, she needed instruction on completing the various computations. Specifically, Mackenzie's problem involved poor computation fluency. Therefore, Mackenzie's Tier 2 intervention would be designed to build these computational skills.

In contrast, Alan had different deficits that hampered his ability to complete the problem-solving activities. While he was quite fluent in computation, the results from his clinical interview suggested that he struggled to identify relevant information in the problem, and he was often confused by irrelevant information. He also sometimes chose the wrong operation for the story problem. Therefore, Mrs. Owens inferred that Alan did not fully comprehend the story problem despite his strong abilities in mathematics computation, and for that reason, his Tier 2 intervention would be designed to provide learning strategy instruction with an emphasis on thinking through the story problem conceptually and developing an equation or set of equations that represented the story problem.

Learning strategy instruction provides exactly the type of intervention Alan requires; it provides students with a strategy that guides their planning and monitoring of the steps necessary for solving problems (Bender, 2009b). In this instructional approach, students must learn the specific strategy and then practice it repeatedly each day (Bender, 2009b). This is especially critical for struggling students who need to be able to employ the strategy effortlessly to be able to then focus on the mathematical learning. It is imperative to provide strategy instruction to the point that the student feels mastery and complete ownership of the strategy. This can best be achieved through carefully designed instruction that provides ample modeling and practice for students. The following examples—Read, Imagine, Decide, and Do and Search, Translate, Answer, Review—both represent learning strategies that help a student cognitively work through the steps in a math problem.

> It is imperative to provide strategy instruction to the point that the student feels mastery and complete ownership of the strategy.

Read, Imagine, Decide, and Do

The *Read, Imagine, Decide, and Do* tactic (RIDD; Jackson, 2002) connects the mathematics planning and problem-solving process to an acronym that represents steps toward problem solution. Each letter in the acronym RIDD stands for a specific step in the problem-solving model. The advantage of this strategy is that this acronym allows students to translate story problems into their own thinking and helps them capitalize on their own problem-solving knowledge.

1. Read the Problem

The first step is to read the problem from beginning to end (Jackson, 2002). While this seems somewhat self-evident, many struggling students search the word problem for key words or phrases that tell them what to do, and they may not carefully read and consider the entire problem. This often misleads the student during the planning process. Clearly reading the problem correctly is critical, and several quick strategies can assist with this. For example, teachers may require students to put a circle (in pencil) around each word in the story problem that suggests a particular mathematical operation. Those circled words might then be compared with a list of such cue words on a poster in the classroom.

Some students get tripped up by unknown words or difficult-to-read numbers. A useful tactic to assist with that problem is word substitution during the reading phase. Teachers show students how to substitute a preselected term for unknown words in the story problem. By providing students with the substitute word, teachers free the student to focus on analyzing the mathematical elements of the word problems. Teachers may use a think-aloud strategy to model this, as in the following example:

> *Lori has 32* . . . *Hmm, I don't know this word, so I'm going to use the word that we selected:* doughnuts. *Lori has 32* doughnuts *and John has 47* . . . *I still don't know that word, so I'm going to say* doughnuts *again so it doesn't stop me from reading the whole problem. That way, I can think more clearly about the mathematics I need to do.*

2. Imagine the Problem

The second step of the RIDD tactic (Jackson, 2002) involves students "imagining the problem." This step of the strategy is especially effective because it guides students to reflectively translate the problem into their own thinking. Students can imagine the problem in pictures or create models with the problem, which is similar to the diagramming strategy discussed later in this chapter. This imagining process activates additional areas of the brain involved with conceptual understanding and spatial reasoning, and allows students to rely on their own areas of relative strength. For example, if a student is visually gifted, his imagine step could result in a "movie in his imagination" that represents the story problem. If another student is gifted musically, she could create short musical lyrics describing the steps for problem solution.

The essential element is that students mentally process the problem and transform that information into their own approach to problem solving (Bender, 2009b).

3. Decide What to Do

The first D in the RIDD acronym signals the students to decide how to do the problem. At this point students bring together their mathematical understanding of the problem, which was facilitated by the imagine activity in the previous step, and begin to sequence the steps for problem completion. As students use the conceptualized image of the problem, they can make connections to the necessary mathematics components in a supported manner. For younger students or struggling students, teachers may wish to support them in this step using questioning or prompting to help them think aloud about the problem. During the decide step, teachers can often determine if students have conceptual understanding of the problem and then differentiate or scaffold their assistance accordingly.

4. Do the Work

The final step of this strategy is for students to complete the planned sequence of steps. At this point, students who have computational fluency should be completely ready to find their solution. Students who have additional difficulties with computation may need differentiated supports like the use of a calculator or peer support to review the work.

This RIDD strategy is particularly effective for students who struggle with processing the tasks embedded in a word problem (Jackson, 2002). The RIDD acronym effectively guides students through the planning and implementing process by providing a way (the acronym) to identify the next step. This strategy is easily learned and can be implemented across grade levels with mathematical story problems. Thus, students may come to use the strategy with automaticity.

Search, Translate, Answer, Review

Within the RTI model, it is important for teachers to be equipped with a variety of strategies to support the varied strengths and needs of students. In fact, students struggle with story problems for a variety of different reasons, and teachers need to recognize that any single strategy is not likely to work for every student. Thus, teachers must make strategic decisions about which and how many strategies to teach students in Tier 2 intervention. Furthermore, caution must be exercised since using too many different strategies may actually confuse those students who don't understand which strategy to use in which situation. For most struggling students, teachers should teach and emphasize only one strategy for solving story problems over a period of weeks to avoid such confusion. By using data they have collected regarding students' strengths and weaknesses, and through close observation of student performance, teachers can make qualified decisions when choosing an appropriate learning strategy for a particular student.

The *Search, Translate, Answer, Review* (STAR) strategy focuses more on linguistic understanding and works well for students who are talented linguistically. This strategy guides the student to translate the story problem into mathematical equations as he or she thinks through it (Foegen, 2008; Gagnon & Maccini, 2001; Maccini & Hughes, 2000). This tactic is another learning strategy represented by an acronym that teaches students to plan their thinking and monitor their completion of the steps in problem solving. Hence, it provides struggling students with scaffolded support. The STAR tactic also capitalizes on the C-R-A sequence of instruction that has been shown to be an effective pedagogical strategy (Foegen, 2008; Witzel et al., 2003). Table 5.5 highlights the steps of the STAR tactic.

> The STAR tactic is another learning strategy represented by an acronym that teaches students to plan their thinking and monitor their completion of the steps in problem solving. Hence, it provides struggling students with scaffolded support.

1. Search the Problem

The first step in the STAR tactic is to search the problem. Students search through the story problem by carefully reading it and identifying what they know and what they need to know. They should be taught to write down these facts before beginning the next step.

Table 5.5: The STAR Tactic for Solving Word Problems

1. Search the problem.   • Carefully read the problem.   • Decide, "What do I know, and what do I need to find out?"   • Write the facts down.
2. Translate the words into a picture equation.   • Find the variable to solve for.   • Use cue words to determine the mathematics operations you need to use.   • Use counters or manipulatives to show the problem.   • Draw a picture of the equation with the facts and operations you know.
3. Answer the problem.   • Solve the problem and find the variables.
4. Review the solution.   • Reread the problem.   • Ask, "Does my answer make sense?"   • Check your answer.

Source: Adapted from Gagnon and Maccini, 2001; Bender, 2009b.

2. Translate the Words Into a Picture Equation

The T step of STAR represents translate; students translate the facts from the first step into a picture equation of the problem. In this step, students would be expected to choose a variable to solve for and use cue words to identify the necessary operation or operations, as well as any sequencing of steps that may be required. Students are encouraged to use counters or pictures to represent the equation, if this strategy assists them. Students should also attempt to draw a picture representing the problem solution and compare it with the various cue words they identified.

3. Answer the Problem

The A step in STAR indicates that students should be prepared to answer the problem by performing the necessary operations they have mapped out. Students should be encouraged to double check their operations and computation at each step.

4. Review the Solution

Finally, students should review their solution in a structured, predictable manner by doing the following:

- Rereading the problem
- Asking themselves, "Does this answer make sense?"
- Checking the answer

In contrast to the RIDD tactic in which the final step is do the work, the final step of the STAR tactic involves reviewing the solution to the problem. For many struggling students, this is a very valuable step as students learn to review their work and consider if their answer makes sense. This provides an excellent opportunity for small-group collaboration through which students can justify their reasoning to their peers.

Similar to the RIDD strategy, STAR serves as a planning system that helps students organize their thoughts and the problem information to prepare for the appropriate (and hopefully correct) solution. Again, teachers should consider if the use of calculators would be appropriate for student use based on student needs and the instructional goals.

Diagramming

One instructional strategy for story problems that has received research support is the use of semantic webs or diagrams that students develop to help solve word problems (Goldman, 1989; Jitendra, 2002; van Garderen, 2007). In essence, this strategy involves teaching students to develop a diagram or "picture" of the problem as an initial step in problem solving. For students who have a strength in spatial thinking or visualization, this diagramming process can be very helpful in thinking through possible problem solutions. This is also one of the steps in the RIDD tactic described previously—drawing a picture of the solution to the story problem.

Figure 5.1 (page 142) presents a simple word problem and several diagrams that students might develop to assist them in formulating an answer. Note how developing a diagram based on the information in the story problem can concretize the metacognitive planning necessary to solve the problem and thereby assist the student in determining the answer.

There are various types of diagrams or semantic webs that students can use as tools to assist them in solving word problems (Goldman, 1989; Jitendra, 2002). For example, some problems involve changes in quantity based on either addition or subtraction, which students can use line diagrams to illustrate. Other story problems may need to be represented as part/whole diagrams or comparison diagrams. (See fig. 5.1 for examples.) Teaching these commonly used diagrams to students can assist them in metacognitively planning the steps toward problem solving.

Jitendra (2002) suggests that students may also use diagramming techniques to solve complex, multistep story problems. Multistep problems require students to complete several distinct steps that each involve one or more mathematics operations. For example, consider once again the problem presented at the beginning of this chapter:

> Two trains departed Philadelphia at 12:00 pm and were traveling 965 miles to St. Louis, Missouri. Train A was carrying 1,622 passengers and 53 tons of cargo. Train B was carrying 2,612 passengers and 29 tons of cargo. If train A traveled at 53 miles per hour and train B traveled 7 miles per hour faster than train A, what time will each train arrive?

In solving this problem, students would have to generate the speed of train B using addition (53 + 7), and then do two division problems (965 ÷ 53 and 965 ÷ 60) to determine the arrival time of trains A and B respectively. As shown in this example, multistep problems often involve performing a mathematics operation to generate some of the information that is then used to solve other aspects of the story problem. Thus, for multistep problems, students would plan several diagrams, and then perform several operations to generate the necessary data. Finally, students would use those data along with other information presented directly within the problem to generate a solution. To use diagrams to complete these multistep problems, students must be taught to recognize the type of information required to answer the question and the steps or operations needed to manipulate that data to determine the answer. Each such step may then be represented by a diagram. Again, for students with a strength in visualization, diagramming even these multistep problems can be of great benefit.

Tactics selected for Tier 2 and Tier 3 interventions must be directly related to students' specific needs and strengths in order to ensure efficacy. We have recommended a variety of highly targeted instructional strategies in this section that are particularly appropriate for students struggling with story problems. All of the instructional strategies recommended for Tier 2 and Tier 3 intervention in this section are also very appropriate for Tier 1 instruction in general education classrooms, and many have been demonstrated as effective in the general education class, as well as with more targeted, smaller groups. Clearly, it is the teacher's responsibility to find strategies that explicitly address the learning needs and strengths of each student.

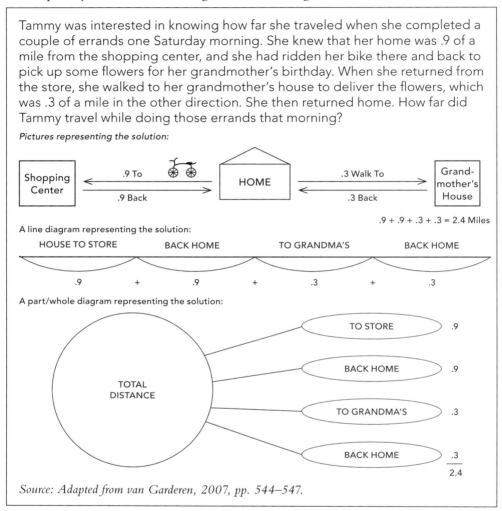

Tammy was interested in knowing how far she traveled when she completed a couple of errands one Saturday morning. She knew that her home was .9 of a mile from the shopping center, and she had ridden her bike there and back to pick up some flowers for her grandmother's birthday. When she returned from the store, she walked to her grandmother's house to deliver the flowers, which was .3 of a mile in the other direction. She then returned home. How far did Tammy travel while doing those errands that morning?

Pictures representing the solution:

A line diagram representing the solution:

A part/whole diagram representing the solution:

Source: Adapted from van Garderen, 2007, pp. 544–547.

Figure 5.1: Sample story problem with diagrams.

Case Study: An RTI for Problem Solving

In this case study example, Anton is a fifth-grade student who is experiencing difficulty in several areas of mathematics, particularly with story problems. Figure 5.2 shows the completed Response to Intervention Documentation Form for Anton.

Student: *Anton Stukes*	Age: *10*	Date: *9/10/08*
Initiating Teacher: *Mr. Henson*	School: *Coopersville Elementary School*	Grade: *5*

1. Student Difficulty and Summary of Tier 1 Instruction:

    I've noticed over the last three weeks that Anton is not successful in the most basic one-step story problems. While he struggles some on certain operations (long division), his most fundamental need is to work to strengthen his problem-solving skills. I've tried to assist him in several ways. First, I had the class work as peer buddies on a set of five word problems daily over a three-day period, and I also tutored him and his peer buddy each day. He still doesn't seem to get it, and his state assessment results from last year do suggest a difficulty in problem-solving applications. On that assessment, he scored 3.1 on mathematics applications, while scoring 5.3 on operations. I conclude that Anton needs more intensive work on solving story problems. I shared these concerns with Ms. Johnson, the school mathematics coach, and requested a Tier 2 intervention on story problems for Anton.

    Mr. Henson, 9/10/08

2. Tier 2 Intervention Plan:

    As the mathematics coach at Coopersville Elementary, I consult with teachers, and in many cases conduct RTI interventions for struggling students. To begin, I will give a pretest to Anton and seven other students that includes five one-step word problems. All of these students need additional assistance on story problems. I will begin with instruction on single-step story problems, and then move into multistep word problems as quickly as possible. I plan on conducting this Tier 2 intervention within Mr. Henson's class four days a week (Monday through Thursday) for fifteen minutes each day with the eight students who need this intervention to move forward in problem-solving skills. I will conduct this intervention when Mr. Henson is leading a class discussion on a topic other than mathematics, and he informs me that he can, in most cases, take the remaining class members to the media center for this fifteen-minute intervention period.

    For the intervention, I will teach the students the STAR tactic to assist them in thinking through and planning their solution to story problems. I plan on reviewing that strategy each day during the intervention, and then demonstrating it prior to having the students practice on a story problem individually. On Friday of each week, I will provide the students with five single-step story problems selected from the school curricula, collect data on their performance, and chart those data. We will continue this intervention for five more weeks, until the end of the current grading period, and then re-evaluate Anton's progress.

Figure 5.2: Response to Intervention Documentation Form for Anton.

continued on next page →

This intervention plan was presented to each student's parents by telephone on 9/11/08, and Anton's mother was glad to see he would receive this additional help.

Ms. Johnson, mathematics coach, 9/12/08

3. Observational Notes of Student in Tier 2 Mathematics Intervention:

    At Coopersville Elementary, observations of Tier 2 interventions are not generally conducted when the reading or mathematics coach does the intervention.

4. Tier 2 Intervention Summary and Recommendations:

    The student support team reviewed Anton's progress on the Tier 2 intervention on story problems [see fig. 5.3 on page 146]. The team noted that Anton was able to master the STAR strategy, though Ms. Johnson reported that it took him a great deal more time than the other students, who were applying STAR in almost every case after the first several days of the intervention. He did attempt to complete those steps in doing his story problems. The data on Anton's performance on single-step word problems suggest that he has progressed a bit, but his progress has been somewhat slower than most of the other students in the group. In my opinion, his progress here will not allow him to catch up with his peers in a reasonable amount of time. Still, given the increased importance of story problems in mathematics in the higher grades, Anton needs more intensive work on story problems. At this point, the other students receiving this Tier 2 intervention need to move on to multistep problems, but Anton needs more work on single-step problems. The team recommends implementation of a Tier 3 intervention for Anton, and Ms. Johnson, as the school mathematics coach, will develop and implement that intervention in the mathematics lab during the daily interventions period.

    Mrs. Bukener, chair of the student support team, 11/12/08

5. Tier 3 Intervention Plan:

    In conducting the Tier 2 intervention with Anton on story problems using the STAR strategy, I noted that Anton seemed to struggle to create a picture of the problem to guide him, and I believe more direct instruction on diagramming story problems may help. I have planned a Tier 3 intervention based on diagramming that I believe will assist Anton in moving from single-step story problems to multistep problems.

    Anton will come to the mathematics lab during the interventions period each day (that period is a forty-five-minute period used for intervention work or for elective subjects). He will continue this intervention for the next two grading periods, and I will chart his progress every two weeks in working on problem solving. We will begin with single-step problems (approximately fourth-grade-level problems) and use the diagramming strategy each day. We will progress to multistep problems with more complex configurations as Anton's progress allows. He will be working in a group of only five students. I also intend to have students spend some time in a computerized curriculum specifically focused on story problems each day, as well as conducting some one-to-one instruction for each student in this cohort.

Ms. Johnson, 11/15/08

6. Observation of Student in Tier 3 Mathematics Intervention:

    It is always wonderful to report a successful intervention! The data from this nine-week grading period on Anton's progress in story problems show a large measure of success [see fig. 5.4 on page 146]. I was able to chart his progress each week, rather than every two weeks as originally planned, during this Tier 3 intervention. His data show success. Anton is feeling much more confident in his ability to work out story problems. The diagramming strategy was exactly what Anton needed to move forward fairly quickly, and I charted his performance on developing diagrams/pictures that accurately presented the concepts in the story problem. Anton was excited to see his own progress on that measure! That roughly paralleled his increased success on story-problem accuracy. This success allowed him to move from single-step problems to multistep problems using all the operations within only four weeks of the beginning date for this intervention.

    Earlier, the student support team recommended that Anton continue this Tier 3 intervention for two grading periods, and I concur with that suggestion. However, based on his clear progress, I do not believe that he will require more intensive instruction or consideration for placement in special education, as he is responding nicely to this intervention. I believe that over the next grading period, Anton's skills in solving problems can be strengthened to a point where his skills on that task will be comparable to most of his peers. It does seem clear that he is making good progress in the current intervention, and we should evaluate his performance data once again at the end of the next grading period.

    While an observation is typically required for students receiving Tier 3 interventions, Anton's progress would seem to make that unnecessary at this time. Of course all student support team members are encouraged to visit the mathematics lab and observe Anton and other students as their time allows.

Ms. Johnson, 12/15/08

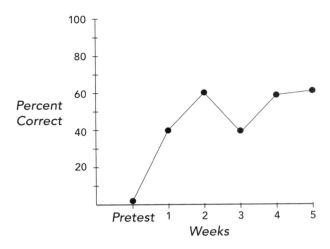

Figure 5.3: Data from Anton's Tier 2 intervention on one-step story problems.

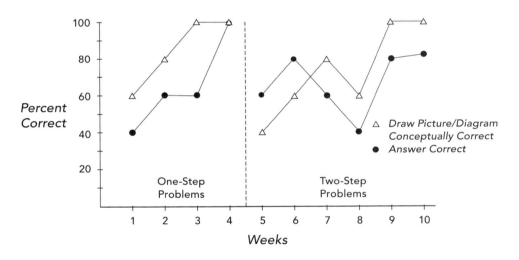

Figure 5.4: Data from Anton's Tier 3 intervention on story problems.

In describing Anton's academic difficulty, Mr. Henson notes that he could have chosen to focus this RTI effort on mathematics operations such as long division rather than on story problems. It is frequently the case in the elementary and middle school grades that students who are experiencing difficulties in mathematics are having multiple difficulties in math, and in this case, Anton showed difficulty in long division as well as story problems. In this case study, Mr. Henson made an informed choice to focus on story problems, since story problems are more heavily emphasized as students move into higher grades. Teachers should realize that in mathematics RTI procedures, perhaps more so than in reading or literacy RTIs, they themselves will often have to make choices for intervention when students show various areas of mathematics deficit. Here, Mr. Henson documented his rationale for that decision. He thought the most important curricular emphasis for Anton's future success overall was story problems, and that is an excellent criterion on which to base such a judgment.

> Teachers should realize that in mathematics RTI procedures, perhaps more so than in reading or literacy RTIs, they themselves will often have to make choices for intervention when students show various areas of mathematics deficit.

Next, note that a mathematics coach delivered the Tier 2 instructional interventions. In some elementary schools, and many middle schools, because of the departmentalized nature of the curriculum, it is common for students to receive Tier 2 instruction from a teacher other than the general education mathematics teacher. This instruction is frequently undertaken in an intervention period or as an assigned class other than the general education mathematics class. While various models of service delivery are used in different schools to facilitate RTI procedures, the use of an intervention period to deliver Tier 2 and Tier 3 interventions is becoming quite common in departmentalized schools, at least in our experience. Given the complexity of this problem-solving skill (single-step versus multistep story problems), it is possible to describe the interventions in terms of several sequenced levels of skill proficiency. Ms. Johnson did so in her description of the Tier 3 intervention by specifying an initial emphasis on single-step story problems and a later emphasis on multistep problems. Of course, such a refined delineation of levels is not possible in certain other areas of mathematics, but when differentiations can be made between levels of instruction that result in a more accurate description of the planned intervention, they should certainly be included in the description of that Tier 3 intervention. These levels are more common in the upper elementary and middle school grades.

Next, notice that time required for progress monitoring of this complex skill requires some consideration. The task of solving story problems involves considerable time to complete only one problem, and thus is similar to the examples presented in the case study in chapter 4. Teachers cannot realistically expect to do progress monitoring using twenty story problems each day, as the time requirements would prohibit even highly successful students from completing that task in a timely fashion. Thus, five or six problems have to be used as the progress-monitoring measure for most RTI procedures on story problems, even though more error is introduced into the measure by virtue of using only a limited number of problems for the progress-monitoring assessments. In RTI procedures with only limited performance data on each day, more progress-monitoring data points are desirable, and in order to generate those additional data points, many, if not most, Tier 2 and Tier 3 interventions in the upper elementary and middle school grades are likely to be extended at least through a nine-week grading period, and perhaps for a longer period of time.

Finally, in this example, Ms. Johnson chose to do an in-term report on Anton's progress, even though the student support team had requested that she complete the Tier 3 intervention for two grading periods. In this case, given Anton's progress in the Tier 3 intervention, it made sense to provide such an interim report on his progress; such a report let the student support team know that the intervention—diagramming to solve story problems—was working for Anton. That report also put to rest any question of his manifesting a learning disability in mathematics, since he was clearly responding to instruction in Tier 3.

Conclusion

In this text, we have described the research supporting the RTI process, the three-tiered model of RTI intervention, and what intervention looks like in each tier. We have emphasized the importance of assessment, describing in detail universal screening and benchmarking, as well as various assessment procedures available to educators for both primary and elementary-level students. We have used NMAP's recommendations (2008) to outline important areas of focus for intervention in elementary mathematics, including number sense and problem solving. We have provided many specific strategies for differentiating instruction at the Tier 1 level and providing student-focused intervention at Tier 2 and 3. We have presented multiple case studies to show what RTI looks like in action. It is our hope that this text allows teams of teachers to develop rigorous RTI procedures in all areas of mathematics so that struggling students achieve success.

However, for this to happen, teachers need support from school leadership, and schools need to be successful in their endeavors to implement RTI on a wide scale. The final chapter of this book presents a variety of specific suggestions for school leaders for beginning a faculty discussion of the RTI process in mathematics at the district and the school level, as well as a variety of planning tools.

PLC Support Strategies for School- and Districtwide RTI Procedures in Mathematics

This chapter provides some guidelines on implementation for RTI in mathematics that come from schools that have undertaken the challenge and found the procedure beneficial to student success, from the available literature, and from our collective experience as we work daily on RTI implementation efforts throughout the United States.

State- and District-Level Leadership

Leadership on RTI procedures from state departments of education varies considerably (Berkeley et al., 2009). Some states have developed either requirements or detailed guidelines for RTI implementation, while others have not. States such as Tennessee, Georgia, and West Virginia have developed fairly specific RTI models and requirements, which may specify how long various interventions must be each day, how many data points constitute appropriate data collection for team decision making on progress-monitoring measures, specific week-by-week time requirements, maximum pupil-teacher ratios for various tiers, and other requirements. While those RTI requirements and guidelines vary a great deal from state to state, they often take the form of general descriptions such as the following:

> All Tier 3 interventions must involve implementation of a research-supported curriculum for an instructional period of at least twenty minutes, four times per week, for a minimum of eight weeks.

Other states—Michigan, California, and Texas, for example—have left development of these RTI particulars up to individual school districts (Berkeley et al., 2009). In such cases, various guideline documents may be available from state departments of education that stipulate much less specific language about what exactly constitutes an appropriate RTI procedure. All RTI efforts should conform to statewide guidelines for RTI, should any be available, and educators at the local district and school levels should seek whatever guidance or specific requirements exist for their locale.

Regardless of the level of guidance from the state department of education, some leadership on RTI procedures must come from the school district office. For example, in states that do not specify time requirements for RTI intervention tiers, school district personnel may wish to develop those guidelines based on the RTI research or based on models from other districts within the state. The issues and processes described in earlier chapters will result in an array of implementation questions from educators, and having some framework for RTI from the school district is not only desirable, but often essential in navigating the waters of RTI implementation.

Bender (2009a) published a Response to Intervention Planning Grid (fig. 6.1) that can be used for initial and early planning for RTI at the various tiers. (See page 174 for a reproducible of this grid. Visit **go.solution-tree.com/rti** for downloadable versions of all reproducibles found in this book.) This grid focuses discussion on the specific details of the RTI planning process. It has been used by many school districts and individual schools in their initial RTI efforts. The main points for discussion are listed across the top of the grid:

- **Person who implements**—Who is responsible for implementing interventions at each tier? What resources can be offered to that person?
- **Pupil-teacher ratio**—What is the maximum number of students in the groups at each tier? Does that number ensure that each intervention is more intensive than the last?
- **Curriculum**—Are our curricula research supported? Should different curricula be used at Tiers 2 and 3 to ensure robust RTI procedures?
- **Intervention time and duration**—How many minutes per day, days per week, and total weeks will each intervention last? Does this ensure progressively increasing intensity?
- **Frequency of performance monitoring**—How often is performance monitored? Daily, weekly, or every other week? Does intensity increase in each tier?
- **Treatment fidelity observation**—Are observations done for each tier? If so, by whom?
- **Notifications**—When does the general education teacher notify the student support team and/or the school administrators? When are parents notified?

Once team members have identified statewide specifics, these items should be removed from the grid. As other issues arise in the initial years of RTI implementation, the grid should be modified to include them, and hopefully this will facilitate discussion of these issues at the district level. This should be a fluid planning grid that can be changed and adapted as schools proceed through their first three to five years of implementation. In short, once a decision is made (such as how frequently teachers

Response to Intervention Planning Grid

	Person Who Implements	Pupil-Teacher Ratio	Curriculum	Intervention Time and Duration	Frequency of Performance Monitoring	Treatment Fidelity Observation	Notifications
Refer for Special Education							
Tier 3 More Intensive Instructions							
Tier 2 Targeted Supplemental Instructions							
Tier 1 General Education							

Figure 6.1: Response to intervention planning grid.

should monitor progress in Tier 2), that question can be taken out of the grid and other issues added as they arise.

School-Level Planning

While guidance from state departments and school districts is critical for effective RTI implementation, we believe that most of the actual RTI implementation issues may be best resolved at the school level. For example, while a school district may wish to institute broad requirements on what constitutes a Tier 3 intervention, various school-level teams can better flesh out the actual implementation details.

We believe that most of the actual RTI implementation issues may be best resolved at the school level.

Following is an example of the type of guideline that a particular school faculty could devise as a starting point for RTI. Note the level of detail that can be achieved via school-based planning for RTIs:

> Tolson Elementary has a math coach for each grade level, and those coaches use *Academy of MATH* as the basis for their remedial mathematics instruction. Our Tier 3 interventions will be conducted by the math coaches four times per week, twenty minutes per day, over two eight-week grading periods, using the *Academy of MATH* curriculum or portions of that curriculum that specifically address the problem or problems of each student. Instruction will take place in groups of no more than three students per teacher. Assessments within the *Academy of MATH* curriculum will be used every two weeks for progress-monitoring purposes.

Clearly, the guidelines developed for RTI implementation at the school level can be much richer and detailed than district guidelines and statements of procedures, as this example shows. In simple terms, educational leadership teams at the school are much more cognizant of the resources available at the school level, and they can apply those resources to maximize them for RTI purposes.

As one example, educators within the school will be able to develop a list of research-supported mathematics curricula that are already available at the school for supplemental instruction. Those educators may be aware of resources that can assist teachers in providing Tier 2 or Tier 3 interventions in mathematics, such as the use of the mathematics coaches in the Tolson Elementary example. Finally, the process of a school-based team fleshing out the specifics of RTI implementation for their faculty can result in increased responsibility for those procedures, increasing the buy-in and facilitating the change process as a faculty collectively moves toward full RTI implementation.

The process of a school-based team fleshing out the specifics of RTI implementation for their faculty can result in increased responsibility for those procedures, increasing the buy-in and facilitating the change process as a faculty collectively moves toward full RTI implementation.

Professional Learning Communities

We strongly support shared decision making, not only for evaluating a child's progress during the actual RTI process in mathematics, but also for overall RTI implementation efforts. On that basis, we recommend that some type of decision-making team at the school level be empowered with the responsibility for RTI implementation in both mathematics and reading, since such shared decision making is likely to result in much greater buy-in on the part of the faculty. This should not be the same group that reviews individual student data (such as the student support team). Rather, the purpose of this group is study and implementation of effective and appropriate RTI procedures at the school level. Of course, schools that have moved forward with RTI procedures in reading may have already formulated such a group, and there is certainly no need to reinvent the wheel.

For schools where no specific group has been formed to study, lead, and oversee RTI implementation, we recommend formation of a professional learning community (PLC), such as that described by DuFour and his colleagues (2004, 2008). PLCs emphasize changing the very culture of the school while demonstrating a long-term commitment to school reform and improvement (DuFour et al., 2008). These facets of PLC operations suggest that the PLC could easily serve as an excellent decision-making team for RTI implementation efforts in both mathematics and reading. Alternatively, in schools where no PLC is functioning, virtually any type of school-based leadership team might well be empowered with this set of responsibilities for RTI implementation.

> For schools where no specific group has been formed to study, lead, and oversee RTI implementation, we recommend formation of a professional learning community.

The RTI implementation process is time consuming, and if PLCs and other leadership teams already have a full plate of activities (and almost all PLCs or school leadership teams do), perhaps formation of another group to oversee RTI planning efforts is warranted. In such situations, Bender (2009a) recommends formation of a schoolwide RTI task force.

Regardless of the title of this team, this group of faculty and administrators should be primarily focused on RTI, and they should manage, over a period of two to three years, the ongoing tasks of implementation of RTI procedures. This team will undertake a wide array of activities focused on implementation of RTI procedures in mathematics, and perhaps reading or other areas also, depending on how the school structures these responsibilities. What is critical is that some team at the school level be empowered to make recommendations on RTI implementation in mathematics.

Team Tasks

The tasks of the PLC or task force will vary depending upon where the school is in their implementation of RTI. In schools that have developed RTI procedures for reading, many decisions have been made that will apply to RTI procedures in mathematics. Regardless of the level of previous RTI implementation, most schools can benefit from a structured planning process. The feature box on page 154 presents a list of activities the PLC/task force might take on in the initial planning phase.

Initial Team Activities for RTI Implementation in Mathematics

1. Conduct a school inventory of curricula, assessments, and teacher training and experiences that can assist with RTI procedures in mathematics. (See fig 6.2, the School Response to Intervention Inventory for Mathematics form, figure 6.2, as a basis for this inventory, and page 175 for a reproducible of this form. Visit **go.solution-tree .com/rti** for downloadable versions of all reproducibles found in this book.)

2. Identify specific individuals to review websites to collect information. State Department of Education websites are excellent places to begin and should be searched thoroughly to ensure that decisions made at the school level are in compliance with newly emerging statewide policies and procedures. (See the list of websites on pages 160–162.)

3. Discuss schoolwide RTI efforts in multiple subjects including reading/literacy, mathematics, writing, and others. Identify resources that might assist in each area.

4. Discuss reshuffling resources at the school level, including, but not limited to, the following:

   • Using paraprofessionals to support RTI mathematics implementation

   • Reallocating technology resources, including both hardware and software (for example, the number of students on site licenses for various instructional software programs)

   • Identifying other resources that might assist implementation

   • Developing personnel requests for new faculty positions to recommend to the administration to facilitate RTI implementation

5. Develop a professional development program for the subsequent year that focuses faculty efforts on RTI issues for mathematics. This might include the following:

   • Determining who might lead in-house workshops on RTI implementation

   • Identifying book study opportunities for faculty focused on RTI

6. Offer to the teachers the option of conducting a classroom walkthrough for mathematics instruction. Use the form in figure 6.3 on page 157 (completed by a member of the RTI PLC or task force) for that walkthrough. (See page 177 for a reproducible of this checklist. Visit **go.solution-tree.com/rti** for downloadable versions of all reproducibles

found in this book.) This should be a formative learning experience for the teacher. The PLC/task force member should review this walkthrough with the teacher and leave the only copy of that walkthrough checklist with the teacher after that discussion.

Hard Copy Supplemental Mathematics Curricula Interventions

List all *supplemental* curricula that are "hard copy" (that is, not primarily computerized curricula, for example, *Algebra 1 Rescue!* and *Saxon Math*). Note the grade range and the areas or subjects for each. Include curricula used by every teacher within the school, including curricula used by particular teachers within specialized programs. Note who is using these and for what group. Also remember to consider any curricula that may be unused in the media center or storage areas in the building.

Computerized Supplemental Curricula Interventions

List all *supplemental* curricula software (for example, *Academy of MATH*). Note the grade range and the areas or subjects for each. Include curricula used by every teacher within the school, including curricula used by particular teachers within specialized programs. Note who is using these and for which students.

Hard Copy Assessments for Universal Screening

List all individual assessments that might be appropriate for universal screening or repeated assessment for performance monitoring (for example, the Number Knowledge Test). Note the grade range and the areas or

Figure 6.2: School response to intervention inventory for mathematics.

continued on next page →

subjects for each. Include curricula used by every teacher within the school, including curricula used by particular teachers within specialized programs. Note who is using these and for which students.

Curricula Recommended for Specific Tiers

Are there reasons for recommending particular curricula for specific tiers? For example, a limited site license for a certain computerized curriculum may suggest use of that curriculum only as a Tier 3 intervention. Explain.

Specialized Training

Have teachers received specialized training for particular supplemental curricula (for example, for *Everyday Mathematics*) or in particular learning strategies (such as *STAR* or *RIDD*, or project-based learning instructional tactics)? Can or will these teachers be responsible for certain tiers of intervention or prepare other teachers for such intervention? Can other teachers receive such training, as necessary?

Source: Adapted from Bender, 2009a, pp. 197–198.

Note that this RTI PLC or task force will at some point undertake the extremely serious responsibility of recommending to the administration and the faculty some type of reshuffling of resources in order to accomplish the goals of RTI procedures in mathematics. This might include reassignment of specific supplemental curricula to different faculty, or it might involve personnel recommendations for new hiring at the school level. In fact, some current professionals within the school may find their job responsibilities changing as a result of implementation of RTI (Bender, 2009a; Cummings et al., 2008), and this can result in serious personnel issues unless the reassignments are managed appropriately.

> The RTI PLC or task force will at some point undertake the extremely serious responsibility of recommending to the administration and the faculty some type of reshuffling of resources in order to accomplish the goals of RTI procedures in mathematics.

Hard feelings can result whenever someone's job description changes, and great care should be taken to avoid this type of problem.

This walkthrough provides informal feedback for teachers and should be completed by a member of the school RTI professional learning community/ task force and/or a school administrator. This is intended as a professional support for mathematics instruction and will highlight various tactics and strategies that are currently recommended for mathematics instruction. This is not a professional evaluation of instruction. It is not likely all indicators will be observed because these indicators encompass a wide variety of instructional practices. Note that some instructional tactics may not be appropriate for some mathematics lessons. The team member conducting the walkthrough should provide this feedback and review it with the teacher in an informal discussion after conducting the walkthrough.

Teacher's Name:	School:
Grade:	RTI Team Member/Observer:

Date of Walkthrough:

Classroom Environment and Instructional Format

_____ Room displays indicate mathematical content appropriate to grade level.

_____ Manipulatives are accessible for student use.

_____ Students are responsible for the management of math materials.

_____ Students are familiar with routines and expectations (for example, they move into small groups quickly, are prepared for activities, and gather appropriate materials with little direction from the teacher).

_____ The teacher effectively uses differentiated instruction, including small groups and individual instruction, as appropriate.

_____ The teacher provides supplemental mathematics activities.

_____ Both the students and the teacher reflect an enthusiasm for mathematics.

Comments:

Figure 6.3: Response to intervention walkthrough checklist.

continued on next page →

Introduction of Mathematical Concepts

_____ Instruction reflects teacher's knowledge of student needs based on formative assessment data.

_____ Relevant precursory skills are reviewed in each lesson.

_____ Teacher provides students struggling with precursory skills with supplemental materials such as scaffolding.

_____ Teacher addresses student learning styles in diversified learning activities.

_____ Teacher presents students with a question or real-world problem to activate math thinking.

_____ Teacher and students raise mathematical questions frequently, and students have multiple opportunities to discuss and share their mathematical thinking.

_____ Teacher has chosen mathematical materials based on concepts as well as student needs.

_____ Materials for the mathematics lesson are organized and prepared.

Comments:

Instructional Activities for Conceptual Understanding

_____ Instructional activities include an appropriate balance of teacher-directed and student-centered activities based on content and student needs.

_____ Students are sufficiently scaffolded to engage successfully in inquiry learning activities.

_____ Students use manipulatives and mathematics tools appropriate to the task.

_____ All students are actively engaged in learning.

_____ Student groups are flexible and frequently change.

_____ Students have choices available in some mathematics activities.

Comments:

Instructional Activities for Automaticity

_____ Teacher identifies skill elements that require practice to build automaticity on a student-by-student basis.

_____ Teacher identifies assessment strategies to identify and increase automaticity.

_____ Students have adequate time and materials to practice skills and build automaticity.

_____ Students utilize available technology to increase automaticity with skills.

Comments:

Problem-Solving Activities

_____ Problem-based learning activities provide the basis for some of the instruction.

_____ Students and teachers frequently discuss problems similar to those being taught to expand applicability of mathematics concepts.

Comments:

Assessment Activities

_____ Teacher asks open-ended questions to extend learning or provide clarification.

_____ Students frequently describe mathematical insights to classmates and teachers.

_____ Student accountability is embedded in various activities.

_____ Teacher interacts with students and monitors understanding.

_____ The classroom structure fosters frequent progress monitoring for struggling students.

Comments:

Closure Activities and Summarization

_____ Students often summarize mathematics content for each other, working in pairs during the middle of a lesson, while the teacher checks for conceptual understanding.

continued on next page →

____	Summaries of activities at the end of the lesson frequently result in some product (for example, a poster summarizing lesson content or bulletin-board notes summarizing content that is then displayed for subsequent days during that instructional unit).
____	Students use the writing process to summarize mathematical thinking (such as the use of a math journal to deepen understanding and serve as informal formative assessment).

Comments:

Signature:

For example, Cummings et al. (2008) describe various changes in the instructional responsibility of special educators during RTI implementation. Many times, guidelines on special education funding do now allow special educators to use their time to instruct students not identified as learning disabled. However, the RTI intervention plan may indicate these teachers are to work with nonidentified students in Tier 2 or 3 interventions. Furthermore, school psychologists, speech language therapists, mathematics instructional coaches, lead teachers, grade-level team leaders, and other support persons may see their roles modified by the implementation of RTI efforts (Bender, 2009a).

There are a variety of resources available to assist the PLC or task force in planning for schoolwide implementation. These include the many Web-based resources mentioned throughout this book and those presented in Web-Based Resources to Support RTI Implementation in Mathematics. Several additional planning tools will help with implementation. These include the following: (1) a School Response to Intervention Inventory for Mathematics (page 175) and (2) a Multiyear RTI Implementation Plan for Mathematics (table 6.1, pages 162–164). At a minimum, these planning documents can serve as discussion starters for the many issues involved in RTI implementation.

Web-Based Resources to Support RTI Implementation in Mathematics

Easy CBM

www.EasyCBM.com

This website provides free access to curriculum-based measures in reading and mathematics for grades K–8. The mathematics items on this assessment are keyed to the focal points of the NCTM (2006). While benchmark scoring information is available for the reading assessments on this site, such scoring information is not yet available for the mathematics assessments. Those scoring data should become available by 2011.

IES What Works Clearinghouse

http://ies.ed.gov/ncee/wwc/publications

This is a clearinghouse sponsored by the U.S. government that describes various research-based instructional curricula in reading and math. Unlike some of the websites dedicated to reporting only on scientifically supported reading curricula, this clearinghouse also reports on new mathematics curricula. While rigorous research standards prevent this site from reporting on some curricula, if such a decision is made, this site will clearly state the rationale and describe the curriculum.

National Association of State Directors of Special Education

www.nasdse.org

This site presents a number of items that will assist educators in implementation of RTI, including various lists of implementation guidelines, position papers, and brief explanations.

National Center on Response to Intervention

www.rti4success.org

The National Center on RTI provides an assortment of briefs, fact sheets, presentations, media, and training modules relevant to RTI that are divided into eighteen separate categories. Many of the current resources were created by other organizations, associations, state departments, or districts, and center-authored resources will be added on a regular basis. Visitors can sign up to receive an online monthly newsletter, the *RTI Responder.*

National Center on Student Progress Monitoring

www.studentprogress.org

This website was established by the U.S. Office of Special Education Programs under funding for the National Center on Student Progress Monitoring. It is structured as a technical assistance center, working in conjunction with Vanderbilt University in Nashville, Tennessee. The site provides a wide array of resources including online discussions, newsletters, and web-based training on monitoring student performance.

continued on next page →

RTI Action Network

www.rtinetwork.org

The RTI Action Network was created by the National Center for Learning Disabilities and is dedicated to the effective implementation of response to intervention in school districts nationwide. The site contains a variety of free resources for districts and other stakeholder groups, including webcasts, national online forums, implementation guidelines, and research summaries. Visitors can also sign up to participate in various webcasts or online workshops.

School-wide Information System

www.swis.org

The School-wide Information System (SWIS) is a Web-based information system developed to facilitate behavioral intervention planning. This system presents options for inputting behavioral data on the number of office referrals to allow school administrators to compile data in a variety of ways. Individual data may be used to support student behavior for particular students, but administrators may also compile data on specific time periods during the day, specific locations within the school, and so on, to analyze and solve behavioral problems throughout the school. According to the website, the system is currently used by more than 3,700 schools in various countries worldwide.

Table 6.1: Multiyear RTI Implementation Plan for Mathematics, Pollocksville Primary

RTI Goals for Academic Year 2010–2011

1. All teachers will receive three hours of in-service on RTI in mathematics. These professional development opportunities will be planned and/or conducted by the PLC and will focus on the following topics:

    a. RTI procedures for our state—in that meeting, the RTI planning grid will be introduced as our primary planning mechanism. This will be completed during the first month of school, and an outside expert (perhaps from the state department of education) will be used to introduce RTI to our faculty.

    b. The use of various screening assessments for performance monitoring in mathematics

    c. Computerized interventions available at our school in mathematics—our mathematics coach will share (for three to five minutes) a bit of information about each

	d.	Research data on efficacy of RTI procedures in reading/literacy and mathematics to serve as advocates for the implementation of RTIs in mathematics
2.		Members of the PLC will select specific professional development opportunities at various state and national conferences on mathematics, and various faculty members will attend these to bring back additional information on RTI implementation for mathematics.
3.		The PLC will develop and present an RTI implementation plan for mathematics to the school faculty. The plan should, to the best degree possible, follow our current RTI practices for reading/literacy. The plan will be discussed at one faculty meeting and then modified as appropriate. Our initial goal is to have these modifications adopted by the end of the 2010–2011 academic year. Current recommendations for the RTI implementation timeline are presented herein.
4.		The PLC will work with the principal and administration on necessary resources for RTI on an ongoing basis. These may include the following:
	a.	Additional professional and/or support staff for RTI interventions
	b.	Purchase of supplemental intervention curricula in mathematics
	c.	Discussions of reallocations of job responsibilities for RTI implementation
5.		The PLC will implement a needs assessment among the faculty focused on RTI procedures in mathematics and how such procedures might differ from RTIs in reading or literacy at the primary level.
6.		The PLC will conduct a school-based inventory to identify assessments, curricula, and specialized staff training at Pollocksville Primary to assist in RTI implementation.
7.		Items on the schoolwide planning grid will be discussed at the end of the year to note any changes from the initial planning session.
8.		Data to document efficacy of our RTI efforts on overall performance in mathematics will be collected from the statewide assessment data. These data from the 2010–2011 academic year will provide a baseline for comparison with subsequent years after RTIs are implemented in mathematics.

RTI Goals for Academic Year 2011–2012

1.	Pollocksville Primary will implement universal screening in mathematics using the Number Knowledge Test (or other appropriate assessment as recommended by the PLC) for all students (kindergarten to grade 3) three times each year, and use those data to determine which students are not on benchmark for appropriate progress in mathematics.
2.	Pollocksville Primary will provide Tier 2 interventions in mathematics for all students requiring more intensive instruction by providing a minimum of thirty minutes of small-group supplemental instruction four times each week.

continued on next page →

3. By January of 2011, Pollocksville Primary will provide Tier 3 interventions in mathematics for students requiring them. These will be provided five days per week for a minimum of thirty minutes per day, and Ms. Surrills, the mathematics coach, will be responsible for instruction during the Tier 3 interventions.

4. The PLC will be expanded to include all former members as well as all grade-level team leaders in an effort to focus more energy on RTI implementation in mathematics.

5. Various teachers will be invited to attend professional development opportunities that address RTI implementation in mathematics and other subjects, as appropriate. Screening instruments in mathematics will be collected and discussed by the PLC for possible use at Pollocksville Primary.

6. The schoolwide planning grid will be used again, in May of each year, specifically to note any changes from the initial planning session.

7. Data on mathematics performance will be collected at the end of this year as a comparison measure on efficacy of RTI in mathematics. These data will be compared to data from the previous year to determine the impact of RTIs in mathematics in our school.

RTI Goals for Academic Year 2012–2013

1. Pollocksville Primary will implement universal screening in mathematics for all students (kindergarten to grade 3) a minimum of three times each year, and use those assessments to determine which students are not on benchmark in mathematics.

2. The PLC at Pollocksville Primary will consider data from the first two years of RTI implementation in mathematics and recommend additional supplemental curricula for purchase.

3. The PLC will consider ongoing training needs for new faculty hired for Pollocksville Primary, as those needs relate to RTI procedures in mathematics, reading/literacy, and other subjects, and make appropriate recommendations to the administration.

Adapted from Bender, 2009a, pp. 62–64.

Conclusion

As virtually every educator knows, the change process is never easy. There are many steps involved in implementing RTI procedures in mathematics at the district and school levels. Communicating with faculty members about the types of issues and challenges involved in implementation can alleviate many problems that could arise later in the change process. In that sense, the planning efforts of an effective PLC or task force whose members are willing to demonstrate their commitment to implementation endeavors will be one of the school's most effective tools as it moves to full RTI implementation. When implemented as described in this text, RTI procedures in mathematics will serve as a supremely effective school improvement mechanism, and they will make it possible for schools to meet the needs of all struggling students in the 21st century.

Reproducibles

Response to Intervention Self-Report Needs-Assessment for Teachers of Elementary Math

Circle one numeral for each descriptive indicator.					
1 = I have little knowledge and want additional in-service on this.					
2 = I have some knowledge, but some additional in-service will be helpful.					
3 = I have a good understanding of this, but I need to put this into practice this year.					
4 = I have complete understanding and have reached proficiency at this practice.					
N/A = Not applicable for our state, school, or school district					
General Understanding of RTI					
1. The pyramid of intervention in our state and district	1	2	3	4	N/A
2. The problem-solving model for our state or district	1	2	3	4	N/A
3. The tiers of intervention in our school	1	2	3	4	N/A
4. The intervention timelines for each intervention tier	1	2	3	4	N/A
5. How RTI applies to all students	1	2	3	4	N/A
6. RTI in mathematics	1	2	3	4	N/A
General Knowledge of Universal Screening and Progress-Monitoring Procedures					
1. The mathematics screening tests used in our school	1	2	3	4	N/A
2. The early mathematics standards	1	2	3	4	N/A
3. The individual mathematics assessments used in our school	1	2	3	4	N/A
4. Progress monitoring in mathematics during Tier 2 and Tier 3 interventions	1	2	3	4	N/A
5. Data-gathering procedures (weekly or daily) for RTI	1	2	3	4	N/A
6. The benchmark scores in mathematics across the grade levels	1	2	3	4	N/A
7. The data-management system for RTI	1	2	3	4	N/A

page 1 of 2

Knowledge of Interventions to Facilitate Student Progress					
1. The supplemental mathematics RTI programs used in our school	1	2	3	4	N/A
2. Frequency and intensity of mathematics interventions	1	2	3	4	N/A
3. How to use flexible grouping for Tiers 1, 2, and 3	1	2	3	4	N/A
4. The technology-based mathematics programs used in our school	1	2	3	4	N/A
5. How to use creative staffing to make time for interventions	1	2	3	4	N/A

My Contributions and Suggestions for RTI in Our School
1. In what RTI areas should we plan further staff development?
2. What suggestions can you offer for making RTI work better for students in our school?

Source: Adapted from Bender, 2009a, pp. 13–14.

Ideas for Using "I Can" Statements

The "I Can" Wall	Post a series of "I can" statements on a bulletin board, and allow students to autograph below the statements once they demonstrate that particular skill.
Peer Reinforcement for "I Can" Statements	Some teachers have a class celebration each time a student demonstrates a skill. The celebration can range from mere applause to a pizza party any time a student accomplishes a particular skill and documents it with an "I can" statement.
"I Can" PowerPoint Presentations	Teachers may encourage students to work either individually or as a team to develop a PowerPoint presentation. The PowerPoint may begin with explicit instructions on how to do a task and should culminate with the "I can" statement.
"I Can" Video	Again, this is a celebration opportunity for students once they accomplish their goal. Students can be videotaped demonstrating use of the mastered skill. The class should watch videos together to celebrate with the student his or her newly learned skill. An additional option is to post the video on a safe site that would allow families to access the learning celebrations.
"I Can" Teams	For certain skills, teachers may have students work in teams to foster differentiation and encourage students to support each other in development of the skill. They should work on the skill until each team member can say, "I can!"
"I Can" T-Shirts	Celebration for accomplishing particularly difficult skills should involve more reinforcement. Some teachers have actually printed "I can" t-shirts as rewards for the class accomplishing difficult mathematics objectives.

Response to Intervention Documentation Form

Student:	Age:	Date:
Initiating Teacher:	School:	Grade:

1. Student Difficulty and Summary of Tier 1 Instruction:

2. Tier 2 Intervention Plan:

3. Observational Notes of Student in Tier 2 Mathematics Intervention:

4. Tier 2 Intervention Summary and Recommendations:

5. Tier 3 Intervention Plan:

6. Observation of Student in Tier 3 Mathematics Intervention:

7. Tier 3 Intervention Summary and Recommendations:

Response to Intervention Planning Grid

	Person Who Implements	Pupil-Teacher Ratio	Curriculum	Intervention Time and Duration	Frequency of Performance Monitoring	Treatment Fidelity Observation	Notifications
Tier 3 More Intensive Instructions							
Tier 2 Targeted Supplemental Instructions							
Tier 1 General Education							

Refer for Special Education

School Response to Intervention Inventory for Mathematics

Hard Copy Supplemental Mathematics Curricula Interventions

List all *supplemental* curricula that are "hard copy" (that is, not primarily computerized curricula, for example, *Algebra 1 Rescue!* and *Saxon Math*). Note the grade range and the areas or subjects for each. Include curricula used by every teacher within the school, including curricula used by particular teachers within specialized programs. Note who is using these and for what group. Also remember to consider any curricula that may be unused in the media center or storage areas in the building.

Computerized Supplemental Curricula Interventions

List all *supplemental* curricula software (for example, *Academy of MATH*). Note the grade range and the areas or subjects for each. Include curricula used by every teacher within the school, including curricula used by particular teachers within specialized programs. Note who is using these and for which students.

Hard Copy Assessments for Universal Screening

List all individual assessments that might be appropriate for universal screening or repeated assessment for performance monitoring (for example, the Number Knowledge Test). Note the grade range and the areas or subjects for each. Include curricula used by every teacher within the school, including curricula used by particular teachers within specialized programs. Note who is using these and for which students.

RTI in Math © 2011 Solution Tree Press • solution-tree.com
Visit **go.solution-tree.com/rti** to download this page.

Curricula Recommended for Specific Tiers

Are there reasons for recommending particular curricula for specific tiers? For example, a limited site license for a certain computerized curriculum may suggest use of that curriculum only as a Tier 3 intervention. Explain.

Specialized Training

Have teachers received specialized training for particular supplemental curricula (for example, for *Everyday Mathematics*) or in particular learning strategies (such as *STAR* or *RIDD*, or project-based learning instructional tactics)? Can or will these teachers be responsible for certain tiers of intervention or prepare other teachers for such intervention? Can other teachers receive such training, as necessary?

Source: Adapted from Bender, 2009a, pp. 197–198.

Response to Intervention Walkthrough Checklist

This walkthrough provides informal feedback for teachers and should be completed by a member of the school RTI professional learning community/ task force and/or a school administrator. This is intended as a professional support for mathematics instruction and will highlight various tactics and strategies that are currently recommended for mathematics instruction. This is not a professional evaluation of instruction. It is not likely all indicators will be observed because these indicators encompass a wide variety of instructional practices. Note that some instructional tactics may not be appropriate for some mathematics lessons. The team member conducting the walkthrough should provide this feedback and review it with the teacher in an informal discussion after conducting the walkthrough.

Teacher's Name:	School:
Grade:	RTI Team Member/Observer:

Date of Walkthrough:

Classroom Environment and Instructional Format

_____ Room displays indicate mathematical content appropriate to grade level.

_____ Manipulatives are accessible for student use.

_____ Students are responsible for the management of math materials.

_____ Students are familiar with routines and expectations (for example, they move into small groups quickly, are prepared for activities, and gather appropriate materials with little direction from the teacher).

_____ The teacher effectively uses differentiated instruction, including small groups and individual instruction, as appropriate.

_____ The teacher provides supplemental mathematics activities.

_____ Both the students and the teacher reflect an enthusiasm for mathematics.

Comments:

Introduction of Mathematical Concepts

____ Instruction reflects teacher's knowledge of student needs based on formative assessment data.

____ Relevant precursory skills are reviewed in each lesson.

____ Teacher provides students struggling with precursory skills with supplemental materials such as scaffolding.

____ Teacher addresses student learning styles in diversified learning activities.

____ Teacher presents students with a question or real-world problem to activate math thinking.

____ Teacher and students raise mathematical questions frequently, and students have multiple opportunities to discuss and share their mathematical thinking.

____ Teacher has chosen mathematical materials based on concepts as well as student needs.

____ Materials for the mathematics lesson are organized and prepared.

Comments:

Instructional Activities for Conceptual Understanding

____ Instructional activities include an appropriate balance of teacher-directed and student-centered activities based on content and student needs.

____ Students are sufficiently scaffolded to engage successfully in inquiry learning activities.

____ Students use manipulatives and mathematics tools appropriate to the task.

____ All students are actively engaged in learning.

____ Student groups are flexible and frequently change.

____ Students have choices available in some mathematics activities.

Comments:

Instructional Activities for Automaticity

_____ Teacher identifies skill elements that require practice to build automaticity on a student-by-student basis.

_____ Teacher identifies assessment strategies to identify and increase automaticity.

_____ Students have adequate time and materials to practice skills and build automaticity.

_____ Students utilize available technology to increase automaticity with skills.

Comments:

Problem-Solving Activities

_____ Problem-based learning activities provide the basis for some of the instruction.

_____ Students and teachers frequently discuss problems similar to those being taught to expand applicability of mathematics concepts.

Comments:

Assessment Activities

_____ Teacher asks open-ended questions to extend learning or provide clarification.

_____ Students frequently describe mathematical insights to classmates and teachers.

_____ Student accountability is embedded in various activities.

_____ Teacher interacts with students and monitors understanding.

_____ The classroom structure fosters frequent progress monitoring for struggling students.

Comments:

RTI in Math © 2011 Solution Tree Press • solution-tree.com
Visit **go.solution-tree.com/rti** to download this page.

Closure Activities and Summarization
_____ Students often summarize mathematics content for each other, working in pairs during the middle of a lesson, while the teacher checks for conceptual understanding.
_____ Summaries of activities at the end of the lesson frequently result in some product (for example, a poster summarizing lesson content or bulletin-board notes summarizing content that is then displayed for subsequent days during that instructional unit).
_____ Students use the writing process to summarize mathematical thinking (such as the use of a math journal to deepen understanding and serve as informal formative assessment).
Comments:
Signature:

References and Resources

Abernathy, S. (2008). *Responsiveness to instruction: An overview.* Accessed at www.ncpublicschools .org/docs/ec/development/learning/responsiveness/rtimaterials/problem-solving/ rtioverview-training-present.ppt on September 9, 2008.

Allsopp, D., Kyger, M., Lovin, L., Gerretson, H., Carson, K., & Ray, S. (2008). Mathematics dynamic assessment: Informal assessment that responds to the needs of struggling learners in mathematics. *Teaching Exceptional Children, 40*(3), 6–16.

Ardoin, S. P., Witt, J. C., Connell, J. E., & Koenig, J. L. (2005). Application of a three-tiered response to intervention model for instructional planning, decision making, and the identification of children in need of services. *Journal of Psychoeducational Assessment, 23,* 362–380.

Asiala, M., Brown, A., DeVries, D., Dubinsky, E., Matthews, D., & Thomas, K. (1996). A framework for research and curriculum development in undergraduate mathematics education. In J. Kaput, A. H. Schoenfeld, & E. Dubinsky (Eds.), *Research in collegiate mathematics education, II* (pp. 1–32). Providence, RI: American Mathematical Society.

Askew, M. (2002). The changing primary mathematics classroom: The challenge of the national numeracy strategy. In L. Haggarty (Ed.), *Aspects of teaching secondary mathematics: Perspectives on practice* (pp. 3–17). New York: RoutledgeFalmer.

AutoSkill. (2004). *Academy of MATH.* Ontario, Canada: Author.

Ball, D. (1991). Research on teaching mathematics: Making subject-matter knowledge part of the equation. In J. Brophy (Ed.), *Advances in research on teaching* (Vol. 2, pp. 1–48). Greenwich, CT: JAI Press.

Barberisi, M. J., Katusic, S. K., Colligan, R. C., Weaver, A. L., & Jacobsen, S. J. (2005). Mathematics learning disorder: Incidence in a population-based birth cohort, 1976–1982, Rochester, Minn. *Ambulatory Pediatrics, 5,* 281–289.

Barton, M. L., & Heidema, C. (2002). *Teaching reading in mathematics* (2nd ed.). Aurora, CO: Mid-continent Research for Education and Learning.

Baskette, M. R., Ulmer, L., & Bender, W. N. (2006). The emperor has no clothes! Unanswered questions and concerns on the response to intervention procedure. *Journal of the American Academy of Special Education Professionals*, 4–24. Accessed at http://aasep.org/aasep-publications/ journal-of-the-american-academy-of-special-education-professionals-jaasep/jaasep-fall-2006/ index.html on October 12, 2006.

Bender, W. N. (2009a). *Beyond the RTI pyramid: Solutions for the first years of implementation.* Bloomington, IN: Solution Tree Press.

Bender, W. N. (2009b). *Differentiating mathematics instruction* (2nd ed.). Thousand Oaks, CA: Corwin Press.

Bender, W. N., & Larkin, M. (2009). *Reading strategies for elementary students with learning difficulties: Strategies for RTI* (2nd ed.). Thousand Oaks, CA: Corwin Press.

Bender, W. N., & Shores, C. (2007). *Response to intervention: A practical guide for every teacher.* Thousand Oaks, CA: Corwin Press.

Berch, D. B. (2005). Making sense of number sense: Implications for children with mathematical disabilities. *Journal of Learning Disabilities, 38,* 333–339.

Berger, A., Tzur, G., & Posner, M. I. (2006). Infant brains detect arithmetic errors. *Proceedings of the National Academy of Sciences, 103,* 12649–12653.

Berkeley, S., Bender, W. N., Peaster, L. G., & Saunders, L. (2009). Implementation of responsiveness to intervention: A snapshot of progress. *Journal of Learning Disabilities, 42*(1), 85–95.

Borasi, R. (1994). Capitalizing on errors as "springboards for inquiry": A teaching experiment. *Journal for Research in Mathematics Education, 25*(2), 166–208.

Bower, K. (2008). Making intervention work for all students: How nontraditional intervention methods work in a traditional mathematics lab. *Principal, 87*(3), 27–30.

Boyer, L. (2008, June). *The West Virginia model for RTI: An update.* Paper presented at the annual Sopris West Educational Conference, Morgantown, WV.

Bradley, R., Danielson, L., & Doolittle, J. (2007). Responsiveness to intervention: 1997–2007. *Teaching Exceptional Children, 39*(5), 8–12.

Brown, R., & Hirst, E. (2007). Developing an understanding of the mediating role of talk in the elementary mathematics classroom. *Journal of Classroom Interaction, 41*(2), 18–28.

Bryant, D. P., Bryant, B. R., Gersten, R. M., Scammacca, N. N., Funk, C., Winter, A., et al. (2008). The effects of tier 2 intervention on the mathematics performance of first-grade students who are at risk for mathematics difficulties. *Learning Disability Quarterly, 31*(2), 47–64.

Buffum, A., Mattos, M., & Weber, C. (2009). *Pyramid response to intervention: RTI, professional learning communities, and how to respond when kids don't learn.* Bloomington, IN: Solution Tree Press.

Burns, M. (2006). *Do the math: Arithmetic intervention by Marilyn Burns—A summary of the research.* New York: Scholastic.

Carpenter, T. P., Hiebert, J., Fennema, E., Fuson, K. C., Wearne, D., & Murray, H. (1997). *Making sense: Teaching and learning mathematics with understanding.* Portsmouth, NH: Heinemann.

Chapin, S., O'Connor, C., & Canavan, A. (2003). *Classroom discussions: Using mathematics talk to help students learn—Grades K–6.* Sausalito, CA: Mathematics Solutions Press.

Chard, D. J., Baker, S. K., Clarke, B., Jungjohann, K., Davis, K., & Smolkowski, K. (2008). Preventing early mathematics difficulties: The feasibility of a rigorous kindergarten mathematics curriculum. *Learning Disability Quarterly, 31*(1), 11–20.

Clark, K. (2010, January). Can school reform ever really work? *U.S. News & World Report, 147,* 23–31.

Colorado, Iowa, & Nebraska Departments of Education. (1996). *Of primary interest.* Colorado, IA: Author.

Cummings, K. D., Atkins, T., Allison, R., & Cole, C. (2008). Response to intervention: Investigating the new role of special educators. *Teaching Exceptional Children, 40*(4), 24–31.

Denton, C. A., Fletcher, J. M., Anthony, J. L., & Francis, D. J. (2006). An evaluation of intensive intervention for students with persistent reading difficulties. *Journal of Learning Disabilities, 39*(5), 447–466.

Devlin, K. (2000). *The mathematics gene: How mathematical thinking evolved and why numbers are like gossip.* New York: Basic Books.

DuFour, R., DuFour, R., & Eaker, R. (2008). *Revisiting professional learning communities at work: New insights for improving schools.* Bloomington, IN: Solution Tree Press.

DuFour, R., DuFour, R., Eaker, R., & Karhanek, G. (2004). *Whatever it takes: How professional learning communities respond when kids don't learn.* Bloomington, IN: Solution Tree Press.

Enochs, L. G., Smith, P. L., & Huinker, D. (2000). Establishing factorial validity of the mathematics teaching efficacy beliefs instrument. *School Science and Mathematics, 100*(4), 194–202.

Fleischner, J., & Manheimer, M. (1997). Mathematics interventions for students with learning disabilities: Myths and realities. *School Psychology Review, 26*(3), 397–414.

Foegen, A. (2008). Algebra progress monitoring and intervention for students with learning disabilities. *Learning Disabilities Quarterly, 31*(2), 65–78.

Fuchs, D., & Deshler, D. D. (2007). What we need to know about responsiveness to intervention (and shouldn't be afraid to ask). *Learning Disabilities Research and Practice, 22*(2), 129–136.

Fuchs, D., & Fuchs, L. S. (2005). Responsiveness to intervention: A blueprint for practitioners, policy makers, and parents. *Teaching Exceptional Children, 41*(1), 93–98.

Fuchs, D., & Fuchs, L. S. (2006). Introduction to response to intervention: What, why, and how valid is it? *Reading Research Quarterly, 40*(1), 93–98.

Fuchs, D., Fuchs, L. S., Thompson, A., Svenson, E., Loulee, V., & Otaiba, S. A. (2001). Peer-assisted learning strategies in reading: Extensions for kindergarten, first grade, and high school. *Remedial and Special Education, 22*(1), 15–21.

Fuchs, L., Fuchs, D., Hamlett, C., Phillips, N., Karns, K., & Dutka, S. (1997). Enhancing students' behavior during peer-mediated instruction with conceptual mathematical explanations. *Elementary School Journal, 17*(3), 223–249.

Fuchs, L. S., Compton, D. L., Fuchs, D., Paulsen, K., Bryant, J., & Hamlett, C. L. (2005). Responsiveness to intervention: Preventing and identifying mathematics disability. *Teaching Exceptional Children, 37*(4), 60–63.

Fuchs, L. S., & Fuchs, D. (2001). Principles for prevention and intervention of mathematics difficulties. *Learning Disabilities Research and Practice, 16*(2), 85–95.

Fuchs, L. S., & Fuchs, D. (2002). Mathematical problem-solving profiles of students with mathematical disabilities with and without co-morbid reading disabilities. *Journal of Learning Disabilities, 35,* 563–573.

Fuchs, L. S., & Fuchs, D. (2007). A model for implementing responsiveness to intervention. *Teaching Exceptional Children, 39*(5), 14–20.

Fuchs, L. S., Fuchs, D., Compton, D. L., Bryant, J. D., Hamlett, C. L., & Seethaler, P. M. (2007). Mathematics screening and progress monitoring at first grade: Implications for responsiveness to intervention. *Exceptional Children, 73*(3), 311–330.

Fuchs, L. S., Fuchs, D., Hamlett, C. L., Hope, S. K., Hollenbeck, K. N., & Capizzi, A. (2006). Extending responsiveness-to-intervention to mathematics problem solving at third grade. *Teaching Exceptional Children, 38*(4), 59–63.

Fuchs, L. S., Fuchs, D., & Hollenbeck, K. N. (2007). Extending responsiveness to intervention to mathematics at first and third grades. *Learning Disabilities Research and Practice, 22*(1), 13–24.

Fournier, D. N. E, & Graves, M. F. (2002). Scaffolding adolescents' comprehension of short stories. *Journal of Adolescent and Adult Literacy, 48*(1), 30–39.

Gagnon, J. C., & Maccini, P. (2001). Preparing students with disabilities in algebra. *Teaching Exceptional Children, 34*(1), 8–15.

Gersten, R., & Dimino, J. A. (2006). RTI (response to intervention): Rethinking special education for students with reading difficulties (yet again). *Reading Research Quarterly, 41*(1), 99–108.

Ginsburg, H. P. (1987). How to assess number facts, calculation, and understanding. In D. D. Hammill (Ed.), *Assessing the abilities and instructional needs of students* (pp. 483–503). Austin, TX: Pro-Ed.

Ginsburg, H. P., & Baroody, A. J. (2003). *Test of early mathematics ability* (3rd ed.). Austin, TX: Pro-Ed.

Goldman, S. (1989). Strategy instruction in mathematics. *Journal of Learning Disabilities, 12,* 43–55.

Greenwood, C. R., Delquadri, J., & Carta, J. J. (1997). *Together we can! Classwide peer tutoring to improve basic academic skills.* Longmont, CO: Sopris West.

Griffin, S. (1998). *Number worlds.* Durham, NH: Number Worlds Alliance.

Griffin, S. (2003). Number worlds: A research based mathematical program for young children. In D. H. Clements & A. DiBiase (Eds.), *Engaging young children in mathematics: Standards for early childhood mathematics education* (pp. 325–342). Mahwah, NJ: Lawrence Erlbaum Associates.

Griffin, S. (2004). Building number sense with number worlds. *Early Childhood Research Quarterly, 19*(1), 173–180.

Good, R. H., & Kaminski, R. (2002). *DIBELS: Dynamic indicators of basic early literacy skills* (6th ed.). Longmont, CO: Sopris West.

Guthrie, J. T. (2001, November). *Engagement and motivation in reading instruction.* Paper presented at the National Invitational Conference on Successful Reading Instruction, Washington, DC.

Hanna, G., & Yackel, E. (2000). White paper on reasoning and proof. In M. Lindquist & G. Martin (Eds.), *The future of the standards.* Reston, VA: National Council of Teachers of Mathematics.

Hughes, C., & Dexter, D. D. (2006). *Universal screening within a response to intervention model.* Accessed at www.rtinetwork.org/learn/research/universal-screening-within-a-rti-model on March 31, 2009.

Hughes, C., & Dexter, D. D. (2008). *Field studies of RTI programs.* Accessed at www.rtinetwork .org on November 20, 2008.

Hutchinson, N. (1987). Strategy instruction research in one knowledge domain: Algebra. *Canadian Journal of Special Education, 5*(2), 169–177.

Hutchinson, N. (1990). Strategies for teaching learning disabled adolescents algebra problems. *Journal of Reading, Writing, and Learning Disabilities Intervention, 3*(1), 63–74.

Howell, R., Patton, S., & Deiotte, M. (2008). *Understanding response to intervention: A practical guide to systemic implementation.* Bloomington, IN: Solution Tree Press.

Jackson, D. T. (2002). Crossing content: A strategy for students with learning disabilities. *Intervention in School and Clinic, 37*(5), 279–283.

Jitendra, A. (2002). Teaching students mathematics problem solving through graphic representations. *Teaching Exceptional Children, 34*(4), 34–38.

Jordan, N. C. (2007). The need for number sense. *Educational Leadership, 65*(1), 63–67.

Jordan, N. C., Kaplan, D., Locuniak, M. N., & Ramineni, C. (2007). Prediction first-grade mathematics achievement from developmental number sense trajectories. *Learning Disabilities Research and Practice, 22*(1), 36–56.

Kame'enui, E. J. (2007). A new paradigm: Responsiveness to intervention. *Teaching Exceptional Children, 39*(5), 6–7.

Kamps, D., Abbott, M., Greenwood, C., Arreaga-Mayer, C., Wills, H., Longstaff, J., et al. (2007). Use of evidence-based, small group reading instruction for English language learners in elementary grades: Secondary-tier intervention. *Learning Disability Quarterly, 30*(3), 153–168.

Kavale, K. A., & Spaulding, L. C. (2008). Is response to intervention good policy for specific learning disability? *Learning Disabilities Research and Practice, 23*(4), 169–179.

Kemp, K. A., Eaton, M. A., & Poole, S. (2009). *RTI & math: The classroom connection.* Port Chester, NY: Dude.

Knowlton, D. (2003). Preparing students for enhanced living. In D. Knowlton & D. Sharp (Eds.), *Problem-based learning for the information age.* San Francisco: Jossey-Bass.

Kulik, C. C., & Kulik, J. A. (1987). Mastery testing and student learning: A meta-analysis. *Journal of Educational Technology Systems, 15*(3), 325–345. (ERIC Document Reproduction Service No. EJ351289)

Kulik, J. (1994). Meta-analytic studies of findings on computer-based instruction. In E. L. Baker and H. F. O'Neil, Jr. (Eds.), *Technology assessment in education and training* (pp. 9–33). Hillsdale, NJ: Lawrence Erlbaum.

Lan, W., & Repman, J. (1995). The effects of social learning context and modeling on persistence and dynamism in academic activities. *Journal of Experimental Education, 64*(1), 53–67.

Lewin, T. (2008, March 14). American students' mathematics achievement. *New York Times,* p. 17.

Linan-Thompson, S., Cirino, P. T., & Vaughn, S. (2007). Determining English language learners' response to intervention: Questions and some answers. *Learning Disability Quarterly, 30*(3), 185–196.

Linan-Thompson, S., Vaughn, S., Prater, K., & Cirino, P. T. (2006). The response to intervention of English language learners at risk for reading problems. *Journal of Learning Disabilities, 39*(5), 390–398.

Lindsley, O. R. (1992). Precision teaching: Discoveries and effects. *Journal of Applied Behavior Analysis, 25,* 51–57.

Locuniak, M. N., & Jordan, N. C. (2008). Using kindergarten number sense to predict calculation fluency in second grade. *Journal of Learning Disabilities, 41*(5), 451–459.

Lovett, M. W., De Palma, M., Frijters, J., Steinbach, K., Temple, M., Benson, N., et al. (2008). Interventions for reading difficulties: A comparison of response to intervention by ELL and EFL struggling readers. *Journal of Learning Disabilities, 41*(4), 333–352.

Mabbott, D. J., & Bisanz, J. (2008). Computational skills, working memory, and conceptual knowledge in older children with mathematics learning disabilities. *Journal of Learning Disabilities, 41*(1), 15–28.

Maccini, P., & Hughes, C. (2000). Effects of a problem-solving strategy on the introductory algebra performance of secondary students with learning disabilities. *Learning Disabilities Research and Practice, 15*(1), 10–21.

Maccini, P., & Ruhl, K. L. (2000). Effects of a graduated instructional sequence on the algebraic subtraction of integers by secondary students with learning disabilities. *Education and Treatment of Children, 23*(4), 465–489.

MacLean, H. E. (2003). *The effects of early intervention on the mathematical achievement of low-performing first grade students.* Unpublished doctoral dissertation, University of Houston.

McCain, T. (2005). *Teaching for tomorrow.* Thousand Oaks, CA: Corwin Press.

McLaughlin, M. W., Shepard, L. A., & O'Day, J. A. (1995). *Improving education through standards-based education reform: A report by the National Academy of Education.* Stanford, CA: National Academy of Education.

Minton, L. (2007). *What if your ABC's were 123's? Building connections between literacy and numeracy.* Thousand Oaks, CA: Corwin Press.

Murphy, M. M., Mazzocco, M. M., Hanich, L. B., & Early, M. C. (2007). Cognitive characteristics of children with mathematics learning disability (MLD) vary as a function of the cutoff criterion used to define MLD. *Journal of Learning Disabilities, 40*(5), 458–478.

National Association of State Directors of Special Education (2006). *Myths about response to intervention implementation.* Accessed at www.rtinetwork.org/Learn/What/ar/MythsAboutRTI on November 21, 2008.

National Council of Teachers of Mathematics. (2000). *Principles and standards for school mathematics.* Reston, VA: Author.

National Council of Teachers of Mathematics. (2006). *Curriculum focal points for mathematics in prekindergarten through grade 8.* Reston, VA: Author.

National Joint Committee on Learning Disabilities. (2005). Responsiveness to intervention and learning disabilities: A report prepared by the National Joint Committee on Learning Disabilities. *Learning Disability Quarterly, 28*(4), 249–260.

National Mathematics Advisory Panel. (2008). *Foundations for success: The final report of the National Mathematics Advisory Panel.* Washington, DC: Author. Accessed at www.ed.gov/MathPanel on December 16, 2008.

O'Connor, R. E., Fulmer, D., Harty, K. R., & Bell, K. (2005). Layers of reading intervention in kindergarten through third grade: Changes in teaching and student outcomes. *Journal of Learning Disabilities, 38,* 440–455.

Partnership for 21st Century Skills. (2007). *21st century curriculum and instruction.* Tucson, AZ: Author. Accessed at www.21stcenturyskills.org/documents/21st_Century_skills_curriculum_and_instruction.pdf on November 19, 2009.

Riccomini, P. (2005). Identification and remediation of systematic error patterns in subtraction. *Learning Disability Quarterly, 28*(3), 233–242.

Rinaldi, C., & Samson, J. (2008). English language learners and response to intervention. *Teaching Exceptional Children, 40*(5), 6–15.

Rosenshine, B., & Meister, C. (1991, April). *Reciprocal teaching: A review of nineteen experimental studies.* Paper presented at the annual meeting of the American Educational Research Association, Chicago, IL.

Scheuermann, A., Deschler, D., & Shumaker, J. (2009). The effects of the explicit inquiry routine on the performance of students with learning disabilities on one-variable equations. *Learning Disability Quarterly, 32*(2), 103–120.

Schleppenbach, M., Flevares, L., Sims, L., & Perry, M. (2007). Teachers' responses to student mistakes in Chinese and U.S. mathematics classrooms. *Elementary School Journal, 108*(2), 131–147.

Silver, E. A., & Lane, S. (1991). Assessment in the context of mathematics instruction reform: The design of assessment in the QUASAR project. In M. Niss (Ed.), *Cases of assessment in mathematics education: An ICMI study* (pp. 59–70). Dordrecht, the Netherlands: Kluwer.

Simmons, D. C., Coyne, M. D., Kwok, O., McDonagh, S., Harn, B. A., & Kame'enui, E. J. (2008). Indexing response to intervention: A longitudinal study of reading risk from kindergarten through third grade. *Journal of Learning Disabilities, 41*(2), 158–173.

Slavin, R. E., & Lake, C. (2007). Effective programs in elementary mathematics: A best-evidence synthesis. *Review of Educational Research, 78*(3), 427–515. Accessed at www.bestevidence.org/word/elem_math_Feb_1_2007.pdf on March 15, 2010.

Sopris West. (2004). *Transitional mathematics program level 1: Developing number sense.* Longmont, CO: Author.

Sousa, D. A. (2005). *How the brain learns to read.* Thousand Oaks, CA: Corwin Press.

Sousa, D. A. (2008). *How the brain learns mathematics.* Thousand Oaks, CA: Corwin Press.

Spectrum K12 School Solutions. (2009). *Response to intervention (RTI) adoption survey 2009.* Washington, DC: Author. Accessed at www.spectrumk12.com/uploads/file/RTI%202009%20Adoption%20Survey%20Final%20Report.pdf on March 15, 2010.

Spectrum K12 School Solutions/Council of Administrators of Special Education. (2008). *RTI adoption survey.* Washington, DC: Author.

Stevens, R. J., & Slavin, R. E. (1995). The cooperative elementary school: Effects on students' achievement, attitudes, and social relations. *American Educational Research Journal, 32(2),* 321–351.

Stiggins, R. (2007). *An introduction to student-involved assessment* for *learning* (5th ed.). Upper Saddle River, NJ: Prentice Hall.

Strauss, M. S., & Curtis, L. E. (1981). Infant perception of numerosity. *Child Development, 52,* 1146–1152.

Strobel, J., & van Barneveld, A. (2008). When is PBL more effective? A meta-synthesis of meta-analyses comparing PBL to conventional classrooms. *Interdisciplinary Journal of Problem-Based Learning, 3(1),* 44–58.

Swan, K. (2002). Building learning communities in online courses: The importance of interaction. *Education, Communication & Information, 2(1),* 23–49.

Thompson, C. J. (2009). The impact of standards-based instruction on mathematics and science achievement. *Research in Education, 81(1),* 53–62.

Tomlinson, C. A. (1999). *The differentiated classroom: Responding to the needs of all learners.* Alexandria, VA: Association for Supervision and Curriculum Development.

Tomlinson, C. A., & McTighe, J. (2006). *Integrating differentiated instruction and understanding by design.* Alexandria, VA: Association for Supervision and Curriculum Development.

Toom, A. (2007). *Word problems in Russia and America: Extended version of a talk at the meeting of the Swedish Mathematical Society, June, 2005.* Recife, Brazil: Federal University of Pernambuco. Accessed at www.de.ufpe.br/~toom/travel/sweden05/WP.PDF on March 15, 2010.

Torgesen, J. K. (2007). *Using an RTI model to guide early reading instruction: Effects on identification rates for students with learning disabilities.* Tallahassee, FL: Florida Center for Reading Research. Accessed at www.fcrr.org on December 12, 2008.

University of Cincinnati. (2008). *Kentucky Center for Mathematics 2007–2008 intervention program evaluations: Summary of results.* Accessed at www.kentuckymathematics.org/research/docs/2009/KCM%20MIT%202007-8%20Final%20Report_cin.pdf on March 15, 2010.

van Garderen, D. (2007). Teaching students with LD to use diagrams to solve mathematical word problems. *Journal of Learning Disabilities, 40(6),* 540–553.

Vellutino, F. R., Scanlon, D. M., Small, S., & Fanuele, D. P. (2006). Response to intervention as a vehicle for distinguishing between children with and without reading disabilities: Evidence for the role of kindergarten and first-grade interventions. *Journal of Learning Disabilities, 39(2),* 157–169.

Vygotsky, L. S. (1978). *Mind and society: The development of higher psychological processes.* Cambridge, MA: Harvard University Press.

Webb, N. M., & Mastergeorge, A. M. (2003). The development of students' helping behavior and learning in peer-directed small groups. *Cognition and Instruction, 2,* 361–428.

What Works Clearinghouse. (2007). *Intervention: Everyday mathematics.* Accessed at www.ies.ed.gov/ncee/wwc/reports/elementary_math/eday_math on March 15, 2010.

White, O. R. (1985). Precision teaching—precision learning. *Exceptional Children, 52,* 522–534.

Witzel, B. S., Mercer, C. D., & Miller, M. D. (2003). Teaching algebra to students with learning difficulties: An investigation of an explicit instruction model. *Learning Disabilities Research and Practice, 18*(2), 121–131.

Wright, R. J. (1992). Number topics in early childhood mathematics curricula: Historical background, dilemmas, and possible solutions. *The Australian Journal of Education, 36,* 125–142.

Wright, R. J. (2003). Mathematics recovery: A program of intervention in early number. *Australian Journal of Learning Disabilities, 8*(4), 6–11.

Wright, R. J. (2009). An overview of mathematics recovery. In A. Dowker (Ed.), *Mathematics difficulties: Psychology, neuroscience and intervention*. San Diego, CA: Elsevier.

Wright, R. J., Martland, J., & Stafford, A. (2006). *Early numeracy: Assessment for teaching and intervention* (2nd ed.). London: Paul Chapman/SAGE.

Wright, R. J., Martland, J., Stafford, A., & Stanger, G. (2006). *Teaching number: Advancing children's skills and strategies* (2nd ed.). London: Paul Chapman/SAGE.

Wright, R. J., Stanger, G., Stafford, A., & Martland, J. (2006). *Teaching number in the classroom with 4- to 8-year-olds*. London: Paul Chapman/SAGE.

Woodward, J., & Brown, C. (2006). Meeting the curricular needs of academically low-achieving students in middle grade mathematics. *Journal of Special Education, 40*(3), 151–159.

Yeh, S. S. (2007). The cost-effectiveness of five policies for improving student achievement. *American Journal of Evaluation, 28*(4), 416–436.

Index

Beyond the RTI Pyramid
Solutions for the First Years of Implementation
William N. Bender
This book helps schools deepen the RTI experience by extending the processes beyond initial implementation and across various content areas and grade levels.
BKF323

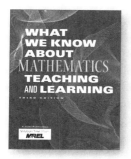

What We Know About Mathematics Teaching and Learning
McREL
Designed for accessibility, this book supports mathematics education reform and brings the rich world of education research and practice to preK–12 educators.
BKF395

Pyramid Response to Intervention: RTI, PLCs, and How to Respond When Kids Don't Learn
Austin Buffum, Mike Mattos, and Chris Weber
Foreword by Richard DuFour
Accessible language and compelling K–12 stories illustrate how RTI is most effective when built on the Professional Learning Communities at Work™ model.
BKF251

Making Math Accessible to Students With Special Needs Series
Practical Tips and Suggestions
r4 Educated Solutions
These manuals offer grade-appropriate research-based strategies for increasing confidence and capability among students with special needs. Each includes reflective questions and tasks for self-guided or group study.

Grades K–2: BKF288 **Grades 3–5: BKF289**
Grades 6–8: BKF290 **Grades 9–12: BKF291**

Solution Tree | Press

a division of
Solution Tree

Visit solution-tree.com or call 800.733.6786 to order.